THE EPISTEMOLOGY OF THE SECRET

In this groundbreaking work, Jean d'Aspremont undertakes the first study of the epistemology of the secret of international law, which is a specific intellectual posture whereby international law is considered to be replete with secrets that international lawyers ought to reveal. In addition to arguing that the epistemology of the secret of international law is everywhere at work in international legal thought and practice, d'Aspremont demonstrates why this posture must be scrutinized, given how much it enables certain sayings, thoughts, perceptions, and actions whilst simultaneously disabling others, making it complicit with the worst forms of capitalism, colonialism, racism, bourgeois ideology, phallocentrism, virilism, and masculinism. This book should be read by anyone interested in how international law comes to do what it does and why it must be rethought.

JEAN D'ASPREMONT is Professor of International Law at Sciences Po Law School and at the University of Manchester. He has written extensively on the theory and philosophy of international law. His work has been translated in several languages including Spanish, Portuguese, Russian, Mandarin Chinese, Hindi, Japanese, and Persian.

THE EPISTEMOLOGY OF THE SECRET

International Law as Revelation

JEAN D'ASPREMONT

Sciences Po, Paris and University of Manchester

CAMBRIDGE
UNIVERSITY PRESS

CAMBRIDGE
UNIVERSITY PRESS

Shaftesbury Road, Cambridge CB2 8EA, United Kingdom

One Liberty Plaza, 20th Floor, New York, NY 10006, USA

477 Williamstown Road, Port Melbourne, VIC 3207, Australia

314–321, 3rd Floor, Plot 3, Splendor Forum, Jasola District Centre, New Delhi – 110025, India

103 Penang Road, #05-06/07, Visioncrest Commercial, Singapore 238467

Cambridge University Press is part of Cambridge University Press & Assessment, a department of the University of Cambridge.

We share the University's mission to contribute to society through the pursuit of education, learning and research at the highest international levels of excellence.

www.cambridge.org
Information on this title: www.cambridge.org/9781009597753

DOI: 10.1017/9781009597739

When citing this work, please include a reference to the DOI 10.1017/9781009597739

First published 2025

A catalogue record for this publication is available from the British Library

A Cataloging-in-Publication data record for this book is available from the Library of Congress

ISBN 978-1-009-59775-3 Hardback

Each generation must discover its mission, fulfil it or betray it, in relative opacity.

—Frantz Fanon, *The Wretched of the Earth*, trans. Richard Philcox, p. 145

CONTENTS

PREFACE

This book is yet another of my attempts to inject a contrast medium into the international legal discourse with a view to having it tell us another story about its own functioning. Making the international legal discourse speak about itself is a scholarly endeavor that, despite the contemporary production of writings about international law at an industrial scale, is far from completion. In my view, fracking the international legal discourse – to use a sinister vocabulary of our era – must be continued at full thrust.[1] This is what this book seeks to contribute to.

As the completion of this book was coming to an end, some parts of the world came to show how much they have morally collapsed, even committing or supporting an abomination that I never thought humanity, in the twenty-first century, would still be capable of (watching silently). On that occasion, the doctrine of statehood,[2] so dear to international law(yers) and already responsible for some of the worst disasters of the past centuries, was, once again, turned into a murderous ideology[3] – and so have some of the other key doctrines of international law. The epistemology of the secret of international law with which this book engages has certainly not been alien to the misery and tragedy unfolding as the final lines of this book were laid down. In fact, and this is something the notebook appended to this volume will revert to, the epistemology of the secret of international law discussed in this book has always been a linchpin of brutal and oppressive colonial enterprises,

[1] On the idea that the fissuring of the Western discourse must be continued at all cost, see Roland Barthes, *Le grain de la voix. Entretiens 1962–1980* (Editions du Seuil, 1981) p. 94 and pp. 139–140. See also Michel Foucault, *Dits et écrits, I (1954–1975)* (Gallimard, 2001) p. 1640.

[2] Because modern statehood has been, in my view, conducive to so much atrocity in the world since its inception, I have always felt it does not deserve a capital S.

[3] Comp. with the concept of 'ideological alibi' of the State by Arjun Appadurai, *Modernity at Large: Cultural Dimensions of Globalization* (University of Minnesota Press, 1996) p. 159.

including those enabled by international law. Shedding light on the complicity between the epistemology of the secret at work in the international legal discourse and some disturbing contemporary invocations of international law is also what this book aims at.

I am aware that persevering, book after book, with the peeling of the international legal discourse in order to grasp how the latter does what it does, especially at a time the world is distressfully caught in an essentialist, nationalist, racist, colonialist, and capitalist turn never witnessed in the lifetime of my generation, could be seen as inglorious, if not obscene.[4] Yet, as I learnt from Homi Bhabha and Louis Althusser, it is damaging and self-defeating to construe theory – and whatever reflection or story that can pejoratively be labelled this way – as necessarily being the elite arcane language of the socially and culturally privileged.[5] Since everything is theory the very moment we start looking at the world and open our mouth, I am convinced that theory is the most decisive site of contestation of all. Even when taking to the streets – which so often seems needed these days – one mobilizes theory. Because it is in (and with) theory that we will repel or stifle all those discourses that separate, discriminate, oppress, exploit, destroy, and exterminate people and the planet, theory must constantly be de-centered, vulgarized, de-Westernized, and surely not construed as a source of rare social capital in the hands of a small and privileged group inhabiting some imperial locations. Showing that theory is simultaneously simple and omnipresent as well as pivotal for all the battles we must urgently fight is similarly part of the ambitions of this book.[6]

Sketching out some of the broad ambitions of this book as well as the context in which it was written does not tell us much about what kind of story this book tries to tell about international law. In a nutshell, what I call in this book the epistemology of the secret of international law is a

[4] I acknowledge that one must enjoy some bourgeois quietness and be spared by bombs as well as starvation to afford probing into discursive mechanisms like the epistemology of the secret of international law like I try to do in this book. On the relationship between scholarly works and the bourgeois way of life, see the remarks of Foucault, *Dits et écrits, I (1954–1975)* p. 685. See also Régis Debray, *Le Scribe* (Editions Grasset et Fasquelle, 1980) pp. 121 and 221.

[5] Homi K. Bhabba, *The Location of Culture* (Routledge, 1994) p. 28; Louis Althusser, *Initiation à la Philosophie pour les Non-Philosophes* (Presses Universitaires de France, 2014) pp. 54–60.

[6] As this book will argue, one way to achieve this is to do away with the distinction between theory and practice that is so common in international legal thought and practice. This is also why I suggest to speak of 'theoractice'. See infra Section 5.4.

specific intellectual posture whereby international law, its texts, its practices, its actors, its effects, its representations, its past, etc. are held as carrying secrets that international lawyers, in whatever capacity, ought to reveal. The epistemology of the secret of international law discussed here is thus a type of epistemology that postulates that there necessarily is hidden, unknown, invisible content in international law's texts, practices, actors, effects, representations, past, etc. and that revealing such hidden, unknown, invisible content necessarily is what engaging with international law is expected to be. In exposing international legal thought and practice as being articulated around an epistemology of the secret, I hope to contradict some of most common representations of international law and especially those that hold that international law conceals and hides a great deal of its meanings, origins, agendas, hierarchies, geographies, histories, etc. In contrast with such common portrayals of international law, this book shows that the secrets of international law are never pre-existing hidden actualities awaiting their revelation but are always produced by international lawyers at the moment they are made known and visible. Questioning such common representations of international law – and the secret-hunting, archaeologist, and speleologist roles that they accordingly assign to international lawyers – is yet another objective of this book.

A preface is often the place where one can say a few words about the making of the book. Whilst this constitutes a very bourgeois and self-centered thing to do, I am going to indulge in this socially accepted genre, for this is a way to expose the errancy of the thought-process that guided some of the inscriptions found in the following pages. The idea of this book came a few years ago when I (finally) ventured in the stunning and world-changing work of Michel Foucault on the *History of Sexuality*. I had always been mindful of the glaring parallels between, on the one hand, the creation of a discourse on sexuality and the setting of a certain ordering normality and, on the other hand, the normality-setting and world-making performances of international law. Yet, what specifically drew my attention then and subsequently gave me the idea of the present book is Foucault's discussion of the technology of confession as a mode of ordering.[7] According to Foucault, following the Fourth Lateran Council (1215), Christianity put in place sophisticated *confession*

[7] See gen. Michel Foucault, *Histoire de la Sexualité 1. La volonté de savoir* (Gallimard, 1976) p. 80; Michel Foucault, *Histoire de la Sexualité IV. Les aveux de la chair* (Gallimard, 2018) p. 100. This is part of Foucault's discussion of the pastoral organization of power. In that

techniques supported by an obligation to truth whose aim was the production of secrets about the soul with a view to having them captured and ordered by the Church apparatus. International law, this book argues, has amply tapped into this technological heritage. Indeed, the epistemology of the secret discussed in the following paragraphs is the manifestation of a specific type of epistemology whereby international law, its texts, its practices, its actors, its effects, its representations, its past, etc. always carry secrets that it behoves international lawyers to locate, unearth, and reveal. In that sense, I could have similarly entitled this book *The Confessionality of International Law* by reference to the abovementioned claim of Foucault that set my project into motion. I decided against this title, for the following discussion, although induced by the work on sexuality by the above-mentioned French philosopher, is not yet another type of Foucauldian discussion about international law, which would be a very unspectacular and banal déjà-vu as well as yet another expression of the Western-centrism of the intellectual references of international law.[8] What is more, the intellectual companions that have driven my thoughts during the preparation of this book are aplenty and much more diverse than what such title would have implied. They come from various parts of the world and areas of the humanities, often holding substantive positions that are hardly reconcilable. Surely, such diversity inevitably creates a cacophony of sort in the references and intellectual sources of inspiration around which this book is articulated.[9] I hope the readers will not bemoan such cacophonic theoretical references and take it as the sign that this book has been informed by a fecund, albeit disorderly, thought-forming process. I also hope that they

regard, see Michel Foucault, *Sécurité, Territoire, Population. Cours au Collège de France. 1977–1978* (Gallimard, 2004) pp. 128–134, 186–188, and p. 241; Michel Foucault, *Naissance de la clinique* (Presses Universitaires de France, 1963) p. 15; Michel Foucault, *Dits et écrits, II* (Gallimard, 2001) pp. 548–549, 560–566, 956–958, and 990; Michel Foucault, *Les anormaux. Cours au Collège de France, 1974–1975* (Gallimard, 1999) pp. 163–172. On the concept of pastoral governance in the specific context of the schooling system, see also Ian Hunter, *Rethinking the School: Subjectivity, Bureaucracy, Criticism* (Allen & Unwin, 1994) pp. 62–92.

8 See the criticisms of Edward Said, *Reflections on Exile and Other Literary and Cultural Essays* (Granta, 2001) p. 196. See also the charge against Foucault for not including the larger world and for not accounting how modern methods of knowledge and power in France and Europe came to be defined as modernity's location by Timothy Mitchell; see Timothy Mitchell, *Questions of Modernity* (University of Minnesota Press, 2000) p. 5.

9 Surely my use of theoretical works amounts to a form of theoretical poaching. I borrow this metaphor from Michel de Certeau's description of Michel Foucault's work; see Michel de Certeau, *Histoire et psychanalyse entre science et fiction* (Gallimard, 2016) p. 215.

will construe such diversity of intellectual companions as a guarantee against a dry transposition, in international legal scholarship, of authors or theoretical frameworks held to belong to an alien world to international law. If anything, the following discussion is not an exercise of transposition, let alone a piece of scholarship driven by any quest for coherence and systematicity.[10] It is only another mesh – of yet another fabric – added to the unsystematic net that my work seeks to compose in order to capture the unthought and the impossible in international law.[11]

Speaking of my past unorderly and unsystematic interventions in international legal thought and practice, I must acknowledge, notwithstanding my detestation for any quest for coherence, that the present book partly continues and prolongs my previous exploration of the meaning-centrism of international legal thought and practice and thus my charge against the belief that international legal texts, forms, and signs carry a determinate or indeterminate meaning.[12] Indeed, by shedding light on what it calls the epistemology of the secret of international law, this book zeroes in on a specific attitude of international lawyers whereby they constantly forage law, legal practices, legal institutions, and, more generally, the world as a whole with a view to locating, finding, and knowing hidden meanings, hidden indeterminacies, hidden practices, hidden rituals, hidden actors, hidden agendas and political projects, hidden powers, hidden hierarchies, hidden discriminations, hidden injustices, hidden configurations of the world, hidden configuration of subjectivities, etc. The epistemology of the secret discussed in the following chapters thus refers to an attitude of international lawyers that goes hand in hand with their belief that texts, forms, and signs always have a signification function and accordingly say something that, albeit

[10] On the idea that it is not possible to think of coherence since Nietzsche's dismantling of the possibility of unity of practice and interpretation, see Michel Foucault, *Le Discours Philosophique* (Gallimard/Seuil, 2023) p. 182. See also Jean d'Aspremont, 'The Chivalric Pursuit of Coherence in International Law' (2024) 37 *Leiden Journal of International Law* 191. See also the remarks of Michelle Staggs, 'Disordering International Law' (2022) 33 *European Journal of International Law* 729.

[11] This is a metaphor I borrowed from François Jullien, *La pensée chinoise. En vis-à-vis de la philosophie* (Gallimard, 2015) p. 370.

[12] See, e.g., Jean d'Aspremont, *After Meaning: The Sovereignty of Forms in International Law* (Edward Elgar, 2021); Jean d'Aspremont, 'Two Attitudes towards Textuality in International Law: The Battle for Dualism' (2022) 42 *Oxford Journal of Legal Studies* 963.

hidden to them, they must locate, find, and know.[13] Likewise, this book resembles my 2021 monograph on *The Discourse on Customary International Law* as well as my 2017 monograph on *International Law as a Belief System*, for it seeks to shed light on some central patterns of thought around which international legal thought and practice are possibly organized. Indeed, like in these previous ventures, the current book captures some key intellectual postures that enables certain claims about international law and disables others.

And yet the present book simultaneously entails a major rupture from my work of the past years. In fact, for last the decade, my scholarship was primarily targeting the modern patterns of thoughts that shape international legal thought and practice[14] and especially modern coherence,[15] modern ontology,[16] modern textuality,[17] modern historicism,[18] modern comparativism,[19] modern consensualism,[20] modern institutionalism,[21]

[13] Such continuity between my earlier critique of meaning-centrism and traditional hermeneutics was noted by one of the anonymous peer-reviewers in the following terms: 'The critique of meaning as pre-given lies at the root of the current project which now extends this aspirational poetics of meaning into a fully-fledged theory of the epistemology of international law as predicated upon a dialectic of the hidden and the visible, the secret and the revealed. These binaries in turn dictate in juridical form what can be spoken and what is excluded, an imperialism of the sayable around which the fragile profession of international lawyering coheres self-protectively.'

[14] Comp. with the idea that the various forms and expressions of modernism have been misunderstood by legal studies and misapplied to the analysis of law. See Peter Goodrich, 'Law and Modernity' (1986) 49 *The Modern Law Review* 545 at 548.

[15] See d'Aspremont, 'The Chivalric Pursuit of Coherence in International Law' 191.

[16] Jean d'Aspremont, 'A Worldly Law in a Legal World', in Andrea Bianchi and Moshe Hirsch (eds.), *International Law's Invisible Frames: Social Cognition and Knowledge Production in International Legal Processes* (Oxford University Press, 2021) pp. 110–123.

[17] d'Aspremont, 'Two Attitudes towards Textuality in International Law' 963.

[18] Jean d'Aspremont, *The Critical Attitude and the History of International Law* (Brill, 2019); Jean d'Aspremont, 'Critical Histories of International Law and the Repression of Disciplinary Imagination' (2019) 7 *London Review of International Law* 89.

[19] Jean d'Aspremont, 'Comparativism and Colonizing Thinking in International Law' (2020) 57 *Canadian Yearbook of International Law* 89.

[20] Jean d'Aspremont, 'Consenting to International Law in Five Moves', in Samantha Besson (ed.), *Consent in International Law* (Cambridge University Press, 2023) pp. 117–134; See also Jean d'Aspremont, 'Current Theorizations about the Treaty', in Duncan B. Hollis (ed.), *The Oxford Guide to Treaties*, 2nd edn (Oxford University Press, 2020) pp. 46–58.

[21] Jean d'Aspremont, 'The Love for International Organizations' (2023) 20 *International Organizations Law Review* 111. See also Jean d'Aspremont, *The Experiences of International Organizations: A Phenomenological Approach to International Institutional Law* (Edward Elgar, 2023).

modern temporality,[22] modern institutionalism,[23] modern scienticism,[24] and modern subjecthood[25] at work in international law. In contrast, the present book, as will be illustrated by Chapter 2, scrutinizes an attitude that has its roots both in Greek philosophy as well as religious modes of governance developed and practiced in the Middle Ages in the tiny part of the world called Europe. In that sense, this book constitutes a venture in the history of ideas that goes back much further than my previous studies of modern thought.[26]

The very resort to a book to speak about the epistemology of the secret in international law warrants an observation. The book – and before it the codex – has long been a tool used by monotheist religions for the sake of a revelation.[27] In that sense, the book, as an object, has long been a tool meant to carry secrets and unknown truths for the reader whose reading thereof could possibly enable their knowledge about what God has to tell them about their existence and their being in the world. With the rise of the bourgeois novel[28] and the popularization of reading within the proletariat,[29] the book did not lose its function of carrying secrets that

[22] Jean d'Aspremont, 'Time Travel in the Law of International Responsibility', in Samantha Besson (ed.), *Theories of International Responsibility Law* (Cambridge University Press, 2022) pp. 252–276.

[23] d'Aspremont, 'The Love for International Organizations' 111; d'Aspremont, *The Experiences of International Organizations.*

[24] Jean d'Aspremont, 'International Law and the Rage against Scienticism' (2022) 33 *European Journal of International Law* 679.

[25] Jean d'Aspremont, 'The Law of Statehood as a Constellation of Hybrids', in Jure Vidmar, Sarah McGibbon, and Lea Raible (eds.), *Research Handbook on Secession* (Edward Elgar, 2022) pp. 29–41. Comp. with Jean d'Aspremont, 'The International Law of Statehood and Recognition: A Post-Colonial Invention', in Thierry Garcia (ed.), *La reconnaissance du statut d'Etat à des entités contestées: Approches de droits international, régional et interne* (Pedone, 2018) pp. 15–28.

[26] Comp with Harold Berman, *Law and Revolution: The Formation of the Western Legal Tradition* (Harvard University Press, 1983); Pierre Legendre, *De la Société comme Texte. Linéaments d'une Anthropologie dogmatique* (Fayard, 2001) esp. pp. 62–67; Alain Supiot, *Homo Juridicus. Essai sur la fonction anthropologique du Droit* (Editions du Seuil, 2005) p. 283.

[27] Guglielmo Cavallo, 'Between Volumen and Codex: Reading in the Roman World', in Guglielmo Cavallo and Roger Chartier (eds.), *A History of Reading in the West*, trans. Lydia G. Cochrane (Polity Press, 1999), pp. 64–88.

[28] Roland Barthes, Leo Bersani, Philippe Hamon, Michael Riffaterre, and Ian Watt, *Littérature et réalité* (Editions du Seuil, 1982) pp. 23, 28, and 34–35. See also Section 2.5.

[29] Reinhard Wittmann, 'Was There a Reading Revolution at the End of the Eighteenth Century', in Guglielmo Cavallo and Roger Chartier (eds.), *A History of Reading in the West*, trans. Lydia G. Cochrane (Polity Press, 1999) pp. 284–311. See also Martyn Lyons, 'New Readers in the Nineteenth Century: Women, Children, Workers', in Guglielmo

the act of reading would reveal to the reader. Scholarly books, which proliferate nowadays, are no exception to that, for they similarly aim at revealing secrets to their readers. Hence, writing a book about the epistemology of the secret of international law is doing exactly what books have always been doing: carrying secrets for the sake of a revelation.[30] In that sense, this book, as it discloses a specific epistemology espoused by international lawyers, is caught in the very epistemology of the secret that it describes. Whether that creates some form of tautology or a performative contradiction does not really matter, unless one naïvely believes in the mathematical order of ideas.[31] In fact, this book does not seek to expunge the epistemology of the secret from international legal thought and practice.[32] Because this book inevitably is a manifestation of the epistemology of the secret with which it grapples, its modest ambition, as was already highlighted above, is solely to make international law tell us a new story about its own functioning.

A final terminological observation is in order. Although the following chapters will commonly refer to 'international legal thought and practice' – mainly to avoid overusing the concept of discourse[33] – in order to designate all that is said, thought, perceived, and actioned through international law, it must be repeated one more time that

Cavallo and Roger Chartier (eds.), *A History of Reading in the West*, trans. Lydia G. Cochrane (Polity Press, 1999) pp. 313–343.

30 See the unease of Roland Barthes about criticizing what books do through writing a book, see Roland Barthes, *La préparation du roman. Cours au Collège de France (1978–1979 et 1979–1980)* (Editions du Seuil, 2015) p. 426.

31 In the same vein, see Jacques Derrida, *Positions* (Editions de Minuit, 1972) pp. 21, 35, and 56; Jacques Derrida, *L'écriture et la différence* (Editions du Seuil, 1967) p. 46; Roland Barthes, *Le degré zéro de l'écriture* (Editions du Seuil, 1972) p. 66; Hayden White, *Tropics of Discourse: Essays in Cultural Criticism* (Johns Hopkins University Press, 1978) pp. 142–143 and 252–253; Paul Ricoeur, *La mémoire, l'histoire, l'oubli* (Editions du Seuil, 2000) p. 399; Jean-François Lyotard, *La Condition Postmoderne* (Editions de Minuit, 1979) p. 107; Edward Said, *The World, the Text, and the Critic* (Harvard University Press, 1983) p. 26; Michel Foucault, *Les mots et les choses* (Gallimard, 1966) p. 12; Michel Foucault, *Naissance de la biopolitique. Cours au Collège de France (1978–1979)* (Gallimard/Seuil, 2004) p. 37.

32 See contra Roland Barthes, for whom one should not seek to find secrets in literary texts, Roland Barthes, *Le bruissement de la langue. Essais critiques IV* (Editions du Seuil, 1984) p. 159; Roland Barthes, *Critique et vérité* (Editions du Seuil, 1999) p. 78. See also contra Bernard Harcourt's calls for resistance to the epistemology of the secret at work in the datafication of contemporary societies in Bernard Harcourt, *Exposed* (Harvard University Press, 2015) pp. 251–283.

33 For an attempt to steer clear of the concept of discourse, see d'Aspremont, *The Experiences of International Organizations.*

I categorically reject the distinction between thought (theory) and practice.[34] In my view, there is neither thought (theory) nor practice but only 'theoractice'.[35]

I want to thank Marianne Nield at Cambridge University Press for her support and guidance as well as Anne Vianin for her important editorial contribution at the final stage of completion of the manuscript. I am grateful to the anonymous peer-reviewers whose comments and feedback have proved immensely perceptive, especially given the half-baked character of the story they had to review back then. I am also indebted to my colleague Mostafa Taherkhani who kindly commented on an earlier version of the manuscript and who decisively contributed to making the following better, sharper, and richer. My greatest gratitude goes to Rebecca Mignot-Mahdavi, especially for her very inspiring insights on what distinguishing between visibility and invisibility does (wrong) to the world, and without whom this book, and the space for writing it, would have remained in the realm of the impossible.

[34] No intellectual figure embodies better the impossibility of distinguishing between theory and practice than Frantz Fanon. On Fanon's life as that of both an intellectual activist and an activist intellectual, see Adam Shatz, *The Rebel's Clinic: The Revolutionary Life of Frantz Fanon* (Farrar, Straus and Giroux, 2024).

[35] See infra Section 5.4.

1

The Epistemology of the Secret of International Law

What is called here the epistemology of the secret of international law is a specific, albeit common, intellectual posture whereby international law – and all that composes it, that is, its texts, its practices, its actors, its effects, its representations, its past, etc. – is considered to be replete with secrets that international lawyers, in whatever capacity, ought to reveal. The epistemology of the secret of international law thus corresponds to the permanent postulation that there necessarily is hidden, unknown, invisible content in international law's texts, practices, actors, effects, representations, past, etc. and that revealing such hidden, unknown, invisible content necessarily is what engaging with international law amounts to.

This book argues that, so construed, the epistemology of the secret of international law is everywhere at work in international legal thought and practice. According to the argument made in the following chapters, there is hardly any engagement with international law that does not seek to unveil some secrets of the latter. For instance, such epistemology of the secret is witnessed when a judicial body or an organ of an international organization interprets an international legal text or ascertains certain facts to which international law is applied. It is patent when an expert opinion on a question of international law or a question of facts relevant for the application of international law is provided to a court, a government, an international organization, or a private actor. It is similarly very manifest in the many ways in which most legal scholars approach the texts, practices, actors, effects, representations, past, etc. of international law. In fact, be they providing an authoritative interpretation of some given international legal rules, commenting on the decision of a court, lamenting the detrimental or unjust effects of international law, shedding light on the main patterns of international legal argumentation, deciphering the possible agendas and vested interests driving certain interpretations or practices, expressing suspicion towards all that international law promises, elucidating the dark histories of international law, bemoaning the methods practiced by international lawyers, etc., legal scholars, just like judges, officers of international organizations, diplomats, counsels, and experts, abide by the epistemology of the secret, which is discussed in this book.[1]

This book also makes the point the epistemology of the secret of international law is intellectually questionable for holding that the hidden, the unknown, the invisible always precedes the revealed, the known, and the visible and for hiding the hidden, the unknown, the invisible, and the revealed, the known and the visible are simultaneously produced. The epistemology of the secret of international law, this book argues, also deserves to be scrutinized given how much it enables certain sayings, thoughts, perceptions, and actions whilst disabling others, being complicit, in doing so, with the worst forms of capitalism, colonialism, racism, bourgeois ideology, phallocentrism, virilism, and masculinism. Ultimately, this book submits that the epistemology of the secret of international law, despite dominating the entirety of international legal thought and practice, can be resisted and that an alternative epistemology, less ordering, less silencing, less centred on the distinction between the hidden, the unknown, and the invisible, on the one hand, and the revealed, the known, and the visible, on the other, can be envisaged.

The very notion of the epistemology of the secret, as it has just been introduced, must, at this stage, be further unpacked. As the foregoing already alludes to, there are two main components of the epistemology of the secret of international law: *secrecy* (i.e., hiddenness) and *revelation* (i.e., the act of revealing the hidden, the unknown, the invisible). An epistemology of the secret, as is understood here, *simultaneously* builds on the postulation of a secret content and a revelation of that content. To put it in more specific terms, the epistemology of the secret of international law, as is construed here, rests on two necessitarian postures. First, it postulates the necessary presence of hidden, unknown, invisible content in the texts, practices, actors, effects, representations, past, etc. of international law – what is called here *the necessity of secret content*. Second, it posits a necessity for international lawyers to reveal such hidden, unknown, invisible content – what is called here *the necessity of revelation*. These two necessities, that is, the necessity of secret content and the necessity of revelation, when taken together, put international lawyers in a position where they are constantly in search of hidden, unknown, invisible content for the sake of revealing a truth about

[1] For further illustrations about how the epistemology of the secret of international law manifests itself in international legal thought and practice, see infra Chapter 4.

international law or the world to which it is applied.[2] The epistemology of the secret examined in the following chapters, so construed, amounts to a permanent truth-telling attitude whereby international lawyers constantly seek to reveal some untold secrets about international law and the world.[3]

If it were limited to two necessitarian postures, that is, the necessity of secret content and the necessity of revelation, the epistemology of the secret would be nothing more than a routine[4] that makes international lawyers constantly revisit the texts, practices, actors, effects, representations, past, etc. of international law for the sake of revealing their hidden, unknown, invisible content. Said differently, if the epistemology of the secret were only about making international lawyers reveal secrets about the texts, practices, actors, effects, representations, past, etc. of international law, it would be nothing more than a speech-producing and discipline-constituting epistemology.[5] Yet the epistemology of the secret discussed here, and the two necessities that compose it, are performing a function that goes well beyond the production of speech and the constitution of the discipline. Indeed, the epistemology of the secret of international law, as it is construed here, is an epistemology that orders what can be said, thought, perceived, and actioned through international law. Through the two abovementioned necessities, the epistemology of the secret of international law enables and disables sayings, thoughts, perceptions, and actions and, in doing so, enables and disables what can be said, thought, perceived, and actioned through international law. The epistemology of the secret of international law, in that sense, is also an

[2] On the relation between the epistemology of the secret of international law and truth, see infra Section 1.1.2.3.

[3] Comp. with the idea of an epistemology of the closet by Eve Kosofsky Sedgwick, *Epistemology of the Closet* (University of California Press, 2008) p. 3. Comp. with the idea of economy of truth of Michel Foucault, see Michel Foucault, *Sécurité, Territoire, Population. Cours au Collège de France. 1977–1978* (Gallimard, 2004) p. 241.

[4] On the idea of routine, which is central in the work of Pierre Schlag, see, e.g., Pierre Schlag, 'Normative and Nowhere to Go' (1990) 43 *Stanford Law Review* 167; Pierre Schlag, 'Spam Jurisprudence, Air Law, and the Rank of Anxiety of Nothing Happening (A Report on the State of the Art)' (2009) 97 *Georgia Law Journal* 803; Pierre Schlag, 'The Law Review Article' (2017) 88 *University of Colorado Law Review* 1043. Comp. with the idea of trope developed by Hayden White, *Tropics of Discourses: Essays in Cultural Criticism* (Johns Hopkins University Press, 1978) pp. 1–3.

[5] On how disciplines legitimize themselves, see Bruno Latour, *La Science en action. Introduction à la sociologie des sciences* (La Découverte, 2005) p. 382. Comp. Pierre Schlag, 'The Aesthetics of American Law' (2002) 115 *Harvard Law Review* 1047.

ordering epistemology that dictates the possible and the impossible in international law.[6]

The rest of this chapter is meant to spell out the various dimensions of the epistemology of the secret of international law as it is understood here. The chapter first unpacks the two necessities that compose the epistemology of the secret of international law, namely the necessity of secret content and the necessity of revelation (Section 1.1) before elaborating on the ordering performed by them (Section 1.2). This chapter ends with a few observations on how the epistemology of the secret of international law, as is understood here, distinguishes itself from an ideology (Section 1.3) and an economy (Section 1.4).

1.1 A Two-pronged Epistemology

As was indicated above, the epistemology of the secret is organized around two co-constitutive and synchronic necessities: the necessary presence of hidden, unknown, invisible content in the texts, practices, actors, effects, representations, past, etc. of international law (what is called here *the necessity of secret content*) and the necessity for international lawyers to reveal such hidden, unknown, invisible content (what is called here *the necessity of revelation*). This section unpacks these two components of the epistemology of the secret one after the other. The attention first turns to the necessity of secret content (Section 1.1.2) and then to the necessity of locating, unearthing, and revealing such hidden, unknown, invisible content (Section 1.1.3). Before shedding light on the various facets of the two necessities that compose the epistemology of the secret of international law, a few important conceptual remarks are in order (Section 1.1.1)

1.1.1 Preliminary Observations

Appreciating how the necessity of secret content and the necessity of revelation do what they respectively do requires that the way they relate to one another is preliminarily elucidated, which in turn calls for a terminological observation.

[6] Comp. with the notion of dark precursor (*précurseur sombre*) of Gilles Deleuze; see Gilles Deleuze, *Différence et répétition* (Presses Universitaires de France, 1968) pp. 156–157. On this notion, see the observations of Ian Buchanan, *Deleuzism* (Duke University Press, 2000) p. 5.

1.1.1.1 Two Synchronous, Coincident, and Mutually Constitutive Necessities

A first preliminary observation is warranted in relation to the way in which the two main components of the epistemology of the secret of international law – namely, the necessity of secret content and the necessity of revelation – relate to one another. It must be emphasized that these two necessities do not constitute two distinct, diachronic, and self-sufficient operations. They are synchronous, coincident, and mutually constitutive. Indeed, there cannot be a necessity of secret content without a necessity of revelation, for, as will be explained below, it is the revelation that creates the hidden, unknown, invisible content.[7] Conversely, there cannot be a necessity of revelation short of the postulation of some hidden, unknown, invisible content in the texts, practices, actors, effects, representations, past, etc. of international law because it is only as long as some hidden, unknown, invisible content is postulated that a necessity to reveal it arises.

It is also important to note that, although the two necessities composing the epistemology of the secret of international law are synchronous, coincident, and mutually supportive, the rest of this section, for didactic reasons, exposes the main patterns of thought of each of the two necessities composing the epistemology of the secret of international law one after the other.

1.1.1.2 Structure and Agency in the Epistemology of the Secret

Before the two necessities composing the epistemology of the secret of international law are unpacked, it must also be preliminarily emphasized that these two necessities cannot be differentiated by associating the necessity of secret content with a question of textual structure and the necessity to reveal such hidden, unknown, invisible content as a question of agency. This can be explained as follows. On the one hand, international lawyers are not autonomous and self-determining actors but are always caught in the epistemology of the secret of international law that makes them experience both the necessity of secret content in the texts, practices, actors, effects, representations, past, etc. of international law and the necessity of revealing such content.[8] On the other hand, the

[7] See infra Section 1.1.3.2.

[8] For some critical remarks on the limitations of the modern idea of an autonomous self, see Emmanuel Levinas, *De l'existence à l'existant* (Vrin, 2013) pp. 100–101; Frédéric Lordon, *La société des affects. Pour un structuralisme des passions* (Editions du Seuil, 2013) p. 274;

epistemology of the secret is no self-sufficient and self-operating textual structure, for it always needs to be set into motion and experienced by international lawyers.[9] To put it differently, in the epistemology of the secret of international law, the revealed (the secret content) and the revealer (the international lawyers) are necessary and co-constitutive components of the epistemology of the secret of international law.[10] This means that the epistemology of the secret of international law, although articulated around the two abovementioned necessities, is a very fluid epistemology where the necessity of secret content in the texts, practices, actors, effects, representations, past, etc. of international law and the necessity of revealing such hidden, unknown, invisible content can only be approached holistically.

1.1.1.3 The Epistemology of the Secret, the Hermeneutics of Suspicion, and Paranoid Reading

The two components of the epistemology of the secret of international law, and the way they work hand in hand, can be reminiscent of what has been called, in the theory of interpretation, the 'school of suspicion'[11] or the 'hermeneutics of suspicion'.[12] The latter refers to a specific attitude of

François Jullien, *La pensée chinoise. En vis-à-vis de la philosophie* (Gallimard, 2015) pp. 25–33; Michel Foucault, *Le Discours Philosophique* (Gallimard/Seuil, 2023) pp. 31–37. On the idea that cultural techniques determine the entire course of action and contradicts the widespread belief that only the subject can carry out actions and rule over things, see Cornelia Vismann, 'Cultural Techniques and Sovereignty' (2013) 30 *Theory, Culture & Society* 83. Comp. with the idea that the modern subject is whoever subjects oneself to the reign of critique, see Laurent de Sutter, *Superfaible. Penser aux XXIe siècle* (Climats, 2023) pp. 56–58.

[9] See Jacques Derrida, *Positions* (Editions de Minuit, 1972) pp. 40–41; See also the idea that performativity always comes with a certain enactment, see Judith Butler, *Notes toward a Performative Theory of Assembly* (Harvard University Press, 2018) pp. 31–32. See also Vincent Forray and Sébastien Pimont, *Décrire le droit . . . et le transformer. Essai sur la décriture du droit* (Dalloz, 2017) pp. 222–223.

[10] On how the revealed and the revealing are interwined in the act of revelation, see the remarks of Jean-Luc Nancy, *Hegel, L'inquiétude du négatif* (Galilée, 2018) p. 79.

[11] Paul Ricoeur, *De l'interprétation. Essai sur Freud* (Editions du Seuil, 1965) pp. 38 and 42–46.

[12] Paul Ricoeur, *Freud and Philosophy: An Essay on Interpretation*, trans. Denis Savage (Yale University Press, 1970) pp. 32–36; Jonathan Culler, *Literary Theory: A Very Short Introduction* (Oxford University Press, 1997) pp. 68–69; Gayatri Chakravorty Spivak, *In Other Worlds: Essays in Cultural Politics* (Routledge, 2006) p. 141; Rita Felski, *The Limits of Critique* (University of Chicago Press, 2015) pp. 1–5. In legal theory and international legal theory, the notion of hermeneutics of suspicion has been given a rather different twist, for it refers to the attitude whereby one interprets one's opponents'

distrust whereby an interpreter or a reader continuously experiences a cartesian[13] moment of doubt towards the truthfulness of the content that is made available to her by a given text.[14] Although the necessity of secret content composing the epistemology of the secret and the idea of suspicion both refer to the possibility of hidden, unknown, invisible content in the object being interpreted, this book, however, prefers the idea of epistemology of the secret to that of hermeneutics of suspicion.[15] Indeed, it is submitted here that the latter puts too much emphasis on the attitude of the reader or interpreter and hence on agency. For sure, as was previously indicated,[16] the epistemology of the secret of international law that is discussed here is put into motion by international lawyers. Yet the idea of suspicion obfuscates the extent to which the necessity of secret content is not only a posture of international lawyers but is also *a condition of international legal texts.*[17] In other words, the necessary presence of hidden, unknown, invisible content in the texts, practices, actors, effects, representations, past, etc. of international law is a condition of any international legal text as much as it is a posture of international lawyers. This is why the more encapsulating and less agency-focused notion of epistemology of the secret is preferred to that of hermeneutics or school of suspicion. All in all, the notion of the epistemology of the secret, as opposed to that of hermeneutics of suspicion,

arguments to be ideologically motivated wrong answers to legal questions. See, e.g., Duncan Kennedy, 'The Hermeneutic of Suspicion in Contemporary American Legal Thought' (2014) 25 *Law Critique* 91. See also Anne Orford, *International Law and the Politics of History* (Cambridge University Press, 2021) pp. 5–6 (for whom the hermeneutics of suspicion refers to the view that legal scholars as partisan actors who interpret legal rules, texts, or processes politically in contrast to empiricist historical research that can offer verifiable and evidence-based interpretations of past legal material). See also the remarks of Fleur Johns, 'Critical International Legal Theory', in Jeffrey L. Dunoff and Mark A. Pollack (eds.), *International Legal Theory: Foundations and Frontiers* (Cambridge University Press, 2022) pp. 3, 133, and 150.

13 This association between the hermeneutics of suspicion and the cartesian doubt is made by Ricoeur, *De l'interprétation* p. 43.

14 Comp. with the idea of suspicion theorized by Nathalie Sarraute, *Tropisms and the Age of Suspicion* (Calder, 1963). For her, suspicion is that of the reader towards the realism of bourgeois novels and the alleged worldliness of the novel's central character.

15 Foucault speaks of the tendency of hermeneutics to make one think that there is language elsewhere than in language. See Michel Foucault, *Dits et écrits, I (1954–1975)* (Gallimard, 2001) p. 593.

16 See Section 1.1.1.2.

17 See the idea of George Steiner that speaking always conceals and leaves things unspoken. See George Steiner, *After Babel: Aspects of Language and Translation*, 3rd edn (Oxford Univeristy Press, 1998) pp. 47, 231, and 240.

allows one to provide a more nuanced and multifaceted account of the discursive practices of international lawyers.[18]

It is noteworthy that the notion of hermeneutics of suspicion has sometimes been described and deplored in critical and queer literary theory as amounting to a mode of 'paranoid reading'.[19] In such literature, paranoid reading has been construed as an attitude towards a text that builds on negative affects, a faith in the possibility of exposure, as well as a constant attempt to ward off humiliation and bad surprises, with a view to deciphering what it is that the text secretly does.[20] Such idea of paranoid reading warrants a terminological observation, given the common denominator it shares with the notion of epistemology of the secret as is understood here. It is submitted here that the idea of paranoid reading, albeit very compelling to describe the hermeneutical presumption of hidden, unknown, invisible content that composes the epistemology of the secret of international law and which is shared with the abovementioned hermeneutics of suspicion, similarly foregrounds too much the attitude of the reader compared to what the text itself does. As is construed here, the epistemology of the secret of international law cannot be reduced to an attitude of the reader but also amounts to a condition of international legal texts. This is why the notion of epistemology of the secret is preferred to that of paranoid reading.

1.1.2 The Necessity of Secret Content

The first of the two necessities composing the epistemology of the secret of international law is the necessary presence of hidden, unknown, invisible content in the texts, practices, actors, effects, representations, past, etc. of international law. This is what is called here *the necessity of secret content*.[21] The necessity of secret content corresponds to the

[18] I owe this argument to one of the anonymous peer-reviewers.

[19] See the criticisms of the hermeneutics of suspicion (which she calls a mode a paranoid reading) by Eve Kosofsky Sedgwick, 'Paranoid Reading and Reparative Reading; or, You're So Paranoid, You Probably Think This Introduction Is about You', in Eve Kosofsky Sedgwick (ed.), *Novel Gazing: Queer Readings in Fiction* (Duke University Press, 1997) pp. 1–38. See the comments of Heather Love, 'Truth and Consequences: On Paranoid Reading and Reparative Reading' (2010) 52 *Criticism* (2010) 235.

[20] Contra Sedgwick, 'Paranoid Reading and Reparative Reading' p. 19.

[21] Comp. with the idea of a metaphysics of presence, that is, the idea that signs are always calling on a pre-existing meaning that they make permanently present. See Jacques Derrida, *De la Grammatologie* (Editions de Minuit, 1967) p. 103; Jacques Derrida, *Marges de la Philosophie* (Editions de Minuit, 1972) pp. 187–188.

permanent postulation of a *presence*. By virtue of such postulation, any of international law's text, practice, actors, effect, representations, past, etc. is supposed to be inhabited by content that is hidden, unknown, invisible to international lawyers.[22] Caught in the necessity of secret content, judges, counsels, experts, legal advisers, scholars, all come to presuppose the necessary presence of secrets in the texts, practices, actors, effects, representations, past, etc. of international law.[23]

The various patterns of thought at work in the necessity of secret content are the postulations of a content that is meaningful (Section 1.1.2.1), in permanent surplus (Section 1.1.2.2), truthful (Section 1.1.2.3), textual (Section 1.1.2.4) and prefigured (Section 1.1.2.5). They are examined in turn.

1.1.2.1 A Meaningful Content

The necessity of secret content at the heart of the epistemology of the secret of international law is premised on the idea that the texts, practices, actors, effects, representations, past, etc. of international law all have a meaningful content, albeit some of it is hidden and ought to be revealed. Ascribing a meaningful content to a text, a form, a practice, a representation, an actor, a past, etc., as the necessity of secret content does, is actually a very common epistemological posture in international legal thought and practice.[24] Such pattern of thought is what I have called elsewhere the meaning-centrism of international legal thought and practice.[25] It corresponds to a well-known and widely studied intellectual attitude that is also named logocentrism.[26] According to such posture,

22 Comp. with the Cornelia Vismann's idea that the authority of the archive in which law grounds itself exists primarily in its invisibility and immateriality, which it creates through secretion and exclusion from the repository. See Cornelia Vismann, *Files: Law and Media, Technology*, trans. Geoffrey Winthrop-Young (Stanford University Press, 2008).

23 Comp. with the claim of Rita Felski for whom suspicion has been routinized in modern thought. See Felski, *The Limits of Critique* p. 47.

24 It must be acknowledged that departing from meaning-centrism was not necessary for these critical works to fulfil their ambitions. For instance, one does not need to de-necessitate meaning-centrism to show the false necessities that these forms induce and rely on or to shed light on their contingency.

25 I have examined this pattern of thought elsewhere. See Jean d'Aspremont, *After Meaning: The Sovereignty of Forms in International Law* (Edward Elgar, 2021). See also Jean d'Aspremont, 'Two Attitudes towards Textuality in International Law: The Battle for Dualism' (2022) 42 *Oxford Journal of Legal Studies* 963.

26 On the idea of logocentrism, see Derrida, *De la Grammatologie* pp. 13, 21–23; Jacques Derrida, *L'Ecriture et la différence* (Editions du Seuil, 1967) p. 23. Such logocentrism of

international law's texts, forms, practices, representations, actors, past, etc. are thought as necessarily having a meaningful content that is always the cause and the origin of such texts, forms, practices, representations, actors, past, etc. It entails that the texts, forms, practices, representations, actors, past, etc. of international law are made of an aggregate of things, ideas, norms, facts, etc., which constitute their meaningful content.

It is probably not difficult to fathom why such postulation of a meaningful content is key to the epistemology of the secret of international law as a whole. In fact, were the texts, practices, actors, effects, representations, past, etc. of international law thought as having either no content at all or no meaningful content, there would not be any secret to reveal for international lawyers and hence no epistemology of the secret possible. This is why the epistemology of the secret of international law can be understood as yet another offspring of international law's more general meaning-centrism.[27]

Whilst the postulation of a meaningful content in all of international law's texts, forms, practices, representations, actors, past, etc. proves a rather intuitive epistemological move, especially for meaning-centric international lawyers, it is important to highlight that such postulation has not gone uncontested. For instance, it has been argued that texts, forms, and simply any representation always postpone meaningful content and defer the latter by constantly passing on the job of signification to other texts, forms, and representations, thereby condemning meaningful content to be permanently absent from forms, texts, and representations.[28] It has also been argued that the postulation of a meaningful content amounts to the failure of the text, form, or representation

Western thought has also been captured through the idea of the eternal journey of the sign as a representative of what it is supposed to represent. See Catherine Malabou and Jacques Derrida, *La Contre-Allée* (La Quinzaine Littéraire, 1999) pp. 44–45. See also Jullien, *La pensée chinoise* pp. 115–119.

[27] Elsewhere I have argued that the meaning-centrism of international law has entailed three main modes of thinking, namely originist thinking, deliverability thinking, and reifying thinking. See d'Aspremont, *After Meaning* pp. 10–14.

[28] Derrida, *De la Grammatologie* pp. 11–126; Derrida, *Marges de la Philosophie* pp. 1–29; Jacques Derrida, *L'écriture et la différence* (Editions du Seuil, 1967) p. 411. On this aspect of the work of Derrida, see the remarks of Peter Salmon, *An Event Perhaps* (Verso, 2020) p. 12. See also Geoffrey Bennington, *Jacques Derrida* (Editions du Seuil, 1991) p. 56. Comp. with Roland Barthes, *Le bruissement de la langue. Essais critiques IV* (Seuil, 1984); Roland Barthes, *S/Z* (Editions du Seuil, 1970) pp. 9–11. For an earlier, albeit less radical, contestation of the idea that language is the instrument of a pre-existing thought, see Edward Sapir, *Language: An Introduction to the Study of Speech* (Ishi Press, 2014) pp. 14–17.

concerned,[29] thereby justifying that one always refuses to seek the secret content of a text.[30] This book is not the place to review such objections. The point made here is rather that such contestations of the postulation of a meaningful content in forms, texts, and representations have not sufficed to seriously challenge meaning-centrism in international legal thought and practice and all the intellectual attitudes that revolve around it. In that sense, the epistemology of the secret of international law can be construed as an offspring of the resilience of meaning-centrism in international legal thought and practice.

1.1.2.2 A Permanent Surplus of Meaningful Content

The necessity of secret content at the heart of the epistemology of the secret of international law does not only rest on the postulation of a meaningful content in international law's texts, forms, practices, representations, actors, past, etc. but also on the idea that there always is more meaningful content to be found than what has already been ascertained, found, and revealed. In fact, from the perspective of the necessity of secret content discussed here, international lawyers are never satisfied with the meaningful content that they read, see, and locate in all of international law's texts, forms, practices, representations, actors, past, etc. because what they read, see, perceive, or place therein can never provide them with a full picture of that meaningful content. For them, just like for speleologists,[31] there is always more meaningful content than what is already known.

Interestingly, this permanent surplus of meaningful content which international law's texts, forms, practices, representations, actors, past, etc. provide beyond what international lawyers can read, and perceive is a surplus without cause. This means that, by virtue of the necessity of secret content, there is no causal explanation for such permanent surplus. International lawyers experience the necessary presence of a surplus of meaningful content without experiencing the need to elucidate why such surplus is not included in what they already read, see, locate in international law's texts, forms, practices, representations, actors, past, etc. In that sense, it does not matter for the epistemology of the secret of

[29] Barthes, *Le bruissement de la langue* p. 109.

[30] Roland Barthes, *Critique et vérité* (Editions du Seuil, 1999) p. 78; Roland Barthes, 'La mort de l'auteur', in R. Barthes (ed.), *Le Bruissement de la langue* (Editions du Seuil, 1984) p. 66.

[31] I borrow this metaphor of the speleologist from de Sutter, *Superfaible* p. 324.

international law whether the secrets of the latter's texts, forms, practices, representations, actors, past, etc. have been caused by some kind of forgetfulness that made them fall into oblivion or whether they are the result of a calculated concealment.[32] The epistemology of the secret is a type of epistemology that is oblivious to the possible causes[33] and origins[34] for there to be hidden meaningful content in international law's texts, forms, practices, representations, actors, past, etc.

1.1.2.3 A Truthful Content

It is important to stress that the hidden, unknown, invisible content located in the texts, practices, actors, effects, representations, past, etc. of international law by virtue of this necessity always constitutes *true* content. In other words, from the perspective of the necessity of secret content, there is not such a thing as an untrue hidden, unknown, invisible content. The necessity of secret content accordingly corresponds to the archaeologist's [35] postulation that what is hidden and to be extracted is a form of truth.[36]

It must be immediately stressed that the truthfulness of the hidden, unknown, invisible content that is postulated by virtue of the necessity of secret content never pre-exists the postulation and revelation of such content. Indeed, it is the postulation and revelation of the hidden, unknown, invisible content of international law's texts, forms, practices,

32 Comp. with the distinction between secret (secretum) and occultation (occulta), in Anne Dufourmantelle, *Défense du secret* (Payot & Rivages, 2019) pp. 34–35.

33 This is very unusual, at least in Western thought, for thinking has often been, since Ancient Greece, as a thinking about causalities. And so is understood what stands as real, namely as something causally explained. On this feature of Western thought, see Jullien, *La pensée chinoise* pp. 16–23.

34 This is a rather spectacular feature, for legal thought is commonly articulated around a very originist type of thinking. Originist thinking refers here to the common understanding of forms, texts, and representations as necessarily having an origin, an author, and a context of making. Said differently, originist thinking corresponds to the experience of a necessity to search for an origin of forms, texts, representations. See gen. Derrida, *Marges de la Philosophie* p. 13; Barthes, *Le bruissement de la langue* pp. 63–69. See also Foucault, *Dits et écrits, I* p. 1007. See also Cornelia Vismann, 'The Archive and the Beginning of Law', in Peter Goodrich, Florian Hoffmann, Michel Rosenfeld and Cornelia Vismann (eds.), *Derrida and Legal Philosophy* (Palgrave, Macmillan, 2008) p. 41.

35 I borrow the metaphor of the archeologists from Rita Felski who speaks of the 'critic-as-archaeologist' who digs deep into a text in order to retrieve a concealed or camouflaged truth. See Felski, *The Limits of Critique* p. 7.

36 Comp. with the argument of Cornelia Vissman according to whom archives, once made invisible, perform a truth-making function in relation to law's self-emergence and self-grounding. See gen. Vismann, *Files.*

representations, actors, past, etc. that make it a truth.[37] Before postulating and revealing such hidden, unknown, invisible content, there is no truth yet but only a postulation that there is a surplus of meaningful content. In that sense, the epistemology of the secret, by virtue of the necessity that there is true content hidden in international law's texts, forms, practices, representations, actors, past, etc. can be characterized as a *truth-making epistemology*.[38] This is the case even if such truth-making is simultaneously a truth-unmaking, that is the repudiation of socially accepted truth by the postulation and revelation of new true content.[39]

That the epistemology of the secret of international law, by virtue of the necessity of secret content, boils down to a truth-making epistemology is no coincidence. In fact, truth-making has long been the primary and most legitimate mode of thinking, especially in the West.[40] Be it as a discourse,[41] a regime,[42] a programme,[43] a system,[44] an ideology,[45] a ritual,[46] a geography,[47] a theatre,[48] a policy,[49] truth is what has long been governing human thought in that part of world. Even though modes and techniques to produce truth have fluctuated over centuries,[50] truth has

[37] Foucault, *Le Discours Philosophique* p. 15.

[38] See the remarks of Jacques Derrida, see Jacques Derrida, *Hospitalité. Volume 1 (Séminaire 1995–1996)* (Editions du Seuil, 2021) p. 211.

[39] See the remarks of Felski, *The Limits of Critique* p. 1. In the same vein, Laurent de Sutter, 'Pour une clinique', in Laurent de Sutter (ed.), *Postcritique* (Presses Universitaires de France, 2019) p. 216. For Foucault, critique is not about seeking to unveil the truth but to shed light on how truth is generated by power and how the former and the latter reinforces one another while questioning the policies of truths practiced in a given society. See Michel Foucault, *Qu'est-ce que la critique?* (Vrin, 2015) p. 39.

[40] Jullien, *La pensée chinoise* p. 258. For further insights on the kinship between the Greek and Christian idea of truth and the epistemology of the secret, see infra Section 2.1.

[41] Michel Foucault, *Dits et écrits, II* (Gallimard, 2001) p. 312.

[42] Michel Foucault, *Naissance de la biopolitique. Cours au Collège de France (1978–1979)* (Gallimard/Seuil, 2004) p. 37.

[43] Paul Veyne, *Les Grecs ont-ils cru à leurs mythes? Essai sur l'imagination constituante* (Editions du Seuil, 1983) p. 137.

[44] Michel Foucault, *Leçons sur la volonté de savoir. Cours au Collège de France 1970–1971* (Seuil/Gallimard, 2011) p. 227.

[45] Veyne, *Les Grecs ont-ils cru à leurs mythes?* p. 128.

[46] Foucault, *Leçons sur la volonté de savoir* p. 227.

[47] Foucault, *Dits et écrits, I (1954–1975)* p. 1561.

[48] Foucault, *Dits et écrits, II* p. 572.

[49] Foucault, *Qu'est-ce que la critique?* p. 39.

[50] See gen. Michel de Certeau, *L'écriture de l'histoire* (Gallimard, 1975) pp. 27–28; Michel Foucault, *L'Herméneutique du Sujet. Cours au Collège de France, 1981–1982* (Editions du Seuil, 2001) p. 19. On the modern assimilation between truth and fact, see Pierre Legendre, *De la Société comme Texte. Linéaments d'une Anthropologie dogmatique*

always been the most important driver of thought and order.[51] The epistemology of the secret of international law is yet another by-product of such widespread and omnipresent truth-centred modes of thinking.[52]

1.1.2.4 A Textual Content

To further unpack the very content that is postulated as being hidden in international law's texts, forms, practices, representations, actors, past, etc. by virtue of the necessity of secret content examined here, a very elementary observation about the textuality of international law must be formulated. It is submitted here that texts[53] are where the practices, actors, effects, representations, past, etc. of international law find their materiality.[54] To put it differently, international law and what it does to the world can only be apprehended through the textual traces it leaves.[55] As a result, engaging with the texts, practices, actors, effects, representations, past, etc. of international law is always a venture into texts.[56] Fighting, reforming, contesting, defending international law are textual

(Fayard, 2001 p. 93. On the elevation of science as the main discourse about truth, see Foucault, *Dits et écrits, II* pp. 158 and 312.

51 Jullien, *La pensée chinoise* p. 258.

52 On the idea that, in the West, Nietzsche offered the very first serious charge against the idea of truth, see Foucault, *Dits et écrits, I (1954–1975)* p. 634. Foucault, *Dits et écrits, II* pp. 30–31. On the idea that Nietzsche showed how science itself has failed to meet its own truth requirement, see Jean-François Lyotard, *La Condition Postmoderne* (Editions de Minuit, 1979) p. 65. On the idea that even poststructuralism has not been able to emancipate us from the idea of truth, see Felski, *The Limits of Critique* pp. 55–57.

53 Text should not be reduced to material inscriptions. Texts are also in the oral language. On the idea of non-material inscriptions, see Jacques Derrida, *Papier Machine* (Galilée, 2001) p. 384. On the idea that language, even oral language, is a type of writing, see Malabou and Derrida, *La Contre-Allée* pp. 73–75. See also the remarks of Peter Goodrich, 'Europe in America: Grammatology, Legal Studies, and the Politics of Transmission' (2001) 101 *Columbia Law Review* (2001) 2033 at 2069–2084; see also Legendre, *De la Société comme Texte*.

54 See gen. Jean d'Aspremont, 'International Law as a Crisis Discourse: The Peril of Wordlessness', in Makane Mbengue and Jean d'Aspremont (eds.), *Crisis Narratives in International Law* (Brill, 2021) pp. 69–84. On the idea of texts as spaces, see Roland Barthes, *L'aventure sémiologique* (Editions du Seuil, 1985) p. 13. See also Barthes, *Le bruissement de la langue* p. 56; Barthes, *S/Z* pp. 10–11.

55 See gen. Legendre, *De la Société comme Texte*. See also d'Aspremont, *After Meaning*. See also gen. Jean d'Aspremont, 'Wording in International Law' (2012) 25 *Leiden Journal of International Law* 575.

56 On the idea that the world is made of all the references enabled by the texts one has read, see Paul Ricoeur, *Temps et récit, Volume 1, L'intrigue et le récit historique* (Editions du Seuil, 1983) p. 17. On the idea that reading is what allows one to experience the real, see Sophie Rabau, *L'intertextualité* (Flammarion, 2002) p. 31.

experiences.[57] Such textual materiality of international law and of any engagement therewith bear important consequences for the way in which the necessity of secret content materializes. Indeed, texts are the very site where the presence of hidden, unknown, invisible content is posited. Said differently, texts are where one finds the traces of the practices, actors, effects, representations, past, etc. of international law. It will be shown later that texts are not only where the postulated hidden, unknown, invisible content is located but are also what the revelation of such content will produce and leave us with.[58]

1.1.2.5 A Prefigured Content

A final dimension of the necessity of secret content composing the epistemology of the secret of international law must be mentioned, namely the prefigured character of what is held as being hidden.[59] In fact, there are only a certain number of possible contents that can be located in the texts, practices, actors, effects, representations, past, etc. of international law by virtue of the necessity of secret content. More specifically, the hidden, unknown, invisible content that international lawyers can possibly locate in the texts, practices, actors, effects, representations, past, etc. of international law is always pre-determined by what can be apprehended through the linguistic and conceptual categories that inhabit international legal thought and practice.[60] Said differently, the content that is posited as being hidden can never be incommensurable to international lawyers' thought categories and unintelligible to them: it always is *at home* and *from home*.[61] This means that

[57] In the same vein, Marielle Macé, *Façons de lire, manières d'être* (Gallimard, 2022) p. 34.

[58] See infra Section 1.1.3.3.

[59] I am thankful to the anonymous peer-reviewer who suggested that I use 'prefigured' instead of 'predetermined'.

[60] On the idea that concepts are deployed as identity checks, see Theodor W. Adorno, *Negative Dialectics* (Continuum, 2007) p. 5. See also Henri Bergson, *La pensée et le mouvant* (Flammarion, 2014) pp. 229 and 240; Gaston Bachelard, *Le nouvel esprit scientifique* (Presses Universitaires de France, 1934) pp. 9 and 15–16.

[61] See the remarks of Jacques Derrida, see Derrida, *Hospitalité* p. 212. This is a claim very common in comparative legal thought. See Pierre Legrand, 'The Same and the Different', in Pierre Legrand and Roderick Munday (eds.), *Comparative Legal Studies: Traditions and Transitions* (Cambridge University Press, 2003) pp. 307–308; Gunter Frankenberg, 'Critical Comparisons: Re-thinking Comparative Law' (1985) 26 *Harvard International Law Journal* 411, esp. pp. 412 and 423; Horatia Muir Watt, 'Globalization and Comparative Law', in Mathias Reimann and Reinhard Zimmermann (eds.), *The Oxford Handbook of Comparative Law* (OUP, 2007), p. 603.

anything that cannot be related back to international lawyers' practical, linguistic, conceptual, cognitive, cultural, imaginary, and emotional universe can never constitute content hidden to them.[62]

The prefigured character of the content posited as being hidden in the texts, practices, actors, effects, representations, past, etc. of international law is certainly not surprising. This aspect of the necessity of secret content is a manifestation of the common finding that language is the seat of any experience of the world and that the visible as well as the experienceable are determined by the sayable.[63] The necessity of secret content is no exception to that. Only what belongs to the practical, linguistic, conceptual, cognitive, cultural, imaginary, and emotional universe of international lawyers can ever qualify as hidden, unknown, invisible content for the sake of the epistemology of the secret examined here.

It must be acknowledged that this dimension of the necessity of secret content, just like the determination of the visible and of the experienceable by the sayable, is often intangible to those that postulate the presence of hidden, unknown, invisible content in the texts, practices, actors, effects, representations, past, etc. of international law. Indeed, international lawyers, when positing that content is being hidden from them, commonly believe in the unbound descriptability[64] of such texts, practices, actors, effects, representations, past, etc., that is, in the unlimited character of the world of possible secrets they can find. That international lawyers are oblivious to the prefigured character of the hidden, unknown, invisible content that can possibly be found in international law's international law's texts, forms, practices, representations, actors, past, etc.

[62] See the remarks of Derrida, *De la Grammatologie* p. 14.

[63] On the constitution of the visible by the sayable, see gen. Legendre, *De la Société comme Texte* p. 17; Gilles Deleuze, *La philosophie critique de Kant* (Presses Universitaires de France, 1963) pp. 22–23; Jacques Rancière, *L'inconscient esthétique* (Galilée, 2001) pp. 21–22; Foucault, *Le Discours Philosophique* p. 248; François Jullien, *L'incommensurable* (L'observatoire, 2022) p. 32. On the idea that any language creates a specific world and geography of remembrance, see Steiner, *After Babel* p. xiv. Comp. with Régis Debray who claims that the moment one stares at the world, one orders the visible and the experience, see Régis Debray, *Vie et mort de l'image* (Gallimard, 1992) p. 56. On the idea that, since the advent of modernity, the visible governs the knowable, see Michel de Certeau, *L'invention du quotidien. 1. Arts de faire* (Gallimard, 1990) p. 272. On the notion of sovereign power of the eye, see Michel Foucault, *Naissance de la clinique* (Presses Universitaires de France, 1963) pp. 11 and 20.

[64] On this notion, see Foucault, *Naissance de la clinique* p. 165.

illustrates the extent to which the epistemology of the secret of international law hides its "legislative power"[65] over the minds of international lawyers.

1.1.3 *The Necessity of Revelation*

The second necessity composing the epistemology of the secret of international law is called *the necessity of revelation*. This refers to the necessity experienced by international lawyers to reveal the hidden, unknown, invisible content that they have posited as being necessarily present in the texts, practices, actors, effects, representations, past, etc. of international law. According to this second necessity, any hidden, unknown, invisible content that they have postulated as being present in the texts, practices, actors, effects, representations, past, etc. of international law must be disclosed for the sake of producing a truth about international law and the world. To put it differently, international lawyers, once they find themselves in the presence of hidden, unknown, invisible content, feel the inescapable necessity to discontinue the self-evidences that have, in the absence of the upcoming act of revelation, dominated international legal thought and practice until then.[66] In that sense, whilst the necessity of secret content corresponds to the necessity of a presence, the necessity of revelation amounts to the necessity of *an event*, that is, the inevitable act of revelation that is about to take place given the presence of hidden,

[65] The expression is from Gilles Deleuze, see Deleuze, *La philosophie critique de Kant* p. 14. See also the remarks of Giorgio Agamben, see Giorgio Agamben, *La puissance de la pensée* (Editions Payot & Rivages, 2021) pp. 30–31; Barthes, *Le bruissement de la langue* pp. 12–18. Bourdieu coined the idea of 'miscognition' (méconnaissance) to seek to capture this induced misunderstanding and self-obfuscation of power, see Pierre Bourdieu, 'A Lecture on the Lecture', in Pierre Bourdieu, *In Other Words: Essays towards a Reflexive Sociology* (Stanford University Press, 1990) pp. 177, 183, and 189. See also Pierre Bourdieu, *Langage et pouvoir symbolique* (Editions du Seuil, 2001) p. 210.

[66] On the idea that the real nowadays is no longer a divine secret that is received but is the product of an event, see Michel de Certeau, *Histoire et psychanalyse entre science et fiction* (Gallimard, 2016) p. 72. Comp. with the idea that understanding always is an event, see Hans-Georg Gadamer, *Truth and Method* (Bloomsbury, 2013) p. 418. On the idea that texts are events, see Edward Said, *The World, the Text, and the Critic* (Harvard University Press, 1983) p. 4. On the idea that a discourse is made of discursive events, see Michel Foucault, *L'ordre du discours* (Gallimard, 1971) p. 59; Foucault, *Dits et écrits, I (1954–1975)* p. 733; Foucault, *Le Discours Philosophique* p. 246; Noam Chomsky and Michel Foucault, *The Chomsky-Foucault Debate on Human Nature* (The New Press, 2006) p. 146.

unknown, invisible content in the texts, practices, actors, effects, representations, past, etc. of international law.[67]

It must be recalled here that the necessity of revelation is not distinct from the necessity of secret content in conceptual, practical, and diachronic terms. In other words, the experience of the necessity of revelation does not follow mechanically the experience of the necessity of secret content. Indeed, and this constitutes a very central aspect of the necessity of revelation that ought to be emphasized right away, the act of revelation is constitutive of the hidden, unknown, invisible content that had been postulated as being present in the texts, practices, actors, effects, representations, past, etc. of international law. The content held to be hidden is actually created at the very moment it is disclosed by the act of revelation. In other words, the content that was held to have been hidden in the past is made hidden, unknown, invisible content by the very act that makes it known and strips its of its secrecy. This is why, as was already indicated, the two necessities composing the epistemology of the secret of international law, namely the necessity of secret content and the necessity of revelation, can be construed as being synchronous, coincident, and mutually constitutive.[68]

The following sections examine the various dimensions of the act of revelation that is made necessary by virtue of the necessity of revelation, namely, the act of revelation as corresponding to an obligation (Section 1.1.3.1), the act of revelation as production (Section 1.1.3.2), and the act of revelation as inscription (Section 1.1.3.3). It is important to highlight that the order in which these various dimensions of the act of revelation are discussed in the following sections does not represent any actual sequence in their experience by in international lawyers when engaging with international law but only follow didactic choices.

1.1.3.1 Revelation as an Obligation to Truth

By virtue of the necessity of revelation that composes the epistemology of the secret of international law, international lawyers come to feel bound to reveal the hidden, unknown, invisible content of the texts, practices,

67 Michel Foucault defines the idea of eventalization as a 'a breach of self-evidence', which means 'making visible a singularity at places where there is a temptation to invoke a historical constant, an immediate anthropological trait, or an obviousness which imposes itself uniformly on all', see Michel Foucault, 'Question of Method', in Graham Burchell, Colin Gordon, and Peter Miller (eds.), *The Foucault Effect: Studies in Governmentality* (University of Chicago Press, 1991) p. 76.

68 See supra Section 1.1.1.1.

actors, effects, representations, past, etc. of international law. The necessity of revelation thus boils down to the experience of a commitment to telling an untold truth about international law.[69] It can be described as *an obligation to truth.*[70]

Provided that the revelation proves socially successful and that what is revealed is accepted as true by one's peers,[71] such obligation of revelation can be experienced as highly satisfactory by those who are committed to it. Indeed, the constant pursuit for the revelation of hidden, unknown, invisible content about international law and the world that is produced by the obligation of revelation can bring about an experience of liberation by those yielding to it. Indeed, the revelation can make one feel that one liberates oneself of all the lies told about international law and to which the revelation comes to put an end. Ironically, it is in emancipating international law and themselves from such lies that international lawyers turn themselves to the simple subjects of an epistemology that constantly makes them experience an obligation to reveal the secrets of the texts, practices, actors, effects, representations, past, etc. of international law.[72]

The foregoing indicates that, notwithstanding the satisfaction and the feeling of emancipation it can generate, the act of revelation, as an obligation, comes with a certain violence for it permanently forces international lawyers to reveal secrets about international law and the world.[73] By virtue of this specific experience, international lawyers are never left in peace. For them, the texts, practices, actors, effects, representations, past, etc. of international law cannot be simply contemplated but must be permanently scrutinized for the sake of revealing their secrets. It could even be said that the obligation of revelation makes the

[69] On the idea that power is not exercised through prohibitions and repressions, see Michel Foucault, *Histoire de la Sexualité 1. La volonté de savoir* (Gallimard, 1976) pp. 57 and 151; Foucault, *Dits et écrits, II* pp. 148–149. See also Michel Foucault, *'Il faut défendre la société'. Cours au Collège de France, 1976* (Gallimard, 1997) p. 18.

[70] The idea of obligation to truth (*obligation de vérité*) is borrow from Foucault, *Dits et écrits, II* p. 176; Foucault, *'Il faut défendre la société'* p. 22.

[71] For some general remarks, see d'Aspremont, 'Wording in International Law' p. 575. See also Olivier Corten, *Sociologies du droit* (Dalloz, 2023) pp. 118–135, 177–195, and 207–264.

[72] Comp. with the irony that Foucault associated with sexual emancipation and sexual desire, see Foucault, *Histoire de la Sexualité 1* pp. 207 and 211.

[73] On the idea that there is always a violence in the sign for the latter forces us to search and never leaves us in peace, see Gilles Deleuze, *Proust et les signes* (Presses Universitaires de France, 1964) p. 20.

epistemology of the secret of international law a fascist[74] epistemology, for it forces international lawyers to constantly speak about the secrets of international law.

1.1.3.2 Revelation as Production of an Invisible-Instantly-Made-Visible

The act of revelation called for by the necessity of revelation is an act of production. This is key in understanding the functioning of the epistemology of the secret of international law as well as the way in which the necessity of secret content and the necessity of revelation work hand in hand and synchronously.[75] Claiming that the act of revelation is an act of production means that, before the revelation, there is no pre-existing hidden, unknown, invisible content awaiting its revelation. The hidden, unknown, invisible content of the texts, practices, actors, effects, representations, past, etc. of international law does not precede its revelation but is produced by it. In that sense, the hidden, unknown, invisible content posited as present in the texts, practices, actors, effects, representations, past, etc. of international law does not have any actuality until they are produced by the act of revelation, which is the very act that invents the secrets concerned.[76] In that sense, *the act of revelation precedes the hidden, unknown, invisible content that it produces.*[77]

The act of revelation is also generative of the secrecy of that content. Although this may look paradoxical, it is the act of revelation that makes the content hidden, unknown, and invisible. In fact, it is only once the hidden, unknown, invisible content has been revealed that it becomes an actual secret. More precisely, the hidden, unknown, invisible content, as hidden, unknown, invisible content, is always born dead, for the act of revelation that produces it is also the act that make it cease to be secret.

[74] I borrow this analogy with fascism from Roland Barthes, see Roland Barthes, 'Lecture in Inauguration of the Chair of Literary Semiology, Collège de France, January 7, 1977', trans. Richard Howard (Collège de France, 1979), pp. 3–16. See also the remarks of Jean-Jacques Lecercle, *De l'interpellation. Sujet, langue, idéologie* (Editions Amsterdam, 2019) p. 90.

[75] See supra Section 1.1.1.1.

[76] On the idea that secrets are produced, see Dufourmantelle, *Défense du secret* pp. 20, 36, 49, and 113; Rancière, *L'inconscient esthétique* p. 22. See also Foucault, *Dits et écrits, II* pp. 554 and 565; Foucault, *Dits et écrits, I (1954–1975)* p. 1562; Foucault, *Histoire de la Sexualité 1* p. 33.

[77] On the idea that truth is produced, see Deleuze, *Proust et les signes* p. 171; Foucault, *Dits et écrits, I (1954–1975)* p. 1562; Foucault, *Dits et écrits, II* pp. 158 and 404; Veyne, *Les Grecs ont-ils cru à leurs mythes?* p. 12.

To put it differently, the revelation does not reveal what was invisible to the international lawyers until the act of revelation but create that invisible content at the moment it makes it visible. The act of revelation is thus an act that simultaneously makes and unmakes the hidden, unknown, invisible content of the texts, practices, actors, effects, representations, past, etc. of international law. In short, the act of revelation always creates *an invisible-instantly-made-visible*.

A – possibly polemic – metaphor can be mobilized to further emphasize the produced character of the hidden, the unknown, the invisible that is postulated by international lawyers by virtue of the epistemology of the secret: since the hidden is always produced for the sake of its revelation, international legal thought and practice could be seen as working as the porn industry. What is held as being happening behind closed doors is staged for the sake of its revelation through screening. In that sense, international lawyers' mass production of speech materials on the hidden, the unknown, and the invisible resemble the mass production of movies in the contemporary porn industry.[78]

Like any act of production, the act of revelation must follow certain protocols. Indeed, producing truth, especially since the modern collapse of the idea that truth is received,[79] commonly requires the compliance with pre-determined methods or rules.[80] The same goes for the revelation of hidden, unknown, invisible content under the regime of secret of international law. Only the use of accepted methods and protocols will allow international lawyers to reveal hidden, unknown, invisible content that can be held true.[81] Unsurprisingly, the potential to produce some kind of truth through the revelation of hidden, unknown, invisible content will also hinge on the social, symbolic, and linguistic capital of

78 I borrow this metaphor from Laurent de Sutter, see de Sutter, *Superfaible* p. 279.

79 On the idea that truth is produced, see Foucault, *Dits et écrits, I (1954–1975)* p. 1562; Foucault, *Dits et écrits, II* pp. 158 and 404; Deleuze, *Proust et les signes* p. 171; Veyne, *Les Grecs ont-ils cru à leurs mythes* p. 12.

80 Legendre, *De la Société comme Texte* p. 19; Foucault, *Dits et écrits, II* pp. 31, 113, and 407.

81 On methods as constituting a socially constrained routine, see Jean d'Aspremont, 'International Legal Methods: Working for a Tragic and Cynical Routine', in Rossana Deplano and Nicholas Tsagourias (eds.), *Handbook on Research Methods in International Law* (Edward Elgar, 2021) pp. 42–59. See also Jean d'Aspremont, *Epistemic Forces in International Law – Foundational Doctrines and Techniques of International Legal Argumentation* (Edward Elgar, 2015) pp. 177–199. See also the remarks of Corten, *Sociologies du droit* pp. 118–135, 177–195, and 207–264.

whomever ventures into the act of revelation.[82] In that sense, it can be said that the act of revelation always takes place in a very hierarchized and socially organized space where the capacity of interpreters to be heard varies greatly.[83] Thus, employing the socially accepted methods and protocols of communication does not in itself offer a guarantee that the hidden, unknown, invisible content that is revealed will be accepted as true.[84] There is, accordingly, always a risk that one seeks to reveal a secret that proves unplausible by the social community to whom it is revealed.[85]

It is noteworthy that, most of the time, the mode of thinking at work in the act of revelation, as act of production, is hypothetical thinking.[86] Given that the hidden, unknown, invisible content that international lawyers can possibly reveal is always pre-determined by what can be apprehended through the linguistic and conceptual categories that inhabit international legal thought and practice, the revelation will always begin with the testing of an hypothetical truth, which, if confirmed by the methods employed on that occasion, will lead to the act of revelation and the production of hidden, unknown, invisible content that is instantly revealed, known, and visible.

1.1.3.3 Revelation as Textual Inscription

It was said earlier that the hidden, unknown, invisible content whose presence is postulated takes its actuality and materiality in a text.[87] The same goes for the act of revelation itself, for the text is also what makes the revelation actual and material. It is through a new inscription that the hidden, unknown, invisible content of the texts, practices, actors, effects, representations, past, etc. of international law is revealed. The act of revelation is an act of inscription.

[82] Pierre Bourdieu, *Ce que parler veut dire. L'économie des échanges linguistiques* (Fayard, 1982) pp. 46, 68, and 109. See also d'Aspremont, 'Wording in International Law' p. 575.
[83] de Certeau, *L'invention du quotidien* pp. 248–249.
[84] Deleuze, *Proust et les signes* p. 39.
[85] In the epistemology of the secret of the Catholic Church, such risk, as Louis Althusser points out, was much more limited, see Louis Althusser, *Initiation à la Philosophie pour les Non-Philosophes* (Presses Universitaires de France, 2014) p. 81. See also infra Chapter 2.
[86] Comp. with the modes of exploration of the unconscious promoted by Freud, see Sigmund Freud, *The Unconscious* (Penguin Classics, 2005).
[87] See supra Section 1.1.2.4.

It is important to stress that text is understood here in a broad sense as any kind of inscription. It is not limited to material inscription and can include oral inscription as well as imagery.[88] For that reason, the act of revelation can be of very different types for international lawyers. It can take the form of an authoritative written decision like a judgement of a court, the resolution of the organ of an international organization, or an expert opinion. It can manifest itself in a pleading or an oral statement, themselves possibly recorded or the object of a transcript. Or it can materialize itself in a piece of legal scholarship, a blog post, an intervention on social media, an op-ed, etc. Teaching output can occasionally also constitute an act of revelation.

That the act of revelation as an act of inscription entails that there always is an act of translation at work in the revelation. In fact, the textual actuality of the hidden, unknown, invisible content ought to be translated in the inscriptions of the act of revelation,[89] which in turn is a superposition of texts over texts.[90] The foregoing also means that the epistemology of the secret is an epistemology that leads to the production of more textual materials. It is an epistemology of textual production. This bears significant consequences, which Section 1.2 sheds light on.

1.2 An Ordering Epistemology

If it were limited to two necessitarian postures, that is, the necessity of secret content and the necessity of revelation, the epistemology of the secret, as was said, would be nothing more than a speech-producing and discipline-justifying epistemology.[91] It is submitted here that the epistemology of the secret of international law simultaneously performs an ordering function: it enables and disables certain sayings, thoughts,

[88] See supra note 89.

[89] On the idea that any act of communication is an act of translation, see Steiner, *After Babel* p. 47.

[90] On the idea that translation always entails the superposition of a sign to another sign, see Jacques Derrida, 'Des Tours de Babel', trans. Joseph F. Graham, in Joseph F. Graham (ed.), *Difference in Translation* (Cornell University Press, 1985) p. 172. See Jacques Derrida, 'Letter to a Japanese Friend', in David Wood and Robert Bernasconi (eds.), *Derrida and Différance* (Northwestern University Press, 1988) p. 5; Roman Jakobson, 'On Linguistic Aspects of Translation', in Achilles Fang and Reuben Brower (eds.), *On Translation* (Harvard University Press, 1959) pp. 232–239, esp. pp. 232–233; Legrand, 'The Same and the Different' pp. 251–252.

[91] On how disciplines legitimize themselves, see Latour, *La Science en action* p. 382. Comp. with Schlag, 'The Aesthetics of American Law' p. 1047.

perceptions, and actions and, in doing so, enables and disables what international law does and can do to the world.[92] Ordering what can be said, thought, perceived, and actioned through international law is what the epistemology of the secret examined here works for.[93]

The claim that the epistemology of the secret of international law orders what can be said, thought, perceived, and actioned through international law is nothing spectacular.[94] This is a feature of any discipline that claims to be so.[95] It is also an epistemological pattern found in most cultures, societies, and more generally in any discourse, for there is no culture, no society, no discourse that does not exclude, limit, prohibit, govern, channel, marginalize, etc. what can be said, thought, experienced, and actioned.[96] In that sense, the epistemology of the secret of international law is an ordering device like those found in many other disciplines, cultures, societies, and discourses in which one is simultaneously caught.[97]

Although performing a function that is rather mundane in any discourse, discipline, culture, and society, the epistemology of the secret of international law performs its ordering function in a very distinctive way, which justifies all the attention devoted to it in this book. The most distinctive feature of the epistemology of the secret of international law probably lies in the dualistic way in which it orchestrates the enabling and disabling of certain sayings, thoughts, perceptions, and actions. Indeed, by constantly producing an invisible-instantly-made-visible, the epistemology of the secret of international law comes to organize sayings, thoughts, perceptions, and actions through a fundamental

[92] For a different take on the idea of secret and the association of the latter with the idea of non-belonging rather than ordering, see Jacques Derrida and Maurizio Ferraris, *A Taste for the Secret* (Polity Press, 2001) p. 59.

[93] Comp. with the ordering function of paranoid reading. See Sedgwick, 'Paranoid Reading and Reparative Reading' p. 9.

[94] See gen. Jean d'Aspremont, 'A Worldly Law in a Legal World', in Andrea Bianchi and Moshe Hirsch (eds.), *International Law's Invisible Frames: Social Cognition and Knowledge Production in International Legal Processes* (Oxford University Press, 2021) pp. 110–123. Jean d'Aspremont, 'International Law, Theory, and History: Ordering through Distinctions', in Jean d'Aspremont (ed.), *The History and Theory of International Law*, vol 1 (Edward Elgar, 2020), pp. 1–27.

[95] On the idea that a discipline is constituted by what it forbids, see White, *Tropics of Discourses* p. 126.

[96] Foucault, *Dits et écrits, I (1954–1975)* pp. 426, 443, and 483. On the use of discursive technologies by religions, see also Legendre, *De la Société comme Texte* p. 95.

[97] On the idea that any act of signification is an act of ordering, see de Certeau, *Histoire et psychanalyse entre science et fiction* p. 74.

distinction that is not systematically found in the technologies of ordering used by other discourses, disciplines, cultures, and societies: the distinction between *the hidden, the unknown, the invisible*, on the one hand, and *the revealed, the known, and the visible*, on the other.[98] Indeed, there cannot be an invisible-instantly-made-visible through the postulation of secret content and the act of revelation as long as the hidden, the unknown, the invisible, on the one hand, and the revealed, the known, and the visible, on the other, are not held as being strictly distinct from one another.[99] Such distinction, as will be further discussed in this section, is what allows the determination of what is sayable, thinkable, perceivable, and actionable, on the one hand, and what is unsayable, unthinkable, unperceivable, and unactionable, on the other hand.

The way in which the epistemology of the secret of international law performs its ordering is distinctive too. Premised on the fundamental distinction between the hidden, the unknown, the invisible, on the one hand, and the revealed, the known, and the visible, on the other, and systematically creating an invisible-instantly-made-visible, the epistemology of the secret of international law comes to constantly produce revealed, known, and visible matter, held as being previously hidden, unknown, invisible. Such revealed, known, and visible matter perpetually generated by the epistemology of the secret of international law materializes itself in speech materials whose format can vary, as will be explained below, a great deal.[100] In other words, the systematic creation of an invisible-instantly-made-visible by the epistemology of the secret of international law manifests itself in a gigantic production of speech materials about international law. International lawyers, in any capacity, speak, and speak again, about the secrets of other texts, practices, actors, effects, representations, past, etc. of international law. For there always is hidden, unknown, invisible content to be revealed, made known, made visible, and international lawyers can never be satisfied with what has already been revealed, made known, and made visible, as speech materials about the secrets of international law are created massively and continuously. It is submitted here that all this revealed, known, and visible matter, held as being previously hidden,

[98] Comp. with the idea of Cornelia Vismann that the legal file is part of an apparatus of governance based on the invisibility of files and archives, see Vismann, *Files*.

[99] Comp. with the idea that truth always supposes that something is kept secret or invisible. See Foucault, *Le Discours Philosophique* p. 15.

[100] See infra Section 1.2.2.

unknown, invisible, is what defines the sayable, thinkable, perceivable, actionable through international law.

As the epistemology of the secret of international law massively produces speech materials thereby defining the sayable, thinkable, perceivable, actionable through international law, it simultaneously suppresses an indefinite amount of sayings, thoughts, perceptions, and actions, which are all those that were not made an invisible-instantly-made-visible and thus not turned into speech materials. Said differently, as it perpetually produces revealed, known, and visible matter, the epistemology of the secret of international law concurrently creates an anti-matter[101] that cannot be said, thought, perceived, and actioned through international law. In that sense, all that has not been made an invisible-instantly-made-visible is turned into the unsayable, unthinkable, unperceivable, and unactionable by the epistemology of the secret of international law.[102]

The foregoing has foregrounded the two main modes of ordering that the epistemology of the secret of international law resorts to: *mass production of speech materials* and *suppression* of all that has not been made an invisible-instantly-made-visible. It is through the mass production of speech materials on the invisible-instantly-made-visible as well as the suppression of all the rest, and thus by defining a matter and an anti-matter, that the epistemology of the secret of international law determines what is sayable, thinkable, perceivable, and actionable through international law as well as what is unsayable, unthinkable, unperceivable, and unactionable through international law.

Articulated around the fundamental distinction between the hidden, the unknown, the invisible, on the one hand, and the revealed, the known, and the visible, on the other, the epistemology of the secret of international law organizes the enabling and disabling of certain sayings, thoughts, perceptions, and actions by virtue of a mass production of speech materials as well as the suppression of all that has not been made an invisible-instantly-made-visible. The rest of this section, after a few preliminary remarks (Section 1.2.1), reviews these two modes of ordering that the epistemology of the secret of international law relies on, namely the mass production of speech materials (Section 1.2.2) and the

101 The expression is from Steiner, *After Babel* p. 238.

102 Comp. with the idea that the epistemology of the known and unknown organized around homo-heterosexual categories has been inexhaustibly productive of modern Western culture and history at large, see Sedgwick, *Epistemology of the Closet* p. 68.

suppression of all that has not been made an invisible-instantly-made-visible (Section 1.2.3).

1.2.1 Preliminary Remarks

A few additional features of the ordering carried out by the epistemology of the secret of international law warrant attention. They pertain to the idea of suppression, the question of agency, and these other possible constraints on one's engagement with international law that the epistemology of the secret of international law can possibly bring about.

1.2.1.1 Suppression as Production

It should be made clear that the suppression of all that has not been made an invisible-instantly-made-visible, which is one of the main modes of ordering of the epistemology of the secret of international law, does not amount to the smothering of something already said, thought, perceived, or actioned. The unsayable, the unthinkable, the unperceivable, and the unactionable that come to be defined by the epistemology of the secret of international law do not pre-exist their suppression but are produced by it.[103] In that sense, just like the sayable, the thinkable, the perceivable, and the actionable are produced by the mass production of speech materials enabled by the epistemology of the secret of international law, the unsayable, the unthinkable, the unperceivable, and the unactionable are produced by their suppression. This dimension of the epistemology of the secret of international law is key to appreciating the ordering function that it performs. It also confirms that the epistemology of the secret of international law is never anchored in anything that is out there in the world but is an irresistible world-making machine that constitutes the hidden, the revealed, the unknown, the known, the invisible, the visible, the sayable, the unsayable, the thinkable, the unthinkable, the perceivable, the unperceivable, the actionable, the unactionable, and all that nourishes it.[104]

1.2.1.2 Ordering as a Non-decisional Practice

It is of the utmost importance to stress that the ordering by the epistemology of the secret of international law, and thus the mass production of speech materials as well as the suppression of all that has not been

[103] I owe this important remark to Rebecca Mignot-Mahdavi.
[104] See also supra Section 1.1.3.2.

made an invisible-instantly-made-visible, did not arise through the conscious agency of international lawyers. Indeed, one ought to resist the idea of a great master plan mindfully designed by international lawyers to make use of specific technologies of ordering in particular in order to define what can be said, thought, perceived, and actioned through international law.[105] Said differently, there has never been a collective decision by certain international lawyers in a certain place and at a certain time to set an epistemology of the secret meant to order what can be said, thought, perceived, and actioned through international law.[106] It is true that, as is described in Chapter 2, the epistemology of the secret of international law bears a lot of resemblance with epistemologies that have been witnessed in certain parts of the world at different times and is part of an old intellectual tradition.[107] Yet, as far as the epistemology of international law is concerned, there has never been a conscious act of borrowing of epistemological devices found elsewhere and that international lawyers deemed efficacious enough for the sake of ordering what can be said, thought, perceived, and actioned through international law.

1.2.1.3 The Literary, Hermeneutical, Critical, Economic, and Ideological Attitudes Incidental to the Epistemology of the Secret

Another feature of the ordering carried out by the epistemology of the secret of international law must be mentioned here as it will not be studied any further in this book. The epistemology scrutinized in this book does not only determine the sayable, the thinkable, the perceivable, and the actionable through international law (which is all that has been made an invisible-instantly-made-visible) as well as the unsayable, the unthinkable, the unperceivable, and the unactionable (which is all that has not been turned into an invisible-instantly-made-visible). The

105 Comp with the idea that ideological devices were not created out of the blue by a decision of the bourgeoisie but are the product of a long-lasting struggle, see Althusser, *Initiation à la Philosophie pour les Non-Philosophes* p. 232. Comp. with the idea that technologies of exclusion or normalization on questions of health and sexuality were not the result of a decision of the bourgeoisie but only of their interest for very efficacious and economically convenient modes of governance, see Foucault, *Dits et écrits, II* pp. 183 and 379; Foucault, *'Il faut défendre la société'* pp. 29–30.

106 Comp with the doubts expressed by Etienne Balibar and Immanuel Wallerstein about the existence of a global bourgeoisie, see Etienne Balibar and Immanuel Wallerstein, *Race, nation, classe. Des identités ambigües* (La découverte, 2018) p. 40.

107 See infra Chapter 3.

epistemology of the secret of international law simultaneously generalizes, universalizes, and imposes a whole range of *literary, hermeneutical, critical, economic, and ideological attitudes* in the field. Indeed, international lawyers speak, write, publish, think, position themselves, dream, nourish ambitions, interact, build a career, live a life, etc. along the lines of the literary, hermeneutical, critical, economic, and ideological prescriptions that come with the epistemology of the secret of international law. In that sense, the way in which the thinking, the speaking, the writing, the publishing, the working about and around international law is practiced, organized, hierarchized, and contested is also, and to a significant extent, the result of the epistemology of the secret of international law studied in this book. In fact, it is because international lawyers are all engaging with international law in a capacity as secret-hunters, speleologists, archaeologists, or porn movie producers in search of revealing what they hold as hidden, unknown, invisible content that they speak, write, think, position themselves, dream, nourish ambitions, interact, build a career, live a life the way they do. These mental, behavioural, scriptural, cognitive, institutional, disciplinary, private, etc. consequences of the epistemology of the secret of international law are obviously part of the ordering generated by it. Yet, such literary, hermeneutical, critical, economic, and ideological attitudes, even if they are occasionally mentioned in the following chapters, will not be scrutinized here.

1.2.2 A Mass Production of Speech Materials

The mass production of speech materials about international law is the first main mode of ordering that the epistemology of the secret of international law resorts to. It has already been indicated how the epistemology of the secret of international law systematically produces an invisible-instantly-made-visible[108] and constantly brings about new inscriptions and the production of textual traces.[109] These new inscriptions and textual traces, whether they take the forms of texts, oral performances, recordings, images, etc., are speech materials whereby international law is talked about. In other words, the epistemology of the secret of international law, and especially the necessity of revelation, induce international lawyers to always speak more about international

[108] See supra Section 1.1.3.2.
[109] See supra Section 1.1.3.3.

law. The epistemology of the secret thus generates a form of *discursive stuffing*,[110] that is a constant overproduction of speech materials of which there can never be enough.[111] In fact, by virtue of the epistemology of the secret discussed here, international lawyers can never have said enough about international law, for there will always be hidden, unknown, invisible content that ought to be revealed. And the more massive the production of new speech materials about the secrets about international law, the more ordering of the sayable, the thinkable, the perceivable, and the actionable is taking place.

It is probably easy to grasp the extent to which the massive production of speech materials using the thought categories of international law perpetuate the existing conceptual order.[112] Everything that is revealed, made known, made visible ends up being said, thought, perceived, and actioned through the very thought categories in place, thereby reaffirming and reinforcing the latter.[113] Indeed, by virtue of the revelation of hidden, unknown, invisible content of the texts, practices, actors, effects, representations, past, etc., speech is produced in accordance with the thought categories espoused and practiced by international lawyers. The epistemology of the secret of international law is thus an epistemology that works for the status quo, one that perpetuates international law as well as the world the latter contributes to shape.[114] Even those revelations of secrets that label themselves

110 Pierre Legendre speaks of 'bourrage de vide', see Pierre Legendre, *Sur la question dogmatique en Occident. Aspect théoriques* (Fayard, 1999) p. 141.

111 Comp. with the idea of over-production of knowledge for the sake of ordering, see Foucault, *Dits et écrits, II* pp. 554–555. See also the idea of discursive eruption ('explosion discursive'), see Foucault, *Histoire de la Sexualité 1* p. 25. The way in which an epistemology of the secret serves a specific discourse ordering through an outpouring of discourse is at the heart of Michel Foucault's first volume on the history of sexuality. See gen. Foucault, *Histoire de la Sexualité 1* esp. pp. 33 and 48–49.

112 Foucault, *Histoire de la Sexualité 1* pp. 48–49. On the idea of writing as a subjection mechanism, see Foucault, *L'ordre du discours* p. 71. On the idea of distinctions and binary categories as powerful modes of ordering, see Gilles Deleuze and Claire Parnet, *Dialogues* (Champs essais, 1996) p. 29; Roland Barthes, *Leçon* (Editions du Seuil, 1978) p. 12; Bruno Latour, *Nous n'avons jamais été modernes. Essai d'anthropologie symétrique* (La Découverte, 1997) pp. 68–69; Michel Foucault, *Les mots et les choses* (Gallimard, 1966) pp. 68–69. On the idea that the hidden, unknown, invisible content is nothing more than what the machine produces, see Jacques Rancière, *Le spectateur émancipé* (La Fabrique éditions, 2008) p. 50.

113 Foucault, *Dits et écrits, II* p. 248.

114 See the remarks of d'Aspremont, 'A Worldly Law in a Legal World' pp. 110–123.

'disruptive' and 'critical' will be reproducing the intelligibility frameworks and thought categories in place.[115]

It is of the utmost importance to distinguish the abovementioned discursive stuffing – and its determination of the sayable, the thinkable, the perceivable, and the actionable – from the mere professional and literary habits that permeate international legal discourse – and that constrains the ways in which claims about international law are made and presented. It is true that international law is the site of a huge variety of disparate habits about the choice of objects of study, the vocabularies, the sources, the literary style, the modes of referencing, the type of reasoning, the narration techniques, the cultural, historical, or symbolic referents being invoked, the problematization, the contextualization, the modes of creation of necessities and ontologies, the relation with practice, the interlocutors, the referencing, the format of outputs, etc. Even if there are significant variations in such habits across traditions, languages, and time,[116] and although they have been the object of occasional contestations,[117] it is fair to say that writing about international law is indeed an

[115] On the idea that critique does not simply cut off, estrange, or isolate but also collects, composes, and gathers together whilst creating imagined or real communities around a sensibility, ethos, and practice of reading, see Felski, *The Limits of Critique* p. 49. On the idea that critique patrols the boundaries of what counts as serious thought, see Fleski, *The Limits of Critique* p. 7. On the idea that distinctions order their own contestation, see gen. Derrida, *L'écriture et la différence* p. 47; Foucault, *Les mots et les choses* p. 12; Latour, *Nous n'avons jamais été modernes* pp. 56–57; Roland Barthes, *Mythologies* (Editions du Seuil, 1957) p. 248. On the inevitable situatedness of critique, see Said, *The World, the Text, and the Critic* p. 26.

[116] Attempts have been made to produce new 'scientific' knowledge about the variations of this routine under the banner of comparative international law, see Anthea Roberts, Paul B. Stephan, Pierre-Hugues Verdier, and Mila Versteeg, 'Comparative International Law: Framing the Field' (2015) 109 *American Journal of International Law* 467; Anthea Roberts, Paul B. Stephan, Pierre-Hugues Verdier, and Mila Versteeg (eds), *Comparative International Law* (Oxford University Press, 2018); Anthea Roberts, *Is International Law International?* (Oxford University Press, 2017). For a criticism of such attempts to universalize differences and the dangers of colonizing thinking, see Jean d'Aspremont, 'Comparativism and Colonizing Thinking in International Law' (2020) 57 *Canadian Yearbook of International Law* 89.

[117] Possibly one of the most powerful contestations of this routine in the international legal literature originates in the rise of a new type of literature that offers a new form of historical-novelist narration. See, e.g., Philippe Sands, *East West Street: On the Origins of Genocide and Crimes Against Humanity* (Weidenfeld & Nicolson, 2016). More serious contestations have been witnessed with respect to domestic law, see, e.g., Fred Rodell, 'Goodbye to Law Reviews' (1936) 23 *Virginia Law Review* 38; Schlag, 'The Law Review Article' p. 1043; Rodell, 'Goodbye to Law Reviews – Revisited' (1962) 48 *Virginia Law Review* 279.

activity saturated with professional and literary habits, which can be construed as a form of routine,[118] very instrumental in the identity of the discipline.[119] Yet, notwithstanding the weight of such professional and literary habits on the ways in which claims about international law are made and presented,[120] the ordering enabled by the mass production of speech materials originating in the epistemology of the secret of international law is much more than the mere pull of a set of habits. The ordering discussed here is not a matter of *how* claims are made but determines *what* claims can possibly be made about international law as well as what thoughts, what perceptions, and what actions are enabled by international law.

1.2.3 *The Suppression of All That Has Not Been Made an Invisible-Instantly-Made-Visible*

There is much more ordering than the mere perpetuation of the thought categories in place – and of the world they enable – that is achieved by the mass production of speech materials about international law as a result of the epistemology of the secret of international law. In fact, the mass production of speech materials prompted by the epistemology of the secret of international law also suppresses what has not been caught by the two necessities of the epistemology of the secret of international law, and thus all that has not been made an invisible-instantly-made-visible. This can be explained as follows. All that falls outside the speech materials produced by the epistemology of the secret, and thus all that has not been turned into an invisible-instantly-made-visible, is condemned to be unsayable, unthinkable, unperceivable, and

118 On the concept of routine, see supra note 40.

119 See gen. Pierre Bourdieu and Loïc J. D. Wacquant, *An Invitation to Reflexive Sociology* (Polity, 1992); Pierre Bourdieu, 'The Force of Law: Toward a Sociology of the Juridical Field', trans. Richard Terdiman (1987) 38 *Hastings Law Journal* 805.

120 It could be said that the habits composing such routines have been reinforced by the digitalization of scholarly production over the last few decades, especially since the latter led to a dramatic increase in scholarly output, thereby allowing international lawyers to repeat the abovementioned habits to an extent and at a rhythm never witnessed before. See gen. Tilmann Altwicker, 'International Legal Scholarship and the Challenge of Digitalization' (2019) 18 *Chinese Journal of International Law* 217. On the idea that the more is produced, the less is happening in legal scholarship, see Schlag, 'Spam Jurisprudence, Air Law, and the Rank of Anxiety of Nothing Happening (A Report on the State of the Art)' pp. 804–805.

unactionable.[121] In that sense, it can be said that the epistemology of the secret of international law, besides generating huge quantities of speech materials about the secrets of international law, simultaneously creates a whole *silence* populated by all that cannot be said, thought, perceived, and actioned through international law.

It is important to recall[122] that the suppression of sayings, thoughts, perceptions and actions – that is, all that has not been made an invisible-instantly-made-visible – does not amount to the stifling of something already said, thought, perceived, or actioned. Indeed, the unsayable, the unthinkable, the unperceivable, and the unactionable do not pre-exist their suppression but are produced by it. The unsayable, the unthinkable, the unperceivable, and the unactionable are produced by their suppression. It is the act of suppression that constitutes what cannot be said, thought, perceived, and actioned through international law.

The effects of such suppression are wide-ranging and probably easy to fathom. Indeed, by muting certain sayings, thoughts, perceptions, and actions, the epistemology of the secret of international law simultaneously suppresses certain meanings, interpretations, geographies, subjectivities, identities, hegemonies, infidelities, discriminations, injustices, equalities, histories, modes of living, possibilities of actions, dreams, hopes, etc.[123] The suppression carried out by the epistemology of the secret is not only about annihilating certain sayings, thoughts, perceptions, and actions. Suppression is also about organizing the possible and impossible contestations of international law.[124] Indeed, disabling certain

[121] Comp with the notion of *non-dit* (non-said) of Michel Foucault, see Foucault, *Dits et écrits, II* p. 54. Comp. with the idea that language conceals more than it confides of George Steiner, see Steiner, *After Babel* pp. 48 and 240. See more gen. de Sutter, *Superfaible* pp. 76 and 170.

[122] See infra Section 1.2.

[123] Comp. with the notion 'institutionalization of ignorance' of Eve Kosofsky Sedgwick, see Sedgwick, *Epistemology of the Closet* p. 78.

[124] On the idea that critique of order is itself determined by order, see Chakravorty Spivak, *In Other Worlds* p. 150; Foucault, *Les mots et les choses* p. 12; Foucault, *L'ordre du discours* p. 23; Régis Debray, *Le Scribe* (Editions Grasset et Fasquelle, 1980) p. 120; Lyotard, *La Condition Postmoderne* p. 107. On the idea that modernity started by identifying itself as critique, see the remarks of Terry Eagleton, *The Function of Criticism* (Verso, 2005) pp. 9–10. Comp. with the notion of autoimmunity of Jacques Derrida, *The Beast and the Sovereign*, vol 2 (University of Chicago Press, 2011) p. 84. For Derrida, autoimmunity consists 'for a living body in itself destroying, in enigmatic fashion, its own immunitary defenses, in auto-affecting itself, then, in an irrepressibly mechanical and apparently spontaneous automatic, fashion, with an ill which comes to destroy what is supposed to protect against ill and safeguard immunity'. See also

sayings, thoughts, perceptions, and actions always determines the *criticability* of international law.[125] The criticability of international law refers to the specific discontent that is enabled by the epistemology of the secret of international law. The suppression of certain sayings, thoughts, perceptions, and actions entails a calibration and allotment of the objects, tools, terminologies, channels, and modes of contestation of international law. Said differently, by virtue of the epistemology of the secret's suppression, only certain struggles and conflicts can be fought, only certain objections and contestations can be made.[126] What has not been made an invisible-instantly-made-visible and is thus left outside the mass of speech materials produced by the epistemology of the secret simply is not contestable and cannot be the object of a discontent.

The foregoing points to the ultimate great conservatism informing international law's epistemology of the secret, and thus the very limited reforms and changes that it leaves space for. Anything that is contested as well as anything that can possibly be reformed or abandoned always lies within the sayings, the thoughts, the perceptions, and the actions enabled by the epistemology of the secret of international law.[127] Such conservatism, and the rehabilitation of capitalism, colonialism, racism, bourgeois ideology, phallocentrism, virilism, and masculinism that it allows is what will lead Chapter 5 to examine the possibilities of resisting the epistemology of the secret of international law.

Derrida, *Hospitalité* p. 254. On the idea that the modes of resistance to colonial power are always formed within the organizational terrain of the colonial state, rather than some wholly exterior social space, see Timothy Mitchell, *Colonising Egypt* (Cambridge University Press, 1991) p. xi; Edward Said, *Reflections on Exile and Other Literary and Cultural Essays* (Granta, 2001) p. 377; Spivak, *In Other Worlds* p. 338. On the idea that culture generates its own mode of repression, see Legendre, *De la Société comme Texte* p. 60. On the idea that contestation is itself a bourgeois concept, see Barthes, *Le bruissement de la langue* p. 116. On the idea that the fate of modern critique is cynicism and disloyalty, see Peter Sloterdijk, *Critique of Cynical Reason* (University of Minnesota Press, 1987) p. 6.

[125] The expression is from Michel Foucault, see Foucault, *'Il faut défendre la société'* p. 7. See also Foucault, *Dits et écrits, II* p. 163.

[126] On the idea that intellectuals are always complicit with the whitewashing of the past, see Debray, *Le Scribe* p. 217.

[127] This is not exclusive, of course, of international lawyers tricking the language and cunningly play with the existing thought categories, see de Certeau, *L'invention du quotidien* p. 249. See also Gilles Deleuze, *Critique et Clinique* (Editions de Minuit, 1993) pp. 9 and 16; Jean-Jacques Lecercle, *De l'interpellation* pp. 97 and 157. Comp. with Judith Butler, *Gender Trouble: Feminism and the Subversion of Identify*, 2nd edn (Routledge, 1990) p. 42.

1.3 The Epistemology of the Secret as an Ideology of Secretism?

It must be acknowledged that the epistemology of the secret of international law, the two necessities around which it is articulated, and the ordering that it performs could be construed as forming an ideological device,[128] something that resembles what could be called an *ideology of secretism*. There are surely solid grounds to espouse such portrayal, some of which can be mentioned here.[129] First, one can construe the epistemology of the secret as a relation of secrets-extraction between a reader and a text, secrets being accordingly understood as valuable commodities whose accumulation reinforces the capital of certain groups. In that sense, the epistemology of the secret of international law could be understood as a form of textuality informed by a capitalist drive for extraction, exploitation, and accumulation. Second, it must be acknowledged that ideology is a descriptive tool commonly used in literature to describe certain attitudes towards texts. Mention can be made of the ideology of the 'reading well',[130] the ideology of the practice of literary

[128] On the inception and origin of the concept of ideology as well as its creation by Pierre-Jean-Georges Cabanis and Antoine Destutt de Tracy in the eighteenth century to refer to the science of ideas treated as natural phenomena, see Georges Canguilhem, *Idéologie et Rationalité. Dans l'Histoire des Sciences de la Vie* (Vrin, 1977), pp. 43–45. For the sake of this section, ideology is understood in a marxist way as a system of thought that make people experience certain realities rather than others. For such understanding of ideology, see Hayden White, *The Content of the Form: Narrative Discourse and Historical Representation* (John Hopkins University Press, 1987) p. 72. Paul de Man, *The Resistance to Theory* (University of Minnesota Press, 1986) p. 11; Althusser, *Initiation à la Philosophie pour les Non-Philosophes* p. 228; Lecercle, *De l'interpellation* pp. 24–25.

[129] For a very refined taxonomy of the traditions of ideology-critique in law, see Justin Desautels-Stein and Akbar Rasulov, 'Deep Cuts: Four Critiques of Legal Ideology' (2021) 31 *Yale Journal of Law & the Humanities* 435. For some illustrations of the resort to ideology critique in the international legal literature, see Ntina Tzouvala, *Capitalism as Civilisation. A History of International Law* (Cambridge University Press, 2020); China Miéville, *Between Equal Rights: A Marxist Theory of International Law* (Haymarket Books, 2006); Liliana Obregon, 'Empire, Racial Capitalism and International Law: The Case of Manumitted Haiti and the Recognition Debt' (2018) 31 *Leiden Journal of International Law* 597; Rose Parfitt, *The Process of International Legal Reproduction. Inequality, Historiography, Resistance* (Cambridge University Press, 2019). For some observations on ideology critique in international law, see Walter Rech, 'Ideology', in Jean d'Aspremont and Sahib Singh (eds.), *Concepts for International Law. Contributions to Disciplinary Thought* (Edward Elgar 2019) pp. 393–412.

[130] George Steiner, *Errata: An Examined Life* (Weidenfeld and Nicholson, 1997) p. 19.

critique,[131] the ideology of the clarity of texts,[132] the ideology of defeat,[133] or the idea of language as constituting an ideology in general.[134] Resorting to the concept of ideology to describe the attitude towards international legal texts that the epistemology of the secret of international law enables would thus not be idiosyncratic. Third, the self-concealing dimension of the epistemology of the secret of international law[135] is a feature that is known to most ideologies. Likewise, the epistemology of the secret of international law, albeit set in motion by the presence of a reader, bears the trappings of an ideology in that it leaves no visible trace of agency, as if it is working self-sufficiently.[136] Finally, the epistemology of the secret can be read as working as an ideology when it demotes engagements with international law that are not at the service of the extraction of secrets to peripheral or irrelevant activities.[137] Motives for approaching the epistemology of the secret of international law as an ideological device and, more specifically, as an ideology of secretism, are thus aplenty.

For the sake of this book, and notwithstanding the reasons to the contrary, the epistemology of the secret of international law is not approached as an ideological device.[138] Indeed, the ambition of this book is not to gauge the extent to which the epistemology examined in this book serves bourgeois, imperialistic, capitalist, racist, phallocentric, virilist, and masculinist ideologies.[139] Surely, the epistemology of the secret

[131] Eagleton, *The Function of Criticism* pp. 21–22 and 98–99; Barthes, *Le bruissement de la langue* p. 116.

[132] Barthes, *Critique et vérité* p. 30.

[133] See Desautels-Stein and Rasulov, 'Deep Cuts: Four Critiques of Legal Ideology' p. 435.

[134] Louis Althusser, *Être Marxiste en Philosophie* (Presses Universitaires de France, 2015) p. 219.

[135] See supra Section 1.1.2.5.

[136] On the idea that ideology leaves no visible trace of an agent, see Althusser, *Initiation à la Philosophie pour les Non-Philosophes* pp. 221–222.

[137] On this dimension of ideology in relation to theoretical enterprises that do not serve the scientistic bourgeois order, see Althusser, *Initiation à la Philosophie pour les Non-Philosophes* p. 200.

[138] For some similar reservations towards the use of ideology in studies of discourse, see the remarks of Michel Foucault, in Chomsky and Foucault, *The Chomsky-Foucault Debate on Human Nature* p. 152. See also Foucault, *Dits et écrits, II* pp. 263–264. See also the remarks of Paul Veyne, *Foucault. Sa pensée, sa personne* (Albin Michel, 2008) pp. 48–49. On the idea that we have already done the critique of ideology, see Roland Barthes, *Le grain de la voix. Entretiens 1962–1980* (Editions du Seuil, 1981) p. 94.

[139] On the idea that all these ideologies are intertwined, see Etienne Balibar and Immanuel Wallerstein, *Race, nation, classe*. See also Colette Guillaumin, *L'idéologie raciste. Genèse et langage actuel* (Gallimard, 2002). For some intellectual perspectives on this point, see

of international law is not innocent and contributes to the making by international law of a bourgeois, imperialistic, capitalist, racist, phallocentric, virilist, and masculinist world, which warrants the greatest scrutiny and resistance.[140] Such complicity is why the question of resisting the epistemology of the secret of international law will be discussed in Chapter 5. That being said, tracing and resisting the (repulsive) ideologies at work in international legal thought and practice always requires that one starts by untangling *how* international law enables and disables what can be said, thought, perceived, and actioned through it, which is the primary ambition of this book. Treating the epistemology of the secret of international law as an epistemology rather than an ideology is a way to maximizes one's understanding of *how* international law does what it does, including all that it should not be doing.[141]

1.4 The Epistemology of the Secret as an Economy of Secrets?

Just like the epistemology of the secret of international law has some of the hallmarks of an ideology, it could be construed as having the characteristics of a specific type of *economy*, at least for three reasons.[142] First, it must be acknowledged that the hidden, unknown, invisible content of the texts, practices, actors, effects, representations, past, etc. of international law that is posited by virtue of the necessity of secret content can constitute a resource that international lawyers constantly seek to extract and exploit for the sake of producing a truth and achieving fame or authority.[143] Surely, there is a social, symbolic, reputational, professional, and even financial value that can be ascribed

Justin Desautels-Stein, *The Right to Exclude. A Critical Race Approach to Sovereignty, Borders, and International Law* (Oxford University Press, 2023).

140 On the idea that the colonial discourse employs a system of representation that is structurally similar to realism and produces a colonized as a social reality which is at once an 'other' and yet entirely knowable and visible, see Homi K. Bhabba, *The Location of Culture* (Routledge, 1994) p. 101.

141 In the same vein, see Barthes, *Le grain de la voix* p. 118.

142 Comp. with Pierre Schlag who speaks of normative legal thought as an 'economy of self-referential instrumentalist rhetorical structures', see Schlag, 'Normative and Nowhere to Go' p. 186. Comp. with Cornelia Vismann who speaks of registers as 'an economy of writing indispensable for the administering of texts', which goes together with 'a new economy of reading', see Vismann, *Files* p. 80.

143 On the idea that we are all compelled to produce truth like we must produce income and wealth, see Foucault, *Dits et écrits, II* p. 176.

to the hidden, unknown, invisible content of the texts, practices, actors, effects, representations, past, etc. of international law and that international lawyers may seek to maximize and take advantage of.[144] In that sense, the epistemology of the secret of international law can be read as a massive extractive industry.[145] Second, the metaphor of an economy can be justified by international lawyers' permanent unsatisfaction of international lawyers with the meaningful content they read, see, perceive, or locate in all of international law's texts, forms, practices, representations, actors, past, etc. as well as their constant postulation of the possibility of more surplus of meaningful content that could potentially be exploited.[146] Indeed, the epistemology of the secret never exhausts itself and is predicated on the idea that secrets can be found *ad infinitum* in all of international law's texts, forms, practices, representations, actors, past, etc. Finally, the mass production of speech materials brought about by the obligation of revelation and their trading on the market of academic publishing are similarly reminiscent of an economy.[147] For all these reasons, the epistemology with which this book engages could be portrayed as functioning like an economy. What is more, such terminological choice would not be unprecedented, for regimes of truth – with which the epistemology of the secret of international law has many common denominators – have sometimes been described as economies of truth.[148]

It is submitted here, however, that the idea of economy, albeit useful to apprehend the many facets of the permanent exploitation of hidden, unknown, and visible content as well as of the market that speech materials produced on that occasion give rise to, the epistemology of the secret of international law, does not provide the appropriate space and vocabulary to dissect the functioning of the two main necessities composing such epistemology, namely the necessity of secret content and

[144] Comp. with the idea that critical theory is a form of cultural capital and prestige-driven commodity, see Felski, *The Limits of Critique* p. 138.

[145] On the idea that modern critique is articulated around intellectual extractivism, see de Sutter, *Superfaible* p. 341. Comp. with the idea of Guy Debord whereby the capitalist society is built on secrets, see Guy Debord, *Commentaires sur la société du spectacle* (Gallimard, 1992) p. 74.

[146] See supra Section 1.1.2.2.

[147] See supra Section 1.2.2.

[148] See the idea of economy of truth of Michel Foucault, see Foucault, *Sécurité, Territoire, Population* p. 241.

the necessity of revelation. What is more, the notion of epistemology has the advantage of putting more emphasis on the enabling and disabling of sayings, thoughts, perceptions, and actions by the abovementioned mass production of speech materials. This is why the notion of epistemology is preferred to that of economy. That being said, the resemblance of the epistemology of the secret of international law to an economy bears some important lessons for the question of resisting to the epistemology of the secret, which Chapter 5 will come back to.

2

Epistemologies of the Secret Elsewhere

Although the present book is only concerned with the epistemology of the secret of international law, this chapter draws attention to other systems of thought that are articulated around a postulation of the necessary presence of some content or substance deemed to be hidden in some way (what is called here the *necessity of secret content*) and/or the necessary performance of an act of revelation of some content or substance previously unknown (what is called here the *necessity of revelation*). The ambition of this chapter is to show that international law can be construed as the receptacle of a very rich, diverse, and long intellectual tradition. In that sense, the various epistemologies of the secret discussed in this chapter provide a novel vantage point from which one can revisit the genealogy of the way in which international law is thought and practiced today. The goal of this chapter is also to shed light on the various roles and functions that epistemologies of the secret have performed over time as well as the different configurations they can take with a view to better appreciating the distinctiveness of the epistemology of the secret of international law.

Before exposing the epistemologies of the secret found in other systems of thought, two fundamental observations are warranted about the exercise carried out in this chapter. First, it must be stressed that this chapter resists any causal and originist narrative. Indeed, the epistemologies of the secret that are examined in the following sections are not approached as *precedents* that would have any kind of causal relationship with the epistemology of the secret of international law and in which the latter would allegedly finds its origins.[1] Second, this chapter mentions epistemologies of the secret that are mostly found in Western systems of

[1] On the precarity of any causal type of thinking, see Michel Foucault, *L'archéologie du savoir* (Gallimard, 1969) p. 34; Michel Foucault, *Dits et écrits, Tome 1 (1954–1975)* (Gallimard, 2001) pp. 607 and 824; Paul Ricoeur, *Histoire et vérité* (Editions du Seuil, 1955) pp. 33–34; Paul Veyne, *Comment on écrit l'histoire* (Editions du Seuil, 1971) p. 195.

thought.[2] Such sampling is primarily informed by practical considerations, which pertain to the linguistic aptitudes of the author of this book as well as the range of accessible textual materials at his disposal. Needless to say that such sampling is highly problematic, for it entails that the following account of the history of ideas – and of the intellectual traditions of which international law is the receptacle – is extremely ethnocentric.[3] It is hoped, however, that the following account will stimulate similar works focused on the epistemologies of the secret at work in systems of thought in other parts of the world.

In this chapter, mention is made of the epistemologies of the secrets at work in Greek logocentric thought (Section 2.1), in the Christian governance of the mind (Section 2.2), in modern thought (Section 2.3), in the more specific idea of critique inherited from modern thought (Section 2.4), in bourgeois literature (Section 2.5), in Freudian psychoanalysis (Section 2.6), and in structuralist thought (Section 2.7). The chapter ends with a few observations on whether poststructuralist charges against logocentrism have compellingly disabled the possibility of an epistemology of the secret, thereby making international law an anomaly from the perspective of the history of thought (Section 2.8).

2.1 The Epistemology of the Secret of Greek Logocentrism

As was stressed above, the epistemology of the secret of international law is predicated on the idea that signs carry a meaningful content that precedes them and of which they are the cause as much as the origin.[4] In that sense, the epistemology of the secret of international law is very dependent on the logocentric tradition that consolidated and generalized itself in Ancient Greece with Aristotle and by virtue of which speaking necessarily entails the meaning of something.[5] For Aristotelian

For an early contestation of causal laws, see David Hume, *A Treatise of Human Nature* (Oxford University Press, 2011).

2 François Jullien has shown that Chinese thought has been rather alien to the idea of revelation as the one around which the epistemology of the secret of international law is articulated, see François Jullien, *La pensée chinoise. En vis-à-vis de la philosophie* (Gallimard, 2015) p. 149.

3 The same charge has been made against the work of Michel Foucault, see Timothy Mitchell, *Questions of Modernity* (University of Minnesota Press, 2000) p. 13.

4 See supra Section 1.1.2.1.

5 In the same vein, see Jullien, *La pensée chinoise* pp. 115–119. He claims that Aristotle defeated the approach of Heraclite and imposed his approach to the logos.

logocentrism, there always is the necessary presence of a content in speaking. Since then, any act of language, and more generally, any form and any sign, have amounted to an act signification of something.[6] Aristotelian logocentrism thus elevated speaking in an act of revelation of a given content, which can itself be the object of a revelation by the recipients of the speech concerned. It is no surprise that, in this context, Western philosophy turn out to be primarily geared towards the interpretation (and the revelation of the hidden, unknown, invisible content) of the signs that populate the world.[7]

Although Greek logocentrism did not build itself as an epistemology of the secret, it had all the rudiments thereof, if only the very precondition without which the necessity of secret content, so central in the epistemology of the secret of international law, would not be a possibility. Without prejudging actual causalities, it goes without saying that the Western epistemologies of the secret that have been experimented and practiced over centuries and that are described in the following sections have been hugely facilitated by this Greek heritage.[8]

2.2 The Epistemology of the Secret of the Christian Governance of the Mind

The parallels between the epistemology of the secret of international law and the techniques of governance of the mind elaborated, honed, and practiced centuries after centuries by Christianity are way too conspicuous for the following account to be anything else than sketchy and cursory. Christianity could even be credited for having designed, in the form of a scheme of permanent scrutiny, revelation, and confession,[9] the most advanced and sophisticated epistemology of the secret in the Western history of thought. What is more, the techniques designed by Christianity to extract and reveal the holy meaning hidden in scripture as well as the techniques of self-interrogation and self-scrutiny are second to

[6] This is what I have called elsewhere the meaning-centric tradition, see Jean d'Aspremont, *After Meaning. The Sovereignty of Forms in International Law* (Edward Elgar, 2021).

[7] Gilles Deleuze, *Proust et les signes* (Presses Universitaires de France, 1964) p. 34; Michel Foucault, *Le Discours Philosophique* (Gallimard/Seuil, 2023) p. 14.

[8] On the idea of Western thought to do away with Greek thought, see Foucault, *Le Discours Philosophique* p. 15.

[9] Michel Foucault, *Naissance de la clinique* (Presses Universitaires de France, 1963) p. 15; Michel Foucault, *Dits et écrits, II* (Gallimard, 2001) p. 564; Michel de Certeau, *Histoire et psychanalyse entre science et fiction* (Gallimard, 2016) p. 72.

none in terms of efficacy. Whether through penance, sacrament of reconciliation, self-examination, confession, pastoral care, the postulation of hidden holy meaning, etc., Christianity has built one of the most highly developed systems of self-revelation ever witnessed.[10] And, in doing so, it has made Christian believers permanently speak about themselves, thereby letting the Christian self be captured and shaped by the Christian discourse,[11] as well as making the Christian disciple a permanent decipherer and revealer.[12] In sum, the necessity of the presence of indefinite hidden holy content and the permanent necessity to reveal it as well as the necessity to reveal how one relates to (and applies) such revealed content are omnipresent in the Christian modes of governance of the mind.[13]

As was said already, the epistemology of the secret of Christianity is of a remarkable refinement. This chapter is not the place to elaborate on all the distinct features thereof. It suffices only to mention a few of the very advanced devices that accompany such epistemology of the secret. For instance, by putting 'the verb' at the start of its Genesis,[14] the Scripture has gone as far as hiding the language and the tools through which holy meaning is extracted as well as revealed.[15] It also comes with a very specific take on temporality. Indeed, the time of the revelation is supposed to be a waiting time, it is a time that will unfold until the return of Christ and the Day of the Judgement.[16] Likewise, the Christian epistemology of the secret has created a subject, the very subject that ought to reveal the holy truth about the Scripture but also the truth about herself.[17] Not to mention the mechanisms of self-referentiality that ensure

[10] Jacques Derrida, *Le dernier des Juifs* (Galilée, 2014) p. 51; de Certeau, *Histoire et psychanalyse entre science et fiction* p. 72; Michel Foucault, *Histoire de la Sexualité IV. Les aveux de la chair* (Gallimard, 2018) pp. 50 and 100–101; Foucault, *Dits et écrits, II* pp. 245 and 564; Michel Foucault, *Sécurité, Territoire, Population. Cours au Collège de France. 1977–1978* (Gallimard, 2004), pp. 186–188; Giorgio Agamben, *La puissance de la pensée* (Editions Payot & Rivages, 2021) pp. 29–30.

[11] Gilles Deleuze, *Critique et Clinique* (Editions de Minuit, 1993) pp. 50–70.

[12] The expression is from Jacques Le Goff, see Jacques Le Goff, 'L'homme médiéval', in Jacques Le Goff (ed.), *L'Homme médiéval* (Editions du Seuil, 1989) p. 38.

[13] de Certeau, *Histoire et psychanalyse entre science et fiction* p. 72.

[14] See the first verse in the opening chapter of the Gospel of John in the New Testament of the Christian Bible 'In the beginning was the Word, and the Word was with God, and the Word was God'.

[15] Agamben, *La puissance de la pensée* pp. 30–31.

[16] François Hartog, *Régime d'historicité. Présentisme et expérience du temps* (Editions du Seuil, 2003) p. 94.

[17] Jullien, *La pensée chinoise* p. 295.

the closure of the whole Christian system of meaning[18] as well as Christian hermeneutic theories, which, despite numerous reforms over the centuries, have remained geared towards the necessary revelation of a necessarily present hidden, unknown, invisible content.[19]

There is yet another feature of the Christian epistemology of the secret that ought to be highlighted here because such mention points to a functional parallel between it and the epistemology of the secret of international law. The goal of the Christian epistemology of the secret is similarly to generate a mass of discursive materials to which Christian thought categories and prescriptions can be applied. In other words, Christianity, through its multiple techniques of extraction, revelation, self-interrogation, and self-scrutiny has created a huge mechanism of discursive ordering,[20] by creating both a world of the sayable and a world of the unsayable.[21] Mass production of discourse for the sake of discursive ordering is certainly a trait common to both Christian and international law's epistemologies of the secret.

2.3 The Epistemology of the Secret of Modern Thought

Modern thought, and its emphasis on 'the real'[22] and 'the visible',[23] has, since its consolidation in the eighteenth and ninetenth century, put in

[18] According to Althusser, this has allowed Christianity to spare a lot of energy seeking to justify that truth revealed through its procedures is guaranteed as truth, see Louis Althusser, *Initiation à la Philosophie pour les Non-Philosophes* (Presses Universitaires de France, 2014) p. 81. On the use of self-referential constructions to preempt foundationalist debates, see Jean d'Aspremont, *International Law as a Belief System* (Cambridge University Press, 2017) pp. 45–54. See also Wouter G. Werner, *Repetition and International Law* (Cambridge University Press, 2022).

[19] On the various mutations in theological modes of reading, see Foucault, *Le Discours Philosophique* p. 83.

[20] Foucault, *Dits et écrits, II* p. 245; Foucault, *Sécurité, Territoire, Population* p. 188; See also Ian Hunter, *Rethinking the School. Subjectivity, Bureaucracy, Criticism* (Allen & Unwin, 1994) pp. xxi and 32–61.

[21] Foucault, *Dits et écrits, II* p. 248.

[22] On the modern primacy of discourses about 'the real', see Michel Foucault, *Les mots et les choses* (Gallimard, 1966) p. 89; Michel Foucault, *'Il faut défendre la société'. Cours au Collège de France, 1976* (Gallimard, 1997) pp. 161–165; Foucault later claimed that determining exactly when discourses about 'the real' became the carrier of a truth is irrelevant, see Foucault, *Naissance de la biopolitique* p. 38. See also Bruno Latour, *Nous n'avons jamais été modernes. Essai d'anthropologie symétrique* (La Découverte, 1997) p. 24, as well as Jürgen Habermas, *The Philosophical Discourse of Modernity: Twelve Lectures*, trans. Frederik Lawrence (Polity Press, 1987) p. 19.

[23] Michel de Certeau, *L'invention du quotidien. 1. Arts de faire* (Gallimard, 1990) p. 272; de Certeau, *Histoire et psychanalyse entre science et fiction* pp. 22 and 207–208; Philippe Descola, *Par-delà nature et culture* (Gallimard, 2005) pp. 121, 1590, and 1605.

place an epistemology of the secret[24] that shares certain attributes with the Christian governance of the mind depicted in Section 2.2.[25] This surely is not a coincidence. Modern thought is not short of Christian pedigree, be it in relation to the very idea of subject, the idea that human beings must look for physical laws, the necessity to know the physical world and exploit nature, the idea that will is the origin, the presumption that the knowledge-holder can act as a therapist, the idea of a world where truth is to be decoded, etc.[26]

The two components of the epistemology of the secret of international law as is understood here, namely a necessity of secret content and a necessity of revelation, are easy to pinpoint in modern thought. Indeed, modern thought, in giving primacy to 'the real',[27] generates a necessity of secret content. Indeed, 'the real' is thought as always being missing and necessitating a search as well as additional scrutiny.[28] For modern thought, there always is an unknown somewhere that ought to

[24] On the kinship between enlightenment and secrecy, see Reinhart Koselleck, *Le Règne de la Critique*, trans. Reinhart Koselleck (Éditions de Minuit, 1979) p. 50.

[25] On the idea that modern forms of governance and the modern governmentalization of the state mimicked the practices of pastoral care developed by Christianity, see Foucault, *Sécurité, Territoire, Population* pp. 128–134; Foucault, *Dits et écrits, II* pp. 548, 560–566, 956–958; Hunter, *Rethinking the School* pp. xxi and 32–61. See also the remarks of Roberto M. Unger, *Law in Modern Society. Toward a Criticism of Social Theory* (The Free Press, 1976) p. 43.

[26] See gen. Descola, *Par-delà nature et culture* p. 132; Alain Supiot, *Homo Juridicus. Essai sur la fonction anthropologique du Droit* (Seuil, 2005) pp. 55–57; Jullien, *La pensée chinoise* p. 150; Foucault, *Dits et écrits, II* p. 312; Derrida, *Le dernier des Juifs* p. 51; Foucault, *Sécurité, Territoire, Population* p. 241; Jullien, *La pensée chinoise* p. 295. On the idea that Augustine is probably the one who conceptualized subjectivity in a way that is very close to the Cartesian cogito, see Jullien, *La pensée chinoise* pp. 294–296. On the idea that the divine prescription that human beings get hold on the universe has been completed with the modern monopoly of the subject over the world and ended up by the sacking of God, see Supiot, *Homo Juridicus* p. 57. On the idea that the cogito is no intellectual accident but builds on a long intellectual tradition as well as a predisposition of European languages, see Jullien, *La pensée chinoise* pp. 284–286. See, however, on the distinction between the Christian conception of time as preparation for judgement and the temporality of modernity, Peter Goodrich, 'Law and Modernity' (1986) 49 *The Modern Law Review* 545 at 558. On the distinct features of modern temporarily, see also Jean d'Aspremont, 'Time Travel in the Law of International Responsibility', in Samantha Besson (ed.), *Theories of International Responsibility Law* (Cambridge University Press, 2022) pp. 252–276.

[27] On the idea that since the advent of modernity, many existing discourses came to revamp their methods and self-representations with a view to securing the venerated status of discourse about 'the real', see Alasdair MacIntyre, *Three Rival Version of Moral Inquiry. Encyclopaedia, Genealogy, and Tradition* (University of Notre Dame Press, 1990) p. 224

[28] Michel de Certeau, *La faiblesse de croire* (Editions du Seuil, 1987) p. 200.

be looked for.[29] Said differently, there always is a surplus of reality in the world that the modern mind can know. In that sense, the unknown, for the modern mind, can never be exhausted.[30] This necessity of the permanent presence of an unknown is exacerbated by the primacy given to scientific discourses,[31] for the latter's function and rationale are premised on the postulation that there always is an unknown that is dormant and that ought to be awaken through the right methods and instruments.[32] This is especially the case with biology, which has elevated itself as the very discourse about the unknown biological content of human bodies.[33]

In the epistemology of the secret of modern thought, the necessity of the presence of an unknown is similarly accompanied by a necessity to reveal such unknown. Indeed, the unknown, for modern thought, is the invisible that ought to be made visible, which is why the permanence of the unknown is systematically accompanied by a necessity to know the unknown, that is, a necessity to make the invisible visible. Indeed, modern thought awards so much discursive, social, symbolic, scientific, market value to the unknown made known that the modern mind constantly seeks to reveal the unknown.[34] It is no coincidence that, since modernity, the unknown made known and visible provides wealth, strength, power, comparative advantages, etc.[35] Knowing the unknown also protects and shields but it also hierarchizes and distributes social capital among people, groups, and institutions.[36] Actually, in the modern system of thought, the act of revelation of the unknown is never a universal possibility and is reserved to the few who master the

[29] On the modern epistemology of the known and unknown, see the remarks of Eve Kosofsky Sedgwick, *Epistemology of the Closet* (University of California Press, 2008) p. 68.

[30] Michel Foucault, *Dits et écrits, I (1954–1975)* (Gallimard, 2001) p. 1561; Foucault, *Le Discours Philosophique* p. 15.

[31] Foucault, *Dits et écrits, II* p. 312. On the idea that philosophy has justified the primacy of the scientific discourse whilst justifying the philosophical discourse through its postulation of a knowing subject, see Foucault, *Le Discours Philosophique* pp. 31, 35–37, and 179–180.

[32] Foucault, *Dits et écrits, I (1954–1975)* p. 1561.

[33] Bruno Latour, *Pasteur: Guerre et paix des microbes* (La Découverte, 2001) p. 71; Supiot, *Homo Juridicus* p. 36.

[34] Michel Foucault, *L'ordre du discours* (Gallimard, 1971) p. 22.

[35] On the idea that modernity came with an institutionalization of ignorance which is never accidental, see Sedgwick, *Epistemology of the Closet* p. 78.

[36] Foucault, *L'ordre du discours* pp. 42–43; Foucault, *Dits et écrits, I (1954–1975)* pp. 29–39.

codes, protocols, and methods of the modern act of revelation of the unknown.[37]

It is noteworthy that, since the consolidation of modern thought, the necessity to reveal the unknown has been amplified by the proliferation of social sciences whose function is commonly understood as producing knowledge about the society to assist lawmakers and policymakers in the enactment of regulations attuned to the actual needs of the political community.[38] The state, by virtue of its governmentalization and pastoral care, has similarly required that more unknown is made known to it.[39] The same necessity of a revelation of the unknown is similarly sustained by modern medical and clinical practices, which, borrowing from the Christian epistemology of the secret and the latter's idea of Christ as a doctor, expect the individual to reveal her inner self to the medical team.[40] This is the reason why it is said that medical and clinical practices have promoted the idea of 'science-confession' for the sake of therapy.[41] In short, the necessity of revelation is in full swing all across modern thought.

In the light of the strong kinship between modern thought and the epistemology of the secret as is understood here, it is no coincidence that, in the last decade, the possible implosion of modern thought under its own weight and contradictions[42] came to be associated with a generalization of suspicion. In fact, what is sometimes construed as the heyday of conspiracism – and all the dramatic consequences that this

[37] On the centrality of method in modern thought, see Jullien, *La pensée chinoise* pp. 93–94.

[38] See gen. Iain McLean and Fiona Hewitt (eds.), *Condorcet: Foundations of Social Choice and Political Theory* (Edward Elgar, 1994). See also Keith Michael Baker, *Origins of Social Science: Condorcet: From Natural Philosophy to Social Mathematics* (University of Chicago Press, 1975). On this function of social sciences, see Bruno Latour, *La fabrique du droit. Une ethnographie du Conseil d'Etat* (La Découverte, 2004) pp. 296–296; Jacques Rancière, *Les mots de l'histoire. Essai de poétique du savoir* (Editions du Seuil, 1992) p. 21; Supiot, *Homo Juridicus* pp. 70–71; Foucault, *Dits et écrits, I (1954–1975)* p. 850; Frédéric Lordon, *La société des affects. Pour un structuralisme des passions* (Editions du Seuil, 2013) pp. 7–8. For some strong charges against the idea of social sciences, see Michel Foucault, *Qu'est-ce que la critique?* (Vrin, 2015) p. 98.

[39] Foucault, *Dits et écrits, II* p. 176; Foucault, *'Il faut défendre la société'* p. 22.

[40] Foucault, *Histoire de la Sexualité IV* pp. 100–101.

[41] Daniele Lorenzini speaks of 'science-aveu', see Daniele Lorenzini, *La force du vrai. De Foucault à Austin* (Le bord de l'eau, 2017) p. 39.

[42] On the idea that modernity was doomed from the start, see gen Peter Sloterdijk, *Critique of Cynical Reason* (University of Minnesota Press, 1987). Comp. with the idea of Erich Fromm according to which modern freedom was bound to turn into anxiety and fear of freedom, see Erich Fromm, *Escape from Freedom* (Henry Holt, 1969).

may have – may be nothing more than the epistemology of the secret of modern thought pushed to a breaking point.[43]

It is interesting to finally note, that, like the Christian governance of the mind, the epistemology of the secret of modern thought hides the language of revelation, as if language had no role in the postulation of an unknown and its revelation. Indeed, for modern thought, knowledge is considered immune to the constitutive character and performativity of language.[44] This also is a feature that the epistemology of the secret of modern thought shares with that of international law, which surely is no coincidence given how much international legal thought and practice have borrowed from modern thought,[45] despite the compelling criticisms which the latter underwent over time.[46]

[43] See the remarks of Bruno Latour, 'Why Has Critique Run out of Steam? From Matters of Facts to Matters of Concern' (2004) 30 *Critical Inquiry* 225, pp. 228–230. See also the essays in Isabelle Alfandary, Anne Emmanuelle Berger, and Jacob Rogozinski (eds.), *Qui a peur de la déconstruction?* (Presses Universitaires de France, 2023).

[44] Roland Barthes, *Le bruissement de la langue. Essais critiques IV* (Editions du Seuil, 1984) pp. 17–18.

[45] For some of remarks on the modernity of international law, see gen. Jean d'Aspremont, 'Consenting to International Law in Five Moves', in Samantha Besson (ed.), *Consent in International Law* (Cambridge University Press, 2023) pp. 117–134; d'Aspremont, *International Law as a Belief System*; Jean d'Aspremont, 'Two Attitudes towards Textuality in International Law: The Battle for Dualism' (2022) 42 *Oxford Journal of Legal Studies* 963; Jean d'Aspremont, 'The Chivalric Pursuit of Coherence in International Law' (2024) 37 *Leiden Journal of International Law* 191; Jean d'Aspremont, 'A Worldly Law in a Legal World', in Andrea Bianchi and Moshe Hirsch (eds.), *International Law's Invisible Frames: Social Cognition and Knowledge Production in International Legal Processes* (Oxford University Press, 2021) pp. 110–123; Jean d'Aspremont, 'International Law and the Rage against Scienticism' (2022) 33 *European Jouranl of International Law* 679. Comp. however, with the idea that the various forms and expressions of modernism have been misunderstood by legal studies and misapplied to the analysis of law, see Goodrich, 'Law and Modernity' p. 548.

[46] On Nietzsche's idea of depth and secret of the text as being just a line on the surface, see the remarks of Foucault, *Dits et écrits, I (1954–1975)* p. 596. For a claim that scientific discourses have failed to meet their own criteria of scientificity, see Jean-François Lyotard, *La Condition Postmoderne* (Editions de Minuit, 1979) pp. 11 and 65; Roland Barthes, *L'aventure sémiologique* (Editions du Seuil, 1985) p. 14. In that regard, it has even been claimed that discourses about 'the real' work as secularized theologies, see Pierre Legendre, *Sur la question dogmatique en Occident. Aspect théoriques* (Fayard, 1999) p. 41. On the idea that what defines the scientificity of discourse is not its object or its content but the primacy that is socially awarded to it, see Barthes, *Le bruissement de la langue* p. 11. On the idea that scientific modes of inquiries have no distinct superiority over literary ones, even when it comes to engaging with 'the real', see gen. Hayden White, *Tropics of Discourses. Essays in Cultural Criticism* (Johns Hopkins University Press, 1986) pp. 121–122 and 142–143; Barthes, *L'aventure sémiologique* p. 14.

2.4 The Epistemology of the Secret of Modern Critique

Whilst modern thought built itself around the necessity of a hidden, of an unknown, of an invisible that were to be permanently looked for and revealed, nowhere is such centrality of the epistemology of the secret more tangible than in the very idea of critique that was born with modern thought.[47] This is why this aspect of modern thought, although it constitutes only a particular offspring of the more general epistemology described Section 2.3, warrants the attention here.

To unpack this claim about the kinship between the modern idea of critique and the epistemology of the secret, it must be recalled that modern thought has always defined itself by its critical questioning of the necessities that govern action, perception, experience, and discourses[48] as well as a contestation of those necessities that are unacknowledged and unconsented. To put it differently, the modern formation of a non-dogmatic subject 'release[d] from his self-incurred tutelage'[49] is the formation of a critical subject. The modern mind even invented a word for such 'critical' consciousness: *Enlightenment*. Enlightenment is synonymous with critique.[50] For the moderns, being enlightened means nothing more than the discovery, awareness, and evaluation of the necessities governing actions, perceptions, experiences, and discourses[51] and the corresponding confidence in one's ability to de-fatalise[52] such necessities. This explains why, since the Enlightenment, everyone has been expected to be critical, such critique being constitutive of the

[47] This is one of the main theses defended by Reinhart Koselleck in *Kritik und Krise* (Verlag Karl Albert, 1959). See also Terry Eagleton, *The Function of Criticism* (Verso 2005) and Laurent de Sutter, *Superfaible. Penser aux XXIe siècle* (Climats, 2023).

[48] Eagleton, *The Function of Criticism* pp. 9–10; White, *Tropics of Discourse* p. 1.

[49] See the famous essay of Immanuel Kant entitled 'What Is Enlightenment?' in the December 1784 issue of the Berlinische Monatsschrift edited by Friedrich Gedike and Johann Erich Biester. On the idea that Kant's 1781 *Critique of Pure Reason* consolidated systematized and formalized two centuries of critical thought, see Habermas, *The Philosophical Discourse of Modernity* p. 16. See also de Sutter, *Superfaible* p. 26. On the idea that Kant should be seen as the inventor of critique, see François Châtelet, *Une histoire de la raison* (Editions du Seuil, 1992) p. 136. On Kant and critique, see gen. Gilles Deleuze, *La philosophie critique de Kant* (Presses Universitaires de France, 1963).

[50] Eagleton, *The Function of Criticism* pp. 9–10.

[51] Michel Foucault, *Le gouvernement de soi et des autres. Cours au Collège de France (1982–1983)* (Gallimard/Seuil, 2008) pp. 15–16.

[52] I borrow this term from Nikolas Rose, *Governing the Soul: The Shaping of the Private Self* (Free Association Books, 1999) p. xii.

modern subject's self-determination.[53] Being a modern subject, in the modern sense, is to live in the permanence of the critical judgement, to live under the reign of critique.[54] Putting the world, oneself, others, the latter's sayings and findings on trial is the way in which the modern mind determines itself. Modernity has thus inaugurated the age of the permanent trial whose critical judgement is determinative of knowledge as the condition of truth that each modern subject ought to police.[55] As a result, critique is constitutive of thought as a whole: there cannot be thought that is not critical.[56]

So construed as a linchpin of modern thought, the idea of critique has reinforced the embedment of modern thought in an epistemology of the secret. Indeed, the idea of critique has dictated the modern mind to organize the permanent trial of the world, of oneself, of others, of the latter's sayings and findings.[57] Yet, no trial, not even the trial permanently conducted by the modern mind, takes place without the finding and revelation of what is being put on trial: facts, physical or social phenomena, patterns of behaviours, patterns of thoughts, norms, beliefs, standards of normality, presuppositions, frameworks of intelligibility, vocabularies, language, etc. The modern trial is always preceded by a postulation of a hidden, an unknown, and an invisible, which, once revealed, can be put on trial. This is why modern thought, for the sake of its permanent critical judgement, always starts by the production of hidden, unknown, invisible content which modern scientific methods simultaneously and immediately allow to turn into a revealed, known, and visible content that is put on trial with a view to creating the critical modern subject that now critically rules the world. In that sense, the idea of critique that was born with modernity has made both the suspicion about the hidden, the unknown, the invisible, and the need for their revelation permanent.[58]

53 Eagleton, *The Function of Criticism*; Lordon, *La société des affects* p. 276.

54 Laurent de Sutter, 'Pour une clinique', in Laurent de Sutter (ed.), *Postcritique* (Presses Universitaires de France, 2019) p. 223; de Sutter, *Superfaible* p. 56.

55 Foucault, *Le gouvernement de soi et des autres* pp. 21–22; Foucault, *Qu'est-ce que la critique?* p. 47.

56 de Sutter, *Superfaible* p. 203.

57 de Sutter, 'Pour une clinique' p. 228.

58 In making this claim, I depart from the claim of Paul Ricoeur according to which the hermeneutics of suspicion was born with Marx, Nietzsche, and Freud. The present section makes the point that what Ricoeur calls the 'school of suspicion' or the 'hermeneutics of suspicion' was born with modernity, see Paul Ricoeur, *De l'interprétation. Essai sur Freud* (Editions du Seuil, 1965) pp. 38 and 42–46. See also Paul Ricoeur, *Freud and*

2.5 The Epistemology of the Secret of Bourgeois Literature

The specific type of bourgeois literature that emerged in the Western world in the seventeenth, eighteenth, and nineteenth century and that seeks to depict the daily life in an individualist and capitalistic society[59] can also be read as being infused with an epistemology of the secret as is understood here.[60] Indeed, such literature shares the same realist ideal as modern thought and always aims at representing 'the real'.[61] It is true that such literature also embraces a novelistic and fictitious form.[62] Yet, such literature, however novelistic and fictitious it turns out to be, commonly seeks to provide the reader with an experience of the actual world.[63] Interestingly, and possibly paradoxically, the modern hierarchy of discourses warrants primacy to scientific discourses because they speak about 'the real',[64] simultaneously demoting literature to a discursive practice for engagement with affects and emotions that are not deemed worthy of scientific studies.[65] It can be argued, however, that despite such modern demotion of bourgeois literature to an unscientific type of

Philosophy: An Essay on Interpretation, trans. Denis Savage (Yale University Press, 1970) pp. 32–36. Comp. with the claim of Erich Fromm according to which Marx, Nietszche and Freud are those thinkers who disturbed the modern confidence in freedom and autonomy, see Fromm, *Escape from Freedom* pp. 6–7.

59 On the idea that such literary genre is a continuation of capitalistic organization of Western societies, see Roland Barthes, Leo Bersani, Philippe Hamon, Michael Riffaterre, and Ian Watt, *Littérature et réalité* (Editions du Seuil, 1982) p. 8. On the idea that the novelistic genre is a transposition to literature of what the daily life is in an individualist society governed by a market economy, see Lucien Goldmann, *Pour une sociologie du roman* (Gallimard, 1964) p. 36.

60 It has been claimed that this form of literature was initiated by authors like Defoe and Richardson, see Barthes, Bersani, Hamon, Riffaterre, and Watt, *Littérature et réalité* pp. 18 and 34.

61 For Alain Supiot, the pursuit of the representation of real has also been witnessed in the practice of painting although it came to be challenged as early as the eighteenth century, see Supiot, *Homo Juridicus* p. 99.

62 See the typology of the novel form by Georg Lukács, *The Theory of the Novel: A Historico-philosophical Essay on the Forms of Great Epic Lterature* (Merlin Press, 1971) esp. pp. 97–154.

63 Barthes, Bersani, Hamon, Riffaterre, and Watt, *Littérature et réalité* pp. 7–8; de Certeau, *Histoire et psychanalyse entre science et fiction* p. 96; White, *Tropics of Discourses* pp. 121–122 and 142–143; Lukács, *The Theory of the Novel* p. 78.

64 Hayden White, *The Content of the Form: Narrative Discourse and Historical Representation* (John Hopkins University Press, 1987) p. 57; Louis Althusser, *Être Marxiste en Philosophie* (Presses Universitaires de France, 2015) pp. 244–255; Althusser, *Initiation à la Philosophie pour les Non-Philosophes* p. 200.

65 See the remarks of de Certeau, *Histoire et psychanalyse entre science et fiction* pp. 94 and 141. On the novel as being the new genre for the description of individual emotions, see

discourse, such literature has always been a discourse about 'the real'.[66] In fact, the daily life depicted in bourgeois literature is never deemed fabulous but always belongs to 'the real world' whose intricacy such literature is supposed to reveal.[67] In a way, it can be said that bourgeois literature, albeit adopting different protocols, methods, and formats,[68] has come to mimic the pursuit of 'the real' at the heart of scientific discourses.[69]

The foregoing explains why bourgeois literature has put in place an epistemology of the secret that is not so different from that of modern thought.[70] Being about the 'real' and the actual world, bourgeois literature always makes the reader presuppose that there is an experience of 'the real world' that the piece of literature concerned can offer and that can be gained through the purchase and reading of such literature.[71] In particular, the reading of bourgeois literature always boils down to an act that reveals something beautiful, subtle, intricate, unjust, unfair, tragic, scandalous, atrocious, etc. about the world. Bourgeois literature thus creates the expectation of a presence of a worldly reality (which corresponds to a necessity of secret content) that the act of reading will help the reader experience (which corresponds to a necessity of revelation) and that justifies the sales of such literature as a basic commodity in

White, *Tropics of Discourses* pp. 122–123; Paul Ricoeur, *Temps et récit, Volume 2, La configuration dans le récit de fiction* (Seuil, 1984) p. 17; Goldmann, *Pour une sociologie du roman* pp. 36–52; Barthes, Bersani, Hamon, Riffaterre, and Watt, *Littérature et réalité* pp. 17 and 35. On the idea that the complex distinctions between passions and affects constitute a product of the eighteenth-century literature to which they had been relegated, see Georges Vigarello, 'Joie, tristesse, terreur . . . La mécanique classique des humeurs', in Georges Vigarello (ed.), *Histoire des émotions. 1. De L'Antiquité aux Lumières* (Editions du Seuil, 2016) pp. 314 and 327.

66 In fact, it is this scienticity-likeness of the literature that allowed it to be insubordinate and subversive at times. Indeed, it is because it allegedly speaks about 'the real' that literature may be perceived as iconoclast and possibly a threat. See Foucault, *Dits et écrits, II* p. 253.

67 Foucault, *Dits et écrits, II* pp. 251–252.

68 Foucault, *Le Discours Philosophique* p. 73.

69 On the similitudes between scientific discourse and literature, see Foucault, *Le Discours Philosophique* p. 24.

70 On the idea that Marie-Henri Beyle (better known by his pen name Stendhal) ought to be considered as the inventor of the genius of suspicion, see Nathalie Sarraute, *L'Ère du Soupçon* (Gallimard, 1987). See also the remarks of Johann Chapoutot, *Le Grand Récit. Introduction à l'histoire de notre temps* (Presses Universitaires de France, 2021) p. 185.

71 For a strong charge against the realism and worldliness of the main characters of bourgeois novels as well as an attempt to promote the 'Nouveau Roman', see Nathalie Sarraute, *Tropisms and the Age of Suspicion* (Calder, 1963).

capitalistic societies. Of course, the extent of the revelation of such worldly experience hidden in the text often depends on the style and accessibility of the text itself as well as the aptitudes and predispositions of the reader. Yet, the act of reading, from the perspective of bourgeois literature, and in contrast with other type of literature like poetry,[72] commonly amounts to an act enabling the revelation of something about the actual world.[73] Literary critique of the bourgeois novel does not escape such conclusion.[74]

The necessity of secret content and the necessity of revelation around which the reading and purchase of bourgeois literature are organized are exacerbated by the idea that texts ought to have well-identified authors. Indeed, from the perspective of bourgeois literature, the author of the text concerned comes to be another layer that ought to be scrutinized for hidden, unknown, invisible content.[75] Once an author is ascribed to a piece of bourgeois literature – as it is in each and every piece of bourgeois literature, there is an intention, a life, a genealogy, a set of influences, biases, sensibilities, etc. that ought to be discovered. Such feature has been even further accentuated with the rise of Romanticism in the nineteenth century as one saw more and more literature where the first person is a narrator who reveals or confesses her inner self.[76] That said, even when what is to be revealed is not the intention, the life, the genealogy, the influences, the biases, the sensibilities, etc. of the author or those of the narrator, such bourgeois literature always seeks to tell us something about 'the real'.[77] Enigmatic styles and staged semantic ambiguities found in such literature are techniques used to provoke the reader

[72] See gen. Jacques Derrida, *L'écriture et la différence* (Editions du Seuil, 1967) p. 24. Foucault, *L'ordre du discours* p. 29; Jullien, *La pensée chinoise* p. 188. On the distinction between poetic attitudes to text and hermeneutical ones, see Jonathan Culler, *Literary Theory: A Very Short Introduction* (Oxford University Press, 1997) p. 62.

[73] On the idea that literary works train their readers in the hermeneutics of suspicion, see Rita Felski, *The Limits of Critique* (University of Chicago Press, 2015) p. 43.

[74] See gen. Roland Barthes, *Critique et vérité* (Editions du Seuil, 1999). The claim could even be made that the *counterpuntal reading* practiced in some streams of postcolonial studies (and whereby one should read and interpret modern literature and culture as being complicit with imperialism) similarly denotes an attitude of suspicion reminiscent of the modern epistemology of the secret. See, e.g., Edward Said, *Culture and Imperialism* (Vintage Books, 1994), esp. 3–61.

[75] On the rise of authored texts, see Foucault, *Dits et écrits, I (1954–1975)* pp. 827 and 850.

[76] Foucault, *Dits et écrits, II* pp. 412–413.

[77] de Certeau, *Histoire et psychanalyse entre science et fiction* p. 74.

into a search for hidden, unknown, invisible content that the act of reading, if performed properly, will reveal.[78]

The account of bourgeois literature that has been provided in the previous paragraphs should suffice to show the way in which it is organized around an epistemology of the secret, one that puts in place a necessity of secret content as well as a necessity of revelation. This is however not where the resemblance with the epistemology of the secret of international law ends. Like other epistemologies of the secret, the epistemology of the secret of the bourgeois literature conceals language and makes it transparent.[79] More importantly, the epistemology of the secret of bourgeois literature, however novelistic and fictitious the latter claims to be, also orders the imaginary, the social space, whilst providing a world of possibility as well as a world of impossibility.[80] In fact, bourgeois literature always tells us, in the name of 'the real' it reveals, what we ought to say, what we ought to believe, what we ought to do or not to do,[81] where we should see ourselves in the world,[82] etc., which is yet another striking parallel with the epistemology of the secret of international law.

2.6 The Epistemology of the Secret of Freudian Psychoanalysis

It is probably easy to fathom the extent to which Freudian psychoanalysis, and especially his concept of unconscious, is constitutive of an epistemology of the secret. In fact, Freudian psychoanalysis postulates a hidden side in the 'self', which is not directly intelligible or cognizable through its external manifestations but that ought to be extracted, which is the work of psychoanalysis. Actually, it could even be said that, because it carries an epistemology of the secret, Freudian psychoanalysis, which has had ramifications in many areas of study and disciplines despite early

[78] Ricoeur, *De l'interprétation* p. 28. Comp. with the idea that the obscurity of a text is what makes us think, see Deleuze, *Proust et les signes* p. 106.

[79] Barthes, Bersani, Hamon, Riffaterre, and Watt, *Littérature et réalité* p. 9. On the idea that the search for truth is bound to be conflated with the sign itself, see Deleuze, *Proust et les signes* p. 21.

[80] de Certeau, *Histoire et psychanalyse entre science et fiction* p. 75; Foucault, *Dits et écrits, II* p. 252.

[81] de Certeau, *Histoire et psychanalyse entre science et fiction* p. 74.

[82] See the very compelling charges of Edward Said about the complicity of modern novels with imperialism and thus with the idea that distant territories and their native peoples should be subjugated, see Said, *Culture and Imperialism* esp. pp. 3–61.

bourgeois and scientist enmity,[83] has contributed to the spread of that type of epistemology across human thought, and especially across the humanities.[84] Freudian psychoanalysis could even be construed as one of the initiators of the so-called hermeneutics of suspicion that it is now frequent to see at work in the humanities[85] and that has much in common with the epistemology of the secret as is understood here.[86]

The epistemology of the secret put in place by Freudian psychoanalysis can be described as follows. For Freud, there always is another signified than the one that is intelligible and accessible to us but that must be extracted and made known for it determines and pathologizes the present.[87] In other words, from the perspective of Freudian psychoanalysis, there always is something hidden, probably located in the past, which retains its grip upon the present and that requires methods of 'interpretation-as-excavation'.[88] Freudian psychoanalysis is thus premised on the necessitarian and permanent presence of a pathological unknown. In that respect, it is no coincidence that Freud, when speaking of the primitive modes of thinking, especially those linked to the murder of the original father, resorts to the metaphor of the vestiges of the city of Pompei.[89]

The resemblance with the epistemology of the secret of international law goes further. Freudian psychoanalysis also elevates the act of

[83] On the idea that Freudian psychoanalysis, because it challenged the scientistic and bourgeois order as well as the embargo on affects and emotions, was demoted to a non-science, see Althusser, *Initiation à la Philosophie pour les Non-Philosophes* p. 200. The same claim is made by de Certeau, *Histoire et psychanalyse entre science et fiction* p. 141.

[84] On the influence of Freud in the humanities in general, see Supiot, *Homo Juridicus* p. 101. See also de Certeau, *La faiblesse de croire* p. 198. On the influence of Freudian psychoanalysis on philosophy, see Emmanuel Levinas, *De l'existence à l'existant* (Vrin, 2013) p. 50. On the idea that it took until Freud (1856–1939) to rehabilitate the scientific study of affects and passions, see the remarks of de Certeau, *Histoire et psychanalyse entre science et fiction* pp. 94 and 141–142.

[85] Paul Ricoeur who coined this notion attributes such suspicious attitude to Freud, see gen. Ricoeur, *Freud and Philosophy* pp. 32–36. On the relation between Freudian psychoanalysis and Ricoeur's hermeneutics of suspicion, see the remarks Felski, *The Limits of Critique* pp. 4 and 58. See also Gayatri Chakravorty Spivak, *In Other Worlds: Essays in Cultural Politics* (Routledge, 2006) p. 141; Culler, *Literary Theory.* pp. 68–69.

[86] On the relation between the epistemology of the secret and the hermeneutics of suspicion, see supra Section 1.1.3.

[87] Freud acknowledges that the possibly of a form of unconscious determinism was already claimed by Descartes as well as Spinoza, each of them in very different terms though, see Sigmund Freud, *Unconscious* (Penguin Classics, 2005).

[88] The expression is from Felski, *The Limits of Critique* p. 58.

[89] Sigmund Freud, *Totem and Tabou*, 2nd edn (Routledge, 2001).

revelation into one of its linchpins. Because, for the sake of Freudian psychoanalysis, the hidden is pathological, it must be revealed to be healed and for the pathology that it causes to be discontinued. In other words, the act of revelation, for Freudian psychoanalysis, is necessary because only the revelation of the pathological hidden will bring an end to the pathology. Possibly in contrast with the epistemology of the secret of international law, it must be emphasized that the Freudian revelation is of an extreme intricacy, for the hidden, and especially the unconscious, cannot be represented through the normal category of language and thought. The hidden not only hides itself but also hides its own modes of signification. This is why Freudian revelation of the hidden always takes the form of a story: Freudian revelation is a form of story-telling.[90] This dimension of Freudian psychoanalysis, as will be shown in Chapter 5, bears important lessons for international legal thought and practice, especially when it comes to resisting the discursive ordering enabled by the epistemology of the secret of international law.[91]

2.7 The Epistemology of the Secret of Structuralist Thought

Structuralism, originally construed as a strand of linguistics and semiotics that emerged following Ferdinand de Saussure's *Course in General Linguistics* published in 1916[92] has ramification in a wide range of fields of study,[93] including anthropology,[94] literary critique,[95] the history of

[90] On this dimension of Freudian psychoanalysis, see Felski, *The Limits of Critique* p. 7; see also de Certeau, *Histoire et psychanalyse entre science et fiction* p. 129.

[91] See infra Chapter 5.

[92] See gen. Ferdinand de Saussure, *Course in General Linguistics*, ed. Charles Bally and Albert Sechehaye (Open Court, 1986). Comp. with Edward Sapir, *Language: An Introduction to the Study of Speech* (Ishi Press International, 1921) p. 22.

[93] On the wide ramifications of structuralist thinking across the humanities, see Culler, *Literary Theory* p. 138. For some insights on why structuralist thought first emerged in relation to linguistics and anthropology, see de Certeau, *Histoire et psychanalyse entre science et fiction* pp. 226–227. On the contemporary fall from grace of structuralism in all such fields, see Etienne Balibar, *Passions du concept. Epistémologie, théologique et politique. Ecrits II* (La découverte, 2020) p. 215.

[94] Claude Lévi-Strauss, *Structural Anthropology, Vol. II*, trans. Monique Layton (University of Chicago Press, 1976); see also Descola, *Par-delà nature et culture* p. 17.

[95] See gen. Barthes, *L'aventure sémiologique*; see also Barthes, *Le bruissement de la langue* pp. 18 and 55. On the ambiguous relationship of Roland Barthes with structuralism, see Barthes, *Le bruissement de la langue* p. 15; see also Barthes, *Critique et vérité* p. 54.

thought,[96] theory of hermeneutics,[97] in the history of myths and religions,[98] in gender critique,[99] in the study of affects,[100] critical legal theory,[101] and even Marxist philosophy.[102] It also deeply permeates international legal thought,[103] which is why it is worthy of mention in this chapter.

There unsurprisingly is an immense variety of structuralist patterns of thought. Yet, for the sake of this chapter it can be said, with some broad

[96] Foucault, like Barthes, had a very ambivalent relationship with structuralism. For some illustration of Foucault's repeated rejection of any espousal of a structuralist type of thinking, see Foucault, *Dits et écrits, I (1954–1975)* pp. 631, 844, 881, and 1077; Foucault, *Dits et écrits, II* pp. 145, 467, and 1254; Noam Chomsky and Michel Foucault, *The Chomsky-Foucault Debate on Human Nature* (The New Press, 2006) p. 147; see also the remarks of Simeon Wade, *Foucault in California* (Heyday, 2019) p. 101. For some illustrations of Foucault flirting with structuralism and of his regular uses of the concept of structure, see Foucault, *Naissance de la clinique* pp. 15–18 and 168; Foucault, *Dits et écrits, I (1954–1975)* pp. 426, 636, 679, and 685; Foucault, *Dits et écrits, II* p. 1055; Foucault, *Sécurité, Territoire, Population* pp. 109 and 186; Foucault, *'Il faut défendre la société'* p. 44. On the relationship of Foucault with structuralism, see the remarks of Paul Veyne, *Foucault. Sa pensée, sa personne* (Albin Michel, 2008) p. 165; see also the remarks of Balibar, *Passions du concept* p. 127.

[97] Stanley Fish, *Is There a Text in This Class?* (Harvard University Press, 1980) p. 356; Ricoeur, *De l'interprétation* pp. 19–22.

[98] Georges Dumézil, *L'Idéologie des trois fonctions dans les épopées des peuples indo-européens* (Gallimard, 1968); Georges Dumézil, *Types épiques indo-européens: un héros, un sorcier, un roi* (Gallimard, 1971); Georges Dumézil, *Histoires romaines* (Gallimard, 1973).

[99] Judith Butler, *Gender Trouble: Feminism and the Subversion of Identify*, 2nd edn (Routledge, 1990) p. xxvi.

[100] See gen. Lordon, *La société des affects*.

[101] See David Kennedy, 'Critical Theory, Structuralism and Contemporary Legal Scholarship' (1985–1986) 21 *New England Law Review* 209.

[102] See, e.g., Althusser, *Être Marxiste en Philosophie* pp. 132–146 and 285–292.

[103] On the structuralist foundations of Martti Koskenniemi's account of international legal argumentation, see Akbar Rasulov, 'From Apology to Utopia and the Inner Life of International Law' (2016) 29 *Leiden Journal of International Law* 641; Sahib Singh, 'International Legal Positivism and New Approaches to International Law', in Jörg Kammerhofer and Jean d'Aspremont (eds.), *International Legal Positivism in a Postmodern World* (Cambridge University Press, 2014) pp. 291–316; Emmanuelle Jouannet comes with a similar but more nuanced account, see Emmanuelle Jouannet, 'A Critical Introduction', in Martti Koskenniemi, *The Politics of International Law* (Hart, 2011) pp. 2 and 7–12. For an overview of the merits of structuralism for international legal thought, see Justin Desautels-Stein, 'International Legal Structuralism: A Primer' (2016) 8 *International Theory* 201–235; and Justin Desautels-Stein, 'Structuralist Legal Histories' (2015) 78 *Law and Contemporary Problems* 37. On the unexploited potential of structuralism in international legal thought, see the remarks by Ntina Tzouvala, *Capitalism as Civilisation: A History of International Law* (Cambridge University Press, 2020) pp. 5–7.

brush strokes, that structuralism boils down to a type of synchronic thinking that focuses on the universality, permanence, and a-historical character of a given structure, system, or totality. According to structuralism, the structure, rather than the agent or the subject, determines the availability of what can be thought, said, seen, and experienced.[104] From the perspective of structuralism, the subject and its agency are displaced by the structure.[105] The subject can simply not constitute the origin[106] of what can be thought, said, seen, and experienced because, from the vantage point of structuralism, it is the structure that produces the subject and not the opposite.[107] To put it differently, structuralism boils down to the permanent negation of the foundational event and of contingency[108] in favour of a permanent referencing system.[109] This is why thinking in terms of structures, rather than subjectivity, is commonly associated with the 'pleasure of systemic thinking'.[110] Thinking in terms of structures entails a systematization and axiomization of relationships,[111] thereby giving rise to an taxonomic mode of thinking[112] that ensures coherence, completion, and totality.[113] Actually, to many, structuralist thought is the climax of modern scientistic thinking that emerged with modern thought,[114] which possibly explains why it became

104 Structuralism's exclusion of agency and historical contingency as well as its turning a blind eye to social conditions of the production of signs has been the object of very severe criticisms, see Balibar, *Passions du concept* p. 216; Descola, *Par-delà nature et culture* p. 170; Pierre Bourdieu, *Ce que parler veut dire. L'économie des échanges linguistiques* (Fayard, 1982) pp. 8–9 and 130; Foucault, *Dits et écrits, I (1954–1975)* p. 1139; Chomsky and Foucault, *The Chomsky-Foucault Debate on Human Nature* p. 147.

105 Foucault, *Dits et écrits, II* p. 871; Balibar, *Passions du concept* p. 219; Kennedy, 'Critical Theory, Structuralism and Contemporary Legal Scholarship' p. 249.

106 Foucault, *Dits et écrits, II* p. 590.

107 Balibar, *Passions du concept* p. 221.

108 Derrida, *L'écriture et la différence* p. 44.

109 On the idea that structure is a mechanism of permanent referencing, see Legendre, *Sur la question dogmatique en Occident* p. 141.

110 Barthes, *L'aventure sémiologique* p. 12.

111 Balibar, *Passions du concept* p. 229.

112 Althusser, *Être Marxiste en Philosophie* p. 105.

113 Derrida, *L'écriture et la différence* pp. 12 and 43.

114 Eagleton, *The Function of Criticism* p. 96. See the remarks of Barthes, *Le bruissement de la langue* p. 15; Balibar, *Passions du concept* pp. 218 and 232; Vincent Descombes, *Le Même et l'Autre. Quarante-cinq Ans de Philosophie Française (1933–1978)* (Editions de Minuit, 1979) p. 125. For Foucault, it is a very advanced mode of formalist thinking, see Foucault, *Dits et écrits, II* p. 1251. For him, it is also a culmination of all that Western philosophy tried to achieve, see Foucault, *Le Discours Philosophique* pp. 211–212.

a very mainstream way of thinking in the humanities in the second half of the twentieth century.[115]

If structuralism is so construed, it may be counter-intuitive to think that structuralist thought hosts an epistemology of the secret as the latter is understood in this book. Indeed, structuralist thought is focused on what enables rather than what is determined. Structuralist thought also is synchronic and does not presuppose a meaning created in the past that would still be hidden in the present. For these reasons, structuralism does not postulate an inherent presence but rather a space of possibility. It must be acknowledged that structuralist thought is built on the theoretical and abstract presupposition of an ultimate foundation – the so-called transcendental signifier – without which the binaries of the structure cannot start to relate to one another. However, this fundamental presupposition of an ultimate and transcendental signified (or origin) on which the whole idea of structure (system) is built cannot be construed as the necessary presence of an ultimate content that would be constitutive of an epistemology of the secret as is understood here.[116] Indeed, by virtue of structuralist thought, this ultimate and transcendental signified is never to be looked for, let alone to be found or revealed.[117] This is precisely what makes structuralism such an efficient and popular mode of thinking: there never is a necessity to search for the (hidden) origin or the foundation of the system concerned. Structuralist thought is a very anti-foundationalist mode of thinking that stifles any possible need for the finding of (hidden) origins or foundations. The structure is left on its feet out of space, out of time, and out of agency without the necessity to postulate, let alone reveal, a hidden origin or foundation.

Whilst the ultimate and transcendental signified (or origin) is not what turns structuralist thought into an epistemology of the secret, another dimension of structuralism ought to be mentioned here as it makes the latter the bearer of an epistemology of the secret reminiscent of the epistemology of the secret of international law: the very code of the structure (system) that is deemed present and which must be searched

[115] On the idea that structuralism is no longer deemed subversive, see Balibar, *Passions du concept* p. 215.

[116] See *contra* the idea that structuralism is built on a metaphysics of presence, see Derrida, *De la Grammatologie* p. 103; Jacques Derrida, *Marges de la Philosophie* (Editions de Minuit, 1972) pp. 187–188.

[117] Barthes, *L'aventure sémiologique* p. 16; Barthes, *Le bruissement de la langue* p. 75. See also Jacques Derrida speaking of the absence of the transcendental signified, see Derrida, *L'écriture et la différence* pp. 410–410.

for. Indeed, thinking in structuralist terms is about breaking the code that is key to its systemic functioning.[118] The quest imposed by structuralist thought is always a quest for revealing the code of the structure, of the system.[119] In other words, structuralist thought is an inquisitory mode of thinking geared towards the elucidation of how the structure of the system constrains and enables. It is submitted here that this presupposition of a fundamental code by virtue of which the structure enables and constrains what can be thought, said, seen, and experienced as well as the necessity to decipher and reveal such code are constitutive of an epistemology of the secret. In fact, being structuralist is to find, elucidate, and reveal the code of the structure in the present. It is true that structuralism may not prove an epistemology of the secret as sophisticated as that of the Christian governance of the mind or that of modern thought, if only because it says very little about the necessity of a revelation as well as the modes of revelation that the act of revelation ought to conform with. Yet, the rudimentary epistemology of the secret that accompanies structuralist thought is a source of valuable insights for this book's venture into the epistemology of the secret of international law given the extent to which structuralist modes of thinking have moulded international legal thought and practice.[120]

2.8 An Epistemology of the Secret after Poststructuralist Thought?

By their rejection of logocentrism[121] and of the idea that texts carry a preexisting meaning that has been loaded unto them to be delivered through the act of interpretation – which is the premise of traditional hermeneutics,[122] poststructuralist thinkers[123] may look like the exterminators of any

118 Bourdieu, *Ce que parler veut dire* p. 13; see also Descombes, *Le Même et l'Autre* pp. 114–115.
119 Kennedy, 'Critical Theory, Structuralism and Contemporary Legal Scholarship' p. 269.
120 See supra Section 1.1.2.1.
121 On the notion of logocentrism, see supra Section 1.2.1.
122 On this traditional mode of thinking, see Derrida, *L'écriture et la différence* pp. 409–410; Jacques Derrida, *The Beast and the Sovereign, Volume 1* (University of Chicago Press, 2011) p. 17; Barthes, *Le bruissement de la langue* pp. 75 and 139.
123 On the distinction between structuralism and poststructuralism, see Jonathan Culler, *On Deconstruction: Theory and Criticism after Structuralism* (Routledge, 2008) pp. 22–30. Comp. with the idea of superstructuralism of Richard Harland to encapsulate the work of both structuralists and poststructuralists as well as to account for the work of those thinkers that do not really fit in either of these categories or have moved between them,

possible epistemology of the secret. From the perspective of post-structuralism, texts never contain a signified – not even one that is indeterminate – but are solely signifiers that bear the traces of other signifiers to which they refer indefinitely, thereby making meaning always absent because constantly deferred.[124] Since all the epistemologies of the secret described in this chapter, as well as the epistemology of the secret of international law introduced in Chapter 1, are premised on the idea that texts have a pre-existing meaning – albeit indeterminate – which they carry but that is hidden and must be revealed, poststructuralist thought can be read as rendering any epistemology of the secret an utter impossibility. In that regard, it is no coincidence to read in post-structuralist literature claims that one must refrain from assigning a secret content to a text[125] or calls to construe texts, not as stone fruits but as onions.[126]

The abovementioned argument that poststructuralist thought inevitably incapacitates any epistemology that, in one way or another, functions as an epistemology of the secret must however be seriously qualified for several reasons. First, it seems fair to say that the poststructuralist objection against logocentrism has had little purchase, except in some circles in literary critique and gender critique.[127] In fact, most of the humanities have continued to be loyal to logocentrism as well as the presupposition of a pre-existing meaning loaded into texts, which can later be delivered or revealed. This has surely been the case in legal studies[128] as well as

see Richard Harland, *Superstructuralism. The Philosophy of Structuralism and Post-Structuralism* (Routledge, 1987).

124 Jacques Derrida, *Positions* (Editions de Minuit, 1972) p. 54; Derrida, *De la Grammatologie* pp. 11–126; Derrida, *Marges de la Philosophie* (Editions de Minuit, 1972) pp. 1–29; Derrida, L'écriture et la différence p. 411. On this aspect of the work of Derrida, see the remarks of Peter Salmon *An Event Perhaps* (Verso, 2020) p. 12; see also Geoffrey Bennington, *Jacques Derrida* (Editions du Seuil, 1991) p. 56. Comp. with Barthes, *Le bruissement de la langue*; Roland Barthes, *S/Z* (Editions du Seuil, 1970) pp. 9–11.

125 See Barthes, *Le bruissement de la langue* p. 66; Barthes, *Critique et vérité* p. 78; Roland Barthes, *Le grain de la voix. Entretiens 1962–1980* (Editions du Seuil, 1981) p. 182.

126 Barthes, *Le bruissement de la langue* p. 159.

127 On how critique has remained attached to the modern distinction between the form and the world, see gen. Mitchell, *Questions of Modernity* p. 20; see also Foucault, *Dits et écrits, II* p. 1266.

128 On the idea that Derrida's has been a fashionable label but was not really read, see Peter Goodrich, Florian Hoffmann, Michel Rosenfeld, and Cornelia Vismann, 'Introduction: A Philosophy of Legal Enigmas', in Peter Goodrich, Florian Hoffmann, Michel Rosenfeld, and Cornelia Vismann (eds.), *Derrida and Legal Philosophy* (Palgrave

international legal studies,[129] including in the most critical strands of legal scholarship.[130] Second, in most humanities, and especially in critical legal studies, poststructuralism thought has been reduced to a question of deconstruction,[131] deflecting the attention away from the charge against logocentrism.[132] Last but not least, poststructuralist thinkers themselves have acknowledged that there may be no way out of logocentrism[133] and that the very texts through which poststructuralist positions are spelled out are themselves caught in logocentrism.[134] This is why, for such

MacMillan, 2008) pp. 4 and 7–10. On the idea that the reception of the work of Derrida and especially the main insights of Grammatology has yet to occur in legal academia, see Peter Goodrich, 'Europe in America: Grammatology, Legal Studies, and the Politics of Transmission' (2001) 101 *Columbia Law Review* 2033 at 2041–2042; see also Vincent Forray and Sébastien Pimont, *Décrire le droit . . . et le transformer. Essai sur la décriture du droit* (Dalloz, 2017).

129 See d'Aspremont, *After Meaning*; see also the remarks of Rose Parfitt, *The Process of International Legal Reproduction: Inequality, Historiography, Resistance* (Cambridge University Press, 2019) p. 21; Tzouvala, *Capitalism as Civilisation* pp. 38–40; Fuad Zarbiyev, *Le Discours interprétatif en droit international* (Bruylant, 2015) pp. 109–118; see also the remarks of Akbar who argues that Martti Koskenniemi engagement with structuralism in *From Apology to Utopia* is much more on the side of traditional French (-speaking) structuralism and that it is more a structuralism *à la Saussure*, see Rasulov, 'From Apology to Utopia and the Inner Life of International Law' p. 641. Comp. with the remarks of China Miéville on the work of Martti Koskenniemi in China Miéville, *Between Equal Rights: A Marxist Theory of International Law* (Haymarket Books, 2006) pp. 55–56. For a similar claim about the meaning-centric use of deconstruction in US legal scholarship, see Pierre Schlag, '"Le Hors de Texte, C'est Moi". The Politics of Form and the Domestication of Deconstruction' (1990) 11 *Cardozo Law Review* 1631 at 1643–1645.

130 See however the use of Derrida by Pierre Schlag, see Schlag, 'Le Hors de Texte, C'est Moi'.

131 For some famous examples of a discussion of Derrida through the sole lens of deconstruction, see Jack M. Balkin, 'Deconstructive Practice and Legal Theory' (1987) 96 *Yale Law Journal* 743; Jack M. Balkin, 'Deconstruction's Legal Career' (2005) 27 *Cardozo Law Review* 719. See the criticisms of Balkin's treatment of Deconstruction by Schlag, '"Le Hors de Texte, C'est Moi"'. On the claim that the attention in legal scholarship was deflected away from Derrida by virtue of the debate on deconstruction, see Goodrich, 'Europe in America' pp. 2037–2042.

132 For an interesting rebuttal by Derrida's himself of the uses of deconstruction in the United States, see Jacques Derrida, 'Letter to a Japanese Friend', in David Wood and Robert Bernasconi (eds.), *Derrida and Différance* (Northwestern University Press, 1988) p. 3.

133 Derrida, *Positions* pp. 21, 35, and 56; see also Derrida, *L'écriture et la différence* p. 46. On the idea that recuperative powers of logocentrism in legal studies must not be underestimated, see Schlag 'Le Hors de Texte, C'est Moi' p. 1649.

134 For some general remarks on the meaning-centric closure of a book, see Derrida, *Positions* p. 11; Derrida, *De la Grammatologie* pp. 30–31; Jacques Derrida, *Papier Machine* (Galilée, 2001) p. 27. On the idea that Derrida's Grammatology is about the

thinkers, de-necessitating logocentrism – and thus the discontinuation of the epistemologies of the secret that the former has enabled – does not entail a neutralization of logocentrism. The very same goes with this book, which is no attempt to unravel and do away with the epistemology of the secret of international law as there may simply be no way out of it. As will be further discussed in Chapter 5, what matters is to be able to resist it.

For all these reasons, it is submitted here that the – very compelling – poststructuralist charges against logocentrism have, overall, remained innocuous and have accordingly not barred the possibility of certain discourses organizing an epistemology of the secret. This is why logocentrism and the epistemologies of the secret that the former enables continue to thrive in human thought. The epistemology of the secret of international law discussed in this book is not an anomaly but only an illustration of the extent to which the dominance of logocentrism and all that it allows have remained unaffected by poststructuralist thought.

That being said, a final observation is in order regarding the possibility of *an epistemology of the secret short of logocentrism*. What if poststructuralism had successfully shown the impossibility of logocentrism and yet preserved the possibility of an epistemology of the secret? The question is warranted following the claim that poststructuralist thought may have convincingly shown that the meaning of text is always absent but left epistemologies of the secret unaltered.[135] According to this argument, the unreliability of meaning-deferring signs postulated by poststructuralist thought secures the permanence of suspicion.[136] From such perspective, poststructuralist thought brings about a second-level hermeneutics that, although it does not focus on an individual text, still perpetuates the search for meaning.[137] From such perspective, poststructuralism can be read as putting in place an epistemology of the secret short of any logocentrism and yet still guaranteeing salient secrets to be discovered.[138]

Let me indicate very clearly that I disagree with such a reading poststructuralist thought, for at least two reasons. First, I continue to think

end of the book, see Goodrich, 'Europe in America' p. 2042; Florian Hoffmann, 'Epilogue: In Lieu of Conclusion' (2005) 6 *German Law Journal* 197 at 197. On the idea that every piece of writing has unity, see Brian Dillon, *Essayism* (Fizcarraldo Editions, 2017) p. 15.

135 See gen. Felski, *The Limits of Critique*.

136 Felski, *The Limits of Critique* pp. 9, 33, and 81.

137 Felski, *The Limits of Critique* p. 55.

138 Felski, *The Limits of Critique* p. 59.

that if poststructuralism has not discontinued all the epistemologies of the secret discussed in this chapter and the previous one, it is because logocentrism has continued to thrive, especially in the humanities. It is therefore difficult to think of a system of thought that has actually done away with logocentrism. Second, and more fundamentally, even if we postulate that logocentrism has been dealt a lethal blow by poststructuralism, it is argued here that in the absence of a logocentric presupposition, it is not possible to experience a necessity of secret content as well as a necessity of revelation in relation to any text, not least because there is no content to be held hidden, unknown, or invisible for that content is always absent and pushed back from one text to another. In other words, there can be no experience of the necessary presence of hidden, unknown, or invisible content and of the necessity of revelation if one denies that texts carry a certain pre-existing content that texts are meant to deliver. In that sense, and as it is understood here, epistemologies of the secret are inseparable from logocentric thought and dependent on there being no poststructuralist revolution.

3

Secrecy and Transparency in International Legal Literature

The epistemology of the secret of international law and the two necessities that compose it, namely the necessity of secret content and the necessity of revelation, as they have been spelled out in Chapter 1, have not been the object of thorough scholarly attention. It is true that international legal scholars have occasionally mobilized the idea of the hermeneutics of suspicion to describe the way in which certain scholars dismiss opponents' arguments to be ideologically or politically motivated postures as opposed to scientifically valid positions.[1] Yet, this has been occasional and at best a convenient tool of description. As a specific intellectual posture of international lawyers whereby the texts, practices, actors, effects, representations, past, etc. of international law are held as carrying secrets that ought to be revealed, the epistemology of the secret of international law has remained outside international lawyers' purview.

This does not mean, however, that the idea of secret has been totally absent from international legal thought and practice. In fact, international lawyers, and especially international legal scholars, have taken a dim look at all the secretive and undisclosed practices that they suppose to be at work in various international legal processes, trying to reveal them for the sake of regulating them. For instance, the practice (and the attempted prohibition) of secret treaties has long been drawing attention.[2] In the context of international legal proceedings, discussions have

[1] See, e.g., Anne Orford, *International Law and the Politics of History* (Cambridge University Press, 2021) pp. 5–6. On the notion of hermeneutics of suspicion and its relation to the idea of an epistemology of the secret, see supra Section 1.1.1.3.

[2] Megan Donaldson, 'The Survival of the Secret Treaty: Publicity, Secrecy, and Legality in the International Order' (2017) 111 *American Journal of International Law* 575; see also Richard Caddell, 'Secret Treaties' (2006) *Max Planck Encyclopedias of International Law* (opil.ouplaw.com); Danae Azaria, 'Secret Treaties in International Law and the Faith of States in Decentralized Enforcement' (2017) *American Journal of International Law Unbound* 469; Vittorio Mainetti, 'Les traités secrets en droit international', in Piermarco Zen Ruffinen (ed.), *Les secrets et le droit* (Schulthess, 2004) pp. 39–417.

been unfolding about the consequence of a non-disclosure or suppression of evidentiary documents,[3] the way in which secrets are divulged,[4] or the production of false secrets.[5] The legality of states' spying practices has also generated an important amount of scholarly debate.[6] Likewise, arguments about a right to secrecy to the benefit of international organizations has also been broached.[7] The secrecy and confidentiality of the choices made by international judges among various custom identification methodologies for the sake of ascertaining the rules of customary

[3] See Anthony Carty, 'The Corfu Channel Case – And the Missing Admiralty Orders' (2004) 3 *The Law and Practice of International Courts and Tribunals* 1; W. Michael Reisman and Christina Parajon Skinner, *Fraudulent Evidence before Public International Tribunals: The Dirty Stories of International Law* (Cambridge University Press, 2014) pp. 54–77; Andrea Gattini, 'Evidentiary Issues in the ICJ's Genocide Case' (2007) 5 *Journal of International Criminal Justice* 889; Andrea Gattini and Giulio Cortesi, 'Some New Evidence on the ICJ's Treatment of Evidence: The Second Genocide Case' (2015) 28 *Leiden Journal of International Law* 899.

[4] Anna Riddell and Brendan Plant, *Evidence before the International Court of Justice* (British Institute of International and Comparative Law, 2016) p. 2; Rüdiger Wolfrum, 'International Courts and Tribunals, Evidence', in Rüdiger Wolfrum (ed.), *Max Planck Encyclopedia of Public International Law* (2012) p. 553; Sara Mansour Fallah, 'The Admissibility of Unlawfully Obtained Evidence before International Courts and Tribunals' (2020) 19 *The Law and Practice of International Courts and Tribunals* 147; Charles N. Brower, 'Evidence Before International Tribunals: The Need for Some Standard Rules' (1994) 28 *International Lawyer* 47; Christopher Gosnell, 'Admissibility of Evidence', in Karim A. A. Khan, Caroline Buisman, and Chris Gosnell (eds.), *Principles of Evidence in International Criminal Justice* (Oxford University Press, 2010) p. 375.

[5] Reisman and Skinner, *Fraudulent Evidence Before Public International Tribunals* pp. 15–54, 90–100, and 163–192.

[6] Matteo Tondini, 'Espionage and International Law in the Age of Permanent Competition' (2018) 57 *The Military Law and the Law of War Review* 17; Christopher D. Baker, 'Tolerance of International Espionage: A Functional Approach' (2003) 19 *American University International Law Review* 1091; Simon Chesterman, 'The Spy Who Came in from the Cold War: Intelligence and International Law' (2006) 27 *Michigan Journal of International Law* 1071; Gérard Cohen-Jonathan and Robert Kovar, 'L'espionnage en temps de paix' (1960) 6 *French Yearbook of International Law* 239; John Kish, *International Law and Espionage* (Martinus Nijhoff, 1995); Fabien Lafouasse, *L'espionnage dans le droit international* (Nouveau Monde Éditions, 2012); Inaki Navarrete, 'L'espionnage en temps de paix en droit international public' (2016) 53 *Canadian Yearbook of International Law* 1. On question of cyber-espionnage, see Thibault Moulin, *Cyber-espionage in International Law: Silence Speaks* (Manchester University Press, 2023); Russell Buchan, *Cyber Espionage and International Law* (Hart, 2018).

[7] Paul Reuter, 'Le droit au secret et les institutions internationales' (1956) 2 *French Yearbook of International Law* 46; see also Hans Morgenthau speaking of the vice of publicity, see Hans Morgenthau, *Politics among Nations* (Alfred A. Knopf, 1950) pp. 431–433.

international law has similarly drawn the attention and been the object of criticism in the international legal scholarship.[8]

In recent years, the possibility of requiring more transparency – understood on that occasion as the opposite of secrecy[9] – in rule-making, policy-making, regulatory, and dispute settlement practices has been the object of extensive scholarly literature. Indeed, notwithstanding the objections that have occasionally been raised against transparency,[10] many international lawyers have come to celebrate and promote transparency,[11] for they deem it instrumental in the legitimacy[12] and accountability[13] of international decision-making processes whilst viewing it as an incentive for compliance.[14] It is in this context that an important body of scholarship has been produced on a possible legal obligation to transparency understood as the obligation, in rule-making and judicial decision-making processes, to provide access to information and produce specific documents. This obligation to transparency has particularly been

[8] Massimo Lando, 'Secret Custom *or* The Impact of Judicial Deliberations on The Identification of Customary International Law' (2022) 81 *The Cambridge Law Journal* 550.

[9] Suzanne J. Piotrowski, *Transparency and Secrecy: A Reader Linking Literature and Contemporary Debate* (Lexington Books, 2010); see Mark Fenster, 'The Opacity of Transparency' (2006) 91 *Iowa Law Review* 885; Ann Florini, 'The End of Secrecy' (1998) 112 *Foreign Policy* 50; Andrea Bianchi, 'On Power and Illusion: The Concept of Transparency in International Law', in Andrea Bianchi and Anne Peters (eds.), *Transparency in International Law* (Cambridge University Press, 2013) p. 2; Anne Peters, 'Towards Transparency as a Global Norm', in Andrea Bianchi and Anne Peters (eds.), *Transparency in International Law* (Cambridge University Press, 2013) p. 534.

[10] Fenster, 'The Opacity of Transparency'; Archon Fung, Mary Graham, and David Weil, *Full Disclosure: The Perils and Promise of* Transparency (Cambridge University Press, 2007); Bianchi, 'On Power and Illusion' p. 1; See Peters, 'Towards Transparency as a Global Norm' pp. 570–574.

[11] On the idea that transparency is now a requirement that dominates Western societies, see Bianchi, 'On Power and Illusion' p. 2; Christopher Hood, 'Transparency in Historical Perspective', in Christopher Hood and David Heald (eds.), *Transparency: The Key to Better Governance?* (Oxford University Press, 2006) pp. 3–23.

[12] Alan Boyle and Kasey McCall-Smith, 'Transparency in International Law-making', in Andrea Bianchi and Anne Peters (eds.), *Transparency in International Law* (Cambridge University Press, 2013) p. 420; Peters, 'Towards Transparency as a Global Norm' pp. 556–558.

[13] Peters, 'Towards Transparency as a Global Norm' p. 534; see also Benedict Kingsbury, Nico Krisch, and Richard B. Stewart, 'The Emergence of Global Administrative Law' (2005) 68 *Law and Contemporary Problems* 15.

[14] Panagiotis Delimatsis, 'Institutional Transparency in the WTO', in Andrea Bianchi and Anne Peters (eds.), *Transparency in International Law* (Cambridge University Press, 2013) p. 114.

discussed in relation to environmental law,[15] international investment law,[16] international economic law,[17] the law of collective security,[18] and in the framework of international judicial proceedings.[19] The customary

[15] See, e.g., the 1998 Convention on Access to Information, Public Participation in Decision-Making and Access to Justice in Environmental Matters (the so-called Aarhus Convention), United Nations, *Treaty Series*, vol. 2161, p. 447. See the remarks of Makane Moïse Mbengue and Mara Tignino, 'Public Participation and Amicus Curiae in Water Disputes', in Edith Brown Weiss, Laurence Boisson de Chazournes and Nathalie Bernasconi-Osterwalder (eds.), *Fresh Water and International Economic Law* (Oxford University Press, 2005) pp. 367–405; Jutta Brunnée and Ellen Hey, 'Transparency and International Environmental Institutions', in Andrea Bianchi and Anne Peters (eds.), *Transparency in International Law* (Cambridge University Press, 2013) p. 23; Jonas Ebbesson, 'Global or European Only? International Law on Transparency in Environmental Matters for Members of the Public', in Andrea Bianchi and Anne Peters (eds.), *Transparency in International Law* (Cambridge University Press, 2013) p. 49.

[16] See Esmé Shirlow, 'Three Manifestations of Transparency in International Investment Law: A Story of Sources, Stakeholders and Structures' (2017) 8 *Göttingen Journal of International Law* 73; Joachim Delaney and Daniel Barstow Magraw, 'Procedural Transparency', in Peter Muchlinski, Federico Ortino, and Christoph Schreuer (eds.), *Oxford Handbook of International Investment Law* (Oxford Universtiy Press, 2008) p. 725; Martins Paparinski, *The International Minimum Standard and Fair and Equitable Treatment* (Oxford University Press, 2013) p. 248; Julie Maupin, 'Transparency in International Investment Law: The Good, the Bad and the Murky', in Andrea Bianchi and Anne Peters (eds.), *Transparency in International Law* (Cambridge University Press, 2013) p. 142.

[17] For a discussion of the obligation to transparency in the context of international economic law, see Carl-Sebastian Zoellner, 'Transparency: An Analysis of an Evolving Fundamental Principle in International Economic Law' (2006) 27 *Michigan Journal of International Law* 579; Lothar Ehring, 'Public Access to Dispute Settlement Hearings in the World Trade Organization' (2008) 11 *Journal of International Economic Law* 1021; J. H. H. Weiler, 'The Rule of Lawyers and the Ethos of Diplomats: Reflections on the Internal and External Legitimacy of WTO Dispute Settlement' (2001) 35 *Journal of World Trade* 191 at 196–197 and 203; Delimatsis, 'Institutional Transparency in the WTO' p. 112; Yves Nouvel, 'Les relations économiques internationales à l'heure de la transparence', in Jean-Marc Sorel (ed.), *Le droit international économique à l'aube du XXIe siècle. En hommage aux professeurs Dominique Carreau et Patrick Juillard* (Pedone, 2009) pp. 177–190.

[18] Antonios Tzanakopoulos, 'Transparency in the Security Council', in Andrea Bianchi and Anne Peters (eds.), *Transparency in International Law* (Cambridge University Press, 2013) p. 392.

[19] See gen. Armin von Bogdandy and Ingo Venzke, 'In Whose Name? An Investigation of International Courts' Public Authority and Its Democratic Justification' (2012) 23 *European Journal of International Law* 7 at 26–30; see also Thore Neumann and Bruno Simma, 'Transparency in International Adjudication', in Andrea Bianchi and Anne Peters (eds.), *Transparency in International Law* (Cambridge University Press, 2013) p. 436.

character of such an obligation[20] as well as its status of general principle of law[21] has also been examined at length. The question has also arisen whether private actors, and notably multinational companies, are held by such requirement.[22] Transparency has similarly been construed as the object of a human right protected by international treaties.[23] In judicial practice, even when transparency is not held to correspond to a specific legal obligation, it has occasionally been used as a yardstick to gauge the behaviour of states and the congruence of such behaviour with their formal and procedural obligations.[24] When it is not understood as a legal obligation, transparency is also sometimes associated, especially in the context of governance beyond the state, with a less formal aspiration for access to information and knowledge, for legitimacy and accountability, or for participatory democracy and good governance.[25]

Engagements by international lawyers with the secretive and undisclosed practices that they suppose to be at work in international legal processes – and which they often deplore – are thus aplenty. Yet, none of these scholarly contributions, as is shown by the short account thereof provided in this chapter, discusses the secret-based discursive patterns

[20] See Peters, 'Towards Transparency as a Global Norm' p. 584; Arnaud de Nanteuil, 'La transparence en droit international: Réflexions sur une exigence encore incertaine' (2015) 61 *French Yearbook of International Law* 809 at 824–826; see also Adel A Hamadi Al Tamimi v. Sultanate of Oman, ICSID Case No. ARB/11/33 para. 399. For a strong contestation of the customary character of the obligation of transparency, see Bianchi, 'On Power and Illusion' p. 5.

[21] See Peters, 'Towards Transparency as a Global Norm' pp. 584–585; See also de Nanteuil, 'La transparence en droit international' pp. 826–829

[22] Peters, 'Towards Transparency as a Global Norm' pp. 551–552

[23] See Jonathan Klaaren, 'The Human Right to Information and Transparency', in Andrea Bianchi and Anne Peters (eds.), *Transparency in International Law* (Cambridge University Press, 2013) p. 223; See Peters, 'Towards Transparency as a Global Norm' pp. 586–587; Marko Milanovic, 'Human Rights Treaties and Foreign Surveillance: Privacy in the Digital Age' (2015) 56 *Harvard International Law Journal* 81.

[24] See International Court of Justice, Whaling in the Antarctic (Australia v. Japan: New Zealand intervening), Judgment of 31 March 2014, para. 195.

[25] On the idea of a 'global administrative law of transparency', see Megan Donaldson and Benedict Kingsbury, 'Power and the Public: The Nature and Effects of Formal Transparency Policies in Global Governance Institutions' in Andrea Bianchi and Anne Peters (eds.), *Transparency in International Law* (Cambridge University Press, 2013) pp. 515–519. On transparency and accountability in global administrative law in general, see Kingsbury, Krisch, and Stewart, 'The Emergence of Global Administrative Law'; see also Luis Miguel Hinojosa Martinez, 'Transparency in International Financial Institutions', in Andrea Bianchi and Anne Peters (eds.), *Transparency in International Law* (Cambridge University Press, 2013) p. 77; Peters, 'Towards Transparency as a Global Norm' p. 534; Bianchi, 'On Power and Illusion' p. 8.

that shape international legal thought and practice, let alone provide insights on the extent to which international lawyers systematically postulate the presence of secret content in international law's texts, practices, actors, effects, representations, past, etc. and feel the need to reveal it. Even the abovementioned scholarly attempts to support an obligation to transparency, although the data whose release such an obligation prescribes is recognized as being produced rather than revealed,[26] are short of any engagement with the epistemology of the secret of international law as it is understood here. What is more, it has been shown earlier that the necessity of revelation is incommensurable with any specific rule or norm of behaviour, whomever it is addressed to, and is thus alien to such a formal obligation to transparency.[27]

Unsurprisingly, all such scholarly examinations, discussions, attempted regulations of the secretive and undisclosed practices unfolding in international legal processes, and which have been cursorily outlined in this chapter, are themselves caught in the epistemology of the secret of international law as is understood here. Indeed, all such scholarly inquiries postulate such secretive and undisclosed practices that they go on revealing for the sake of ordering and regulating them. In that sense, international lawyers' engagements with the secretive and undisclosed practices of international legal processes constitute a very germane illustration of how the epistemology of the secret of international law functions and plays out in international legal thought and practice. In that sense, the account of international lawyers' inquiries into questions of secrets provided in the present chapter anticipates Chapter 4 whose ambition is to offer a broader and more comprehensive picture of all the manifestations of the epistemology of the secret of international law.

A final observation is warranted. The fact that the epistemology of the secret of international law and its two main necessities permeate those abovementioned inquiries about the secretive and undisclosed practices

[26] On the idea that data and information that are the object of an obligation to transparency are not revealed but produced, see Fenster, 'The Opacity of Transparency'; see also Bianchi, 'On Power and Illusion' pp. 10–15. On the idea that, within the epistemology of the secret of international law, the hidden, the unknown, the invisible content is produced at the moment of its revelation, see supra Section 1.1.3.2.

[27] See supra Section 1.1.3.1. On the idea that power is not exercised through prohibitions and repressions, see Michel Foucault, *Histoire de la Sexualité 1. La volonté de savoir* (Gallimard, 1976) pp. 57 and 151; Michel Foucault, *Dits et écrits, II* (Gallimard, 2001) pp. 148–149; see also Michel Foucault, *'Il faut défendre la société'. Cours au Collège de France, 1976* (Gallimard, 1997) p. 18.

of international legal processes without disclosing themselves to the authors of such studies is but the very work of that epistemology. As was already indicated,[28] the epistemology of the secret of international law always hides its power.[29] The present chapter's account of international lawyers' engagements with the secretive and undisclosed practices that they suppose to be at work in various international legal processes, like the following chapters on the manifestations of the epistemology of the secret of international law, shed light on the extent to which the necessity of secret content as well as the necessity of revelation self-obfuscate.

[28] See supra Section 1.1.2.5.

[29] See the remarks of Giorgio Agamben, *La puissance de la pensée* (Editions Payot & Rivages, 2021) pp. 30–31; Roland Barthes, *Le bruissement de la langue. Essais critiques IV* (Seuil, 1984) pp. 12–18; Pierre Bourdieu, 'A Lecture on the Lecture', in Pierre Bourdieu, *In Other Words: Essays towards a Reflexive Sociology* (Stanford University Press, 1990) pp. 177, 183, and 189; Pierre Bourdieu, *Langage et pouvoir symbolique* (Editions du Seuil, 2001) p. 210.

4

Manifestations of the Epistemology of the Secret of International Law

This chapter exposes some concrete and contemporary manifestations of the epistemology of the secret of international law. It particularly sheds light on the way in which the postulation of a hidden, unknown, invisible content (what is called here *the necessity of secret content*) as well as the experience of the necessity to reveal such content (what is called *the necessity of revelation*) play out in international legal thought and practice, for the sake of ordering what can be said, thought, perceived, and actioned through international law. This chapter is patterned after the three dimensions of the epistemology of the secret of international law that have been spelled out in Chapter 1. The attention first turns to some actual manifestations of the necessity of secret content (Section 4.1) and then to a few concrete examples of the necessity of revelation (Section 4.2). The chapter then illustrates how such two necessities come to enable a mass production of speech materials which, in turn, determines what can possibly be said, thought, perceived, and actioned through international law (Section 4.3).

Before developing such an account of the materializations of the epistemology of the secret of international law, three caveats must be formulated. First, as was indicated above, the epistemology of the secret of international law found its most tangible expressions in texts. Texts are the very site where the presence of hidden, unknown, invisible content is posited.[1] Likewise, it is through texts that the hidden, unknown, invisible content of the texts, practices, actors, effects, representations, past, etc. of international law is revealed, the act of revelation being an act of textual inscription.[2] By the same token, it is through the mass production of speech materials, which are, most of the time, textual materials, that the epistemology of the secret of international law performs its ordering

[1] See supra Section 1.1.2.4

[2] See supra Section 1.1.3.3.

function.[3] This is why the manifestations of the epistemology of the secret of international law presented here are primarily of a textual character and originate in textual works.

Second, the following account of the concrete manifestations of the epistemology of the secret of international law is necessarily selective. Given that the latter informs the entirety of international legal thought and practice and, as has been argued here, drives the engagements with international law of legal scholars, judges, officers of international organizations, diplomats, counsels, experts, activists, etc., it is not materially possible to offer, in this chapter, a comprehensive exposition of all the ways in which the epistemology of the secret of international law manifests itself. This is why the following account zeroes in only on two specific discursive outputs where the epistemology of the secret of international law is most tangible, namely *judicial decisions* and *scholarly literature*. Although the argument can be made that the distinction between these two types of output is very feeble as they both constitute legal discourse, the following account of the manifestations of the epistemology of the secret of international law distinguishes between them for didactic reasons.

Third, it has already been indicated how much the necessity of secret content and the necessity of revelation hang together and work synchronously.[4] Indeed, the experience of the necessity of revelation does not follow mechanically the experience of the necessity of secret content, for the act of revelation is constitutive of the hidden, unknown, invisible content that has been postulated as being present in the texts, practices, actors, effects, representations, past, etc. of international law. As was said, the content held to be hidden, unknown, invisible is actually created at the very moment it is disclosed by the act of revelation.[5] Such synchronicity is very tangible in the account of the manifestations of the epistemology of the secret of international law provided in the present chapter. In fact, it will be very clear to the reader that judges and scholars come to postulate the presence of hidden, unknown, invisible content for the sake of the revelation that is expected from them. What is more, the act of revelation being constitutive of the hidden, unknown, invisible content so revealed, there is a great degree of artificiality in presenting the materializations of the necessity of secret content before those of the necessity of

[3] See supra Section 1.2.2.
[4] See supra Section 1.1.1.1.
[5] See supra Section 1.1.3.2.

revelation. Actually, there surely is a case to expose expressions of the necessity of revelation in international legal thought and practice before introducing manifestations of the necessity of secret content therein. Yet, the following account, in order to maximize its legibility, is patterned after the sequence of Chapter 1's presentation of the main components of the epistemology of the secret of international law. It accordingly reviews the discursive practice of international judges and international legal scholars in relation to the necessity of secret content before examining those pertaining to the necessity of revelation.

4.1 The Postulation of the Necessary Presence of Hidden, Unknown, Invisible Content

The following paragraphs shed light on the immense variety of hidden, unknown, invisible content that international judges (Section 4.1.1) and international legal scholars (Section 4.1.2) deem possible to locate and find in the texts, practices, actors, effects, representations, past, etc. of international law with which they are confronted. It must be noted that the following sample of judicial practice is restricted to the practice of the International Court of Justice, which is seen as sufficiently illustrative of the wide variety of hidden, unknown, invisible contents that are posited to be necessarily located in the texts, practices, actors, effects, representations, past, etc. of international law when an international court or tribunal is solicited.

4.1.1 The Many Hidden, Unknown, Invisible Contents for Which the International Court of Justice Is Solicited

There is a wide range of specific contents that international courts and tribunals can potentially locate and find in the texts, practices, actors, effects, representations, past, etc. that come within their purview.[6] If one takes only the judgements and advisory opinions delivered by the International Court of Justice (hereafter the Court), the hidden, unknown, invisible contents whose presence in the texts, practices, actors, effects, representations, past, etc. of international law is posited

[6] On how the determination of the existence of a dispute as well as the affirmation of jurisdiction shape what comes within the purview of international courts and tribunals, see Jean d'Aspremont, 'The Control over Knowledge by International Courts and Arbitral Tribunals', in Thomas Schultz and Federico Ortino (eds.), *Oxford Handbook of International Arbitration* (Oxford University Press, 2020) p. 338.

by the Court and all those soliciting it include the actuality of a legal dispute,[7] the existence or absence of an intention to be legally bound,[8] the scope and content of a treaty provision,[9] the actual content of the Court's past decision,[10] whether a given treaty provision has a customary

[7] See, e.g., Dispute over the Status and Use of the Waters of the Silala (Chile v. Bolivia), Judgment of 1 December 2022, para. 101 and para. 59, 65, and 147; Application of the International Convention on the Elimination of All Forms of Racial Discrimination (Qatar v. United Arab Emirates), Judgement of 4 February 2021, para. 69–70; Obligations concerning Negotiations relating to Cessation of the Nuclear Arms Race and to Nuclear Disarmament (Marshall Islands v. Pakistan), Judgment of 5 October 2016, para. 33–55; Obligations concerning Negotiations relating to Cessation of the Nuclear Arms Race and to Nuclear Disarmament (Marshall Islands v. United Kingdom), Judgement of 5 October 2016, para. 33–58; Obligations concerning Negotiations relating to Cessation of the Nuclear Arms Race and to Nuclear Disarmament (Marshall Islands v. India), Judgment of 5 October 2016, para. 33–55; Request for Interpretation of the Judgment of 15 June 1962 in the Case concerning the Temple of Preah Vihear (Cambodia v. Thailand) (Cambodia v. Thailand), Judgment of 11 November 2013, para. 37–45; South West Africa (Ethiopia v. South Africa; Liberia v. South Africa), Preliminary Objections, Judgment, I.C.J. Reports 1962, p. 328; Interpretation of Peace Treaties with Bulgaria, Hungary, and Romania, First Phase, Advisory Opinion, I.C.J. Reports 1950, p. 74; Application of the International Convention on the Elimination of All Forms of Racial Discrimination (Georgia v. Russian Federation), Preliminary Objections, Judgment, I.C.J. Reports 2011 (I), p. 84, para. 30; P.C.I.J., Interpretation of Judgments Nos. 7 and 8 (Factory at Chorzów) (Germany v. Poland), Judgment No. 11, 1927, P.C.I.J., Series A, No. 13, pp. 10–11

[8] Military and Paramilitary Activities in and against Nicaragua (Nicaragua v. United States of America), Judgment of 27 June 1986, p. 43, para. 71; Frontier Dispute (Burkina Faso/Republic of Mali), Judgment, I.C.J. Reports 1986, p. 573, para. 39; Obligation to Negotiate Access to the Pacific Ocean (Bolivia v. Chile), Judgment, I.C.J. Reports 2018 (II), p. 555, para. 146; Nuclear Tests (Australia v. France), Judgment, I.C.J. Reports 1974, p. 267, para. 44; Nuclear Tests (New Zealand v. France), Judgment, I.C.J. Reports 1974, p. 473, para. 47; Frontier Dispute (Burkina Faso/Republic of Mali), Judgment, I.C.J. Reports 1986, p. 573, para. 39; Nuclear Tests (Australia v. France), Judgment, I.C.J. Reports 1974, p. 269, para. 48; Nuclear Tests (New Zealand v. France), Judgment, I.C.J. Reports 1974, p. 474, para. 50; Dispute over the Status and Use of the Waters of the Silala (Chile v. Bolivia), Judgment of 1 December 2022, para. 230; Maritime Delimitation in the Indian Ocean (Somalia v. Kenya), Judgment of 2 February 2017, para. 47

[9] Jadhav (India v. Pakistan), Judgment of 17 July 2019, para. 75; Immunities and Criminal Proceedings (Equatorial Guinea v. France), Judgment of 11 December 2020, para. 76–118; Certain Activities Carried Out by Nicaragua in the Border Area (Costa Rica v. Nicaragua), Judgment of 16 December 2015, para. 164; Whaling in the Antarctic (Australia v. Japan: New Zealand intervening), Judgement of 31 March 2014, para. 51–97; Application of the Convention on the Prevention and Punishment of the Crime of Genocide (Croatia v. Serbia), Judgment of 3 February 2015, para. 124–166; Frontier Dispute (Burkina Faso/Niger), Judgment of 16 April 2013, para. 60–69.

[10] Request for Interpretation of the Judgment of 15 June 1962 in the Case concerning the Temple of Preah Vihear (Cambodia v. Thailand) (Cambodia v. Thailand), Judgment of 11 November 2013, para. 58–107.

nature,[11] the content of customary international law,[12] the existence and content of a right under international law,[13] the norm-creating character of a treaty provision,[14] whether a given provision has the status of a

[11] See, e.g., Dispute over the Status and Use of the Waters of the Silala (Chile v. Bolivia), Judgment of 1 December 2022, para 117; Alleged Violations of Sovereign Rights and Maritime Spaces in the Caribbean Sea (Nicaragua v. Colombia), 21 April 2022, para 155; Alleged Violations of Sovereign Rights and Maritime Spaces in the Caribbean Sea (Nicaragua v. Colombia), 21 April 2022, para. 101 and para 185; Question of the Delimitation of the Continental Shelf between Nicaragua and Colombia beyond 200 Nautical Miles from the Nicaraguan Coast (Nicaragua v. Colombia), Preliminary Objections, Judgment, I.C.J. Reports 2016 (I), p. 116, para. 33; Application of the Convention on the Prevention and Punishment of the Crime of Genocide (Croatia v. Serbia), Judgment of 3 February 2015, para. 128; Dispute regarding Navigational and Related Rights (Costa Rica v. Nicaragua), Judgment, I.C.J. Reports 2009, p. 237, para. 47; Questions relating to the Obligation to Prosecute or Extradite (Belgium v. Senegal), Judgment of 20 July 2012, para. 113; Application of the Convention on the Prevention and Punishment of the Crime of Genocide (Bosnia and Herzegovina v. Serbia and Montenegro), Judgment of 26 February 2007, I.C.J. Reports 2007 (I), pp. 109–110, para. 160, 385, and 398; Territorial Dispute (Libyan Arab Jamahiriya/Chad), Judgment, I.C.J. Reports 1994, pp. 21–22, para. 41; Oil Platforms (Islamic Republic of Iran v. United States of America), Preliminary Objection, Judgment, I.C.J. Reports 1996 (II), p. 812, para. 23

[12] Corfu Channel (United Kingdom v. Albania), Merits, Judgment, I.C.J. Reports 1949, p. 22; Fisheries (United Kingdom v. Norway), Judgment, I.C.J. Reports 1951, p. 131; Pulp Mills on the River Uruguay (Argentina v. Uruguay), Judgment, I.C.J. Reports 2010 (I), pp. 55–56, para. 101; Legality of the Threat or Use of Nuclear Weapons, Advisory Opinion, I.C.J. Reports 1996 (I), p. 242, para. 29; Certain Activities Carried Out by Nicaragua in the Border Area (Costa Rica v. Nicaragua) and Construction of a Road in Costa Rica along the San Juan River (Nicaragua v. Costa Rica), Judgment, I.C.J. Reports 2015 (II), p. 706, para. 104; Jurisdictional Immunities of the State (Germany v. Italy: Greece intervening), Judgment of 3 February 2012, para 78 and 91. Gabčíkovo-Nagymaros Project (Hungary/Slovakia), Judgment, I.C.J. Reports 1997, p. 56, para. 78; Question of the Delimitation of the Continental Shelf between Nicaragua and Colombia beyond 200 nautical miles from the Nicaraguan Coast (Nicaragua v. Colombia), Judgement of 13 July 2023, para. 45; Dispute over the Status and Use of the Waters of the Silala (Chile v. Bolivia), Judgment of 1 December 2022, para. 97; See, e.g., Alleged Violations of Sovereign Rights and Maritime Spaces in the Caribbean Sea (Nicaragua v. Colombia), 21 April 2022, para 56, 100, 216–217, 233, 244; Accordance with international law of the unilateral declaration of independence in respect of Kosovo, Advisory Opinion of 22 July 2010, para. 78–121; Legality of the Threat or Use of Nuclear Weapons, Advisory Opinion of 8 July 1996, para. 64–89.

[13] Question of the Delimitation of the Continental Shelf between Nicaragua and Colombia beyond 200 nautical miles from the Nicaraguan Coast (Nicaragua v. Colombia), Judgement of 13 July 2023, para. 163; Obligation to Negotiate Access to the Pacific Ocean (Bolivia v. Chile), Judgment of 1 October 2018, para. 175.

[14] North Sea Continental Shelf (Federal Republic of Germany/Netherlands), Judgment of 20 February 1969, para 72; Military and Paramilitary Activities in and against Nicaragua (Nicaragua v. United States of America), Judgment of 27 June 1986, para. 259–261; Oil

peremptory norm of international law,[15] whether a provision has the status of an *erga omnes* or *erga omnes partes* obligation,[16] the existence or absence of a breach of an international legal rule,[17] the compatibility of a factual or claimed situation with customary international law,[18] the accordance of a legal definition with customary international law,[19] the status of a property,[20] the history of certain institutions or international relations,[21] etc.

It is submitted here that there is no need to extend such list of illustrations any further. The foregoing suffices to show the diversity of contents whose presence in the texts, practices, actors, effects, representations, past, etc. of international law is posited by the Court and all those soliciting its services.

Platforms (Islamic Republic of Iran v. United States of America), Judgment of 12 December 1996, para. 28 and 31

15 Questions relating to the Obligation to Prosecute or Extradite (Belgium v. Senegal), Judgment of 20 July 2012, para 99.

16 Questions relating to the Obligation to Prosecute or Extradite (Belgium v. Senegal), Judgment of 20 July 2012, para. 103 Legal Consequences of the Construction of a Wall in the Occupied Palestinian Territory, Advisory Opinion of 9 July 2004, para 155–156; East Timor (Portugal v. Australia), Judgment of 30 June 1995, para 29.

17 See, e.g., Armed Activities on the Territory of the Congo (Democratic Republic of the Congo v. Uganda), Judgment, I.C.J. Reports 2005, p. 280, para. 345; Dispute over the Status and Use of the Waters of the Silala (Chile v. Bolivia), Judgment of 1 December 2022, para. 128; Question of the Delimitation of the Continental Shelf between Nicaragua and Colombia beyond 200 nautical miles from the Nicaraguan Coast (Nicaragua v. Colombia), Judgement of 13 July 2023, para. 144 and 195

18 Question of the Delimitation of the Continental Shelf between Nicaragua and Colombia beyond 200 nautical miles from the Nicaraguan Coast (Nicaragua v. Colombia), Judgement of 13 July 2023, para. 164, para 196; Alleged Violations of Sovereign Rights and Maritime Spaces in the Caribbean Sea (Nicaragua v. Colombia), 21 April 2022, para 245 and 260.

19 Dispute over the Status and Use of the Waters of the Silala (Chile v. Bolivia), Judgment of 1 December 2022, para. 92; Immunities and Criminal Proceedings (Equatorial Guinea v. France), Judgment of 11 December 2020, para. 41–74

20 Immunities and Criminal Proceedings (Equatorial Guinea v. France), Judgment of 11 December 2020, para. 76–118

21 Obligation to Negotiate Access to the Pacific Ocean (Bolivia v. Chile), Judgment of 1 October 2018, para 16–83; Request for Interpretation of the Judgment of 15 June 1962 in the Case concerning the Temple of Preah Vihear (Cambodia v. Thailand) (Cambodia v. Thailand), Judgment of 11 November 2013, para. 14–29; Legal Consequences of the Construction of a Wall in the Occupied Palestinian Territory, Advisory Opinion of 9 July 2004, para. 70–85.

4.1.2 *The Vast Hidden, Unknown, Invisible Universe of International Legal Scholars*

The contents that international legal scholars posit as being hidden in the texts, practices, actors, effects, representations, past, etc. of international law are even more copious than those postulated by the International Court of Justice and those soliciting the latter. Indeed, such postulated secret contents include the meaning of treaty provisions,[22] the content of certain legal regimes,[23] the nature of international law and of the international legal order,[24] the new complexities of the international legal order,[25] the traditions that international law allegedly draws on and flows from,[26] the contents and contours of certain judicial practices,[27]

[22] See the practice of commentaries of major conventions. See, e.g., Andreas Zimmermann, Christian J. Tams, Karin Oellers-Frahm, and Christian Tomuschat (eds.), *The Statute of the International Court of Justice* (Oxford University Press, 2019); Pierre Klein and Olivier Corten (eds.), *Les Conventions de Vienne sur le Droit des Traités. Commentaire article par article* (Bruylant, 2006); Jean-Pierre Cot, Alain Pellet, and Mathias Forteau, *La Charte des Nations Unies, Commentaire article par article*, 3rd edn (Economica, 2005).

[23] Christine Gray, *International Law and the Use of Force*, 3rd edn (Oxford University Press, 2008); Jure Vidmar, *Democratic Statehood in International Law: The Emergence of New States in Post-Cold War Practice* (Hart, 2013); David Raič, *Statehood and the Law of Self-Determination* (Kluwer, 2002).

[24] Hilary Charlesworth and Christine Chinkin, *The Boundaries of International Law: A Feminist Analysis* (Manchester University Press, 2000) p. 21; Philip Allott, 'Language, Method and the Nature of International law' (1971) 45 *British Yearbook of International Law* 79; Frédéric Megret, 'International Law as Law', in James Crawford and Martti Koskenniemi (eds.), *Cambridge Companion to International Law* (Cambridge University Press, 2012) p. 64; Stephen C. Neff, *Justice among Nations: A History of International Law* (Harvard University Press, 2014) p. 2; Ingo Venzke, 'International Law as an Argumentative Practice: On Wohlrapp's *The Concept of Argument*' (2016) 7 *Transnational Legal Theory* 9; Jean d'Aspremont, *International Law as a Belief System* (Cambridge Univerisity Press, 2017).

[25] Richard Falk, *The End of World Order: Essays on Normative International Relations* (Holmes & Meier, 1983) p. 25

[26] Hersch Lauterpacht, 'The Grotian Tradition in International Law' (1946) 23 *The British Yearbook of International Law* 1; John Tasioulas, 'Customary International Law and the Quest for Global Justice', in Amanda Perreau-Saussine and James B. Murphy (eds.), *The Nature of Customary Law* (Cambridge University Press, 2007) p. 307; John Tasioulas, 'In Defence of Relative Normativity: Communitarian Values and the Nicaragua Case' (1996) 16 *Oxford Journal of International Law* 85; Fernando R. Tesón, 'The Kantian Theory of International Law' (1992) 92 *Columbia Law Review* 53.

[27] Jean d'Aspremont and Makane M. Mbengue, 'Strategies of Engagement with Scientific Fact-finding in International Adjudication' (2014) 5 *Journal of International Dispute Settlement* 240; Francis G. Jacobs, 'Judicial Dialogue and the Cross-Fertilization of Legal System: The European Court of Human Rights' (2008) 38 *Texas International Law Journal* 547; Charles H. Koch Jr., 'Judicial Dialogue for Legal Multiculturalism' (2004) 25 *Michigan Journal of International Law* 979; Jean d'Aspremont, 'The

the contours and content of an international legal concept[28] or of a theoretical notion,[29] the foundations of international

Recommendations Made by the International Court of Justice' (2007) 56 *International and Comparative Law Quarterly* 185; Samantha Besson, 'International Courts and the Jurisprudence of Statehood' (2019) 9 *Transnational Legal Theory* 30.

28 Philip Allott, 'The Concept of International Law' (1999) 10 *European Journal of International Law* 31; Jan Klabbers, *The Concept of Treaty in International Law* (Kluwer, 1996) p. 8; Jean d'Aspremont, 'The Idea of "Rules" in the Sources of International Law' (2014) 84 *British Yearbook of International Law* 103; Anthony D'Amato, *The Concept of Custom in International Law* (Cornell University Press, 1971); Godefridus J. H. Van Hoof, *Rethinking the Sources of International Law* (Kluwer, 1983); Mario Prost, *The Concept of Unity in Public International Law* (Hart, 2012); Eric Suy, *Les actes juridiques unilatéraux en droit international public* (LGDJ, 1962); Philippe Gautier, *Essai sur la définition des traités entre Etats* (Bruylant, 1993); Olivier Barsalou, 'La doctrine de l'objecteur persistant en droit international' (2006) 19 *Revue Québécoise de droit international* 1; Patrick Dumberry, 'Incoherent and Ineffective: The Concept of Persistent Objector Revisited' (2010) 59 *International and Comparative Law Quarterly* 779; Jean-Paul Jacqué, *Elements pour une théorie de l'acte juridique en Droit international public* (LGDJ, 1972); Alexandre-Charles Kiss, 'Les traités-cadres: Une technique juridique caractéristique du droit international de l'environnement' (1993) 39 *French Directory of International Law* 792; Joe Verhoeven, *Droit international 1. Les nullités du droit des gens* (Pedone, 1981). For some classical works on this topic, see Robert Y. Jennings, 'Nullity and Effectiveness in International Law', in *Cambridge Essays in International Law: Essays in honour of Lord McNair* (Stevens & Sons, Ltd, 1965) pp. 64–87; Gaetano Arangio-Ruiz, 'Le domaine reservé. L'organisation internationale et le rapport entre le droit international et le droit interne. Cours général de droit international public' (1990-IV) 225 *Collected Courses* 29; Michel Virally, 'A Propos de la "Lex Ferenda"', in Daniel Bardonnet (ed.), *Mélanges Reuter: Le droit international: Unité et diversité* (Pedone, 1981) pp. 521–533; Mathias Forteau, 'L'Etat selon le droit international: Une figure à géométrie variable' (2007) 4 *Revue générale de droit international public* 737; Ian Brownlie, 'Recognition in Theory and Practice', in Ronald St. John Macdonald and Douglas M. Johnston (eds.), *The Structure and Process of International Law: Modern Essays in Legal Philosophy, Doctrine and Theory* (Brill, 1983) p. 197; Jean d'Aspremont, 'Softness in International Law: A Self-serving Quest for New Legal Materials' (2008) 19 *European Journal of International Law* 1075; Thomas Skouteris, *The Notion of Progress in International Law Discourse* (T.M.C. Asser Press, 2010); Benedict Kingsbury, 'The Concept of "Law" in Global Administrative Law' (2009) 20 *European Journal of International Law* 1; Michel Virally, 'La notion de fonction dans la théorie de l'organization internationales', in *Mélanges Offerts à Charles Rousseau: La Communauté Internationale* (Pedone, 1974), pp. 277–300; Christiane Ahlborn, 'The Rules of International Organizations and the Law of International Responsibility' (2011) 8 *International Organizations Law Review* 397; Blanca Montejo, 'The Notion of "Effective Control" under the Articles on the Responsibility of International Organizations', in Maurizio Ragazzi (ed.), *Responsibility of International Organizations: Essays in Memory of Sir Ian Brownlie* (Martinus Nijhoff, 2013) pp. 389–404.

29 Jean d'Aspremont and Frédéric Dopagne, 'Two Constitutionalisms in Europe: Pursuing an Articulation of the European and International Legal Orders' (2008) 68 *Heidelberg Journal of International Law (ZaÖRV)* 939.

law,[30] what constitutes the universality and unity of international law,[31] the future of international legal thought and practice,[32] the functions of international law,[33] the actual dysfunctionality of international law,[34] the past and the history of international law[35], the past and present 'turns' in

[30] Jean d'Aspremont, 'The Foundations of the International Legal Order' (2007) 18 *Finnish Yearbook of International Law* 219.

[31] Pierre-Marie Dupuy, 'L'unité de l'ordre juridique international: Cours général de droit international public' (2002) 297 *Collected Courses* 9; Bruno Simma, 'Universality of International Law from the Perspective of a Practitioner' (2009) 20 *European Journal of International Law* 265. For an illustration, see Jonathan I. Charney, 'Universal International Law' (1993) 87 *American Journal of International Law* 529; Clarence W. Jenks, *The Common Law of Mankind* (Stevens & Sons, Ltd, 1958).

[32] Gilbert Guillaume, 'La Cour Internationale de Justice. Quelques propositions concrètes à l'occasion du cinquantenaire' (1996) 100 *Revue générale de droit International Public* 323; Mahnoush H. Arsanjani, Jacob K. Cogan, Robert Sloane, and Siegfried Wiessner (eds.), *Looking to the Future: Essays on International Law in Honor of W. Michael Reisman* (Brill, 2011); David P. Fidler, 'Revolt against or from within the West? TWAIL, the Developing World, and the Future Direction of International Law' (2003) 2 *Chinese Journal of International Law* 29; Sam Muller, David Raic, and J. M. Thuránszky, (eds.), *The International Court of Justice: Its Future Role after Fifty Years* (Martinus Nijhoff, 1997); Myres S. McDougal, 'International Law and the Future' (1979) 50 *Mississippi Law Journal* 259; Nico J. Schrijver, 'The Future of the United Nations' (2006) 10 *Max Planck Yearbook of United Nations Law* 1; Colin B. Picker, Isabella Bunn, and Douglas Arner (eds.), *International Economic Law – The State and Future of the Discipline* (Hart, 2008); Anne-Marie Slaughter, 'The Liberal Agenda for Peace: International Relations Theory and the Future of the United Nations' (1994) 4 *Transnational Law and Contemporary Problems* 377.

[33] Allott, 'The True Function of Law in the International Community' p. 391; Martti Koskenniemi, 'What Is international Law For?', in Malcolm D. Evans, *International Law* (Oxford University Press, 2003) pp. 89–114.

[34] Anthony Carty, *The Decay of International Law: A Reappraisal of the Limits of Legal Imagination in International Affairs, with a new Introduction* (Manchester University Press, 2019); Anthony Carty, *The Philosophy of International Law* (Edinburgh University Press, 2007).

[35] See, e.g., Wilhelm Grewe, *The Epochs of International Law*, trans. Michael Byers (de Gruyter, 2000); Neff, *Justice among Nations*; Bardo Fassbender and Anne Peters, *The Oxford Handbook of the History of International Law* (Oxford University Press, 2012); Matthew Craven, Malgosia Fitzmaurice, and Maria Vogiatzi (eds.), *Time, History and International Law* (Brill, 2007); David J. Bederman, *International Law in Antiquity* (Cambridge University Press, 2004); Randall Lesaffer, 'The Classical Law of Nations (1500–1800)', in Alexander Orakhelashvili (ed.), *Research Handbook on the Theory and History of International Law* (Edward Elgar, 2011) p. 410; Slim Laghmani, 'Les Origines du droit international public et le concept de discours fondateur', in Pierre-Marie Dupuy and Vincent Chetail (eds.), *The Roots of International Law. Liber Amicorum Peter Haggenmacher* (Martinus Nijhoff, 2014) pp. 449–464; C. H. Alexandrowicz, *An Introduction to the History of the Law of Nations in the East Indies* (Clarendon, 1967); Charles H. Alexandrowicz, *The Law of Nations in Global History* (Oxford University Press, 2017); Taslim Olawale Elías, *Africa and the Development of International Law*

international legal thought,[36] the fundamental tensions at work in international legal thought and practice,[37] the genealogy of certain scholarly attitudes,[38] the forebears, trailblazers, and architects of the

(Sijthoff, 1972); Ram P. Anand, *Origin and Development of the Law of the Sea: History of International Law Revisited* (Martinus Nijhoff, 1983). On the idea that international lawyers are constantly historicizing past texts, doctrines, concepts, and practices, see Anne Orford, 'On International Legal Method' (2013) 1 *London Review of International Law* 166 at 172 and 175 ('After all, as lawyers, particularly those of us with common law backgrounds, we are trained in the art of making meaning move across time'); see also Anne Orford, 'International Law and the Limits of History', in Wouter Werner, Marieke de Hoon, and Alexis Galan (eds.), *The Law of International Lawyers: Reading Martti Koskenniemi* (Cambridge University Press, 2015) p. 297; Thomas Kleinlein, 'International Legal Thought: Creation of a Tradition and the Potential of Disciplinary Self-Reflection' in Giuliana Ziccardi Capaldo, *The Global Community: Yearbook of International Law and Jurisprudence 2016* (Oxford University Press, 2016) p. 812; see also Matthew Craven, 'The Invention of a Tradition: Westlake, The Berlin Conference and the Historicisation of International Law' in Luigi Nuzzo and Miloš Vec (eds.), *Constructing International Law: The Birth of a Discipline* (Klostermann, 2012) p. 4; Kate Purcell, 'Faltering at the Critical Turn to History: "Juridical Thinking" in International Law and Genealogy as History, Critique, and Therapy' (2016) 2/15 *Jean Monnet Working Paper Series* 1 at 13–15.

36 On the 'turn to history' in contemporary international legal scholarship, see Matt Craven, 'Theorizing the Turn to History in International Law', in Anne Orford and Florian Hoffmann (eds.), *The Oxford Handbook of the Theory of International Law* (Oxford University Press, 2016) pp. 21–37; see also George R. B. Galindo, 'Martti Koskenniemi and the Historiographical Turn in International Law' (2005) 16 *European Journal of International Law* 539. For some general observations on the 'linguistic turn' in international legal thought, see Ingo Venzke, 'Contemporary Theories and International Lawmaking', in Catherine Brölmann and Yannick Radi (eds.), *Research Handbook on the Theory and Practice of International Lawmaking* (Edward Elgar, 2016) pp. 66–84.

37 Jan Klabbers, 'Two Contending Approaches to the Law of International Organizations', in Jan Klabbers and Åsa Wallendahl (eds.), *Research Handbook on International Organizations Law: Between Functionalism and Constitutionalism* (Edward Elgar, 2010) pp. 3–30; see also Jan Klabbers, 'Two Concepts of International Organization', 2 *International Organizations Law Review* (2005) 277; Olivier Corten, *Sociologies du droit* (Dalloz, 2023).

38 Akbar Rasulov, 'New Approaches to International Law: Images of a Genealogy', in Jose Maria Beneyto and David Kennedy (eds.), *New Approaches to International Law: The European and the American Experiences* (TMC Asser/Springer, 2012) pp. 151–191; Andrea Bianchi and Fuad Zarbiyev, *Demystifying Treaty Interpretation* (Cambridge University Press, 2024) pp. 49–84; Richard Collins, 'Classical Positivism in International Law Revisited', in Jean d'Aspremont and Jörg Kammerhofer (eds.), *International Legal Positivism in a Post-Modern World* (Cambridge University Press, 2014) pp. 23–49; Jochen von Bernstorff, 'German Intellectual Historical Origins of International Legal Positivism', in Jean d'Aspremont and Jörg Kammerhofer (eds), *International Legal Positivism in a Post-Modern World* (Cambridge University Press, 2014) p. 50.

discipline,[39] the emergence of new law-governed world practices,[40] the coherence of legal argumentation and legal practices,[41] the modes of distinction between law and non-law,[42] the terms of a

[39] David Kennedy, 'Tom Franck and the Manhattan School' (2003) 35 *NYU Journal of International Law and Politics* 397; Jeffrey Dunoff, 'From Interdisciplinarity to Counter disciplinarity: Is There Madness in Martti's Method?' (2013) 27 *Temple Journal of International and Comparative Law* 309; Wouter Werner, Marieke de Hoon, and Alexis Galán (eds.), *The Law of International Lawyers: Reading Martti Koskenniemi* (Cambridge University Press, 2018); Jean d'Aspremont, 'Martti Koskenniemi, the Mainstream and Self-Reflectivity' (2016) 29 *Leiden Journal of International Law* 625; John Haskell, 'Hugo Grotius in the Contemporary Memory of International Law: Secularism, Liberalism, and the Politics of Restatement and Denial', in José M. Beneyto, David Kennedy, Justo Corti Varela, and John Haskell (eds.), *New Approaches to International Law: The European and the American Experiences* (T.M.C Asser/Springer, 2012) pp. 123–150; Martti Koskenniemi, 'Into Positivism: Georg Friedrich von Martens (1756–1821) and Modern International Law' (2008) 15 *Constellations* 189; H. Thierry, 'The European Tradition of International Law: Georges Scelle' (1990) 1 *European Journal of International Law* 193; Frédéric Dopagne, 'Retour sur un "Classique" – M. Virally, 'La notion de fonction dans la théorie de "l'organization internationale"' (2011) *Revue Générale de Droit International Public* (2011) 285.

[40] Vidmar, *Democratic Statehood in International Law*; Marcelo G. Kohen (ed.), *Secession: International Law Perspectives* (Cambridge University Press, 2006); Jean d'Aspremont, *L'Etat non-démocratique en droit international* (Pedone, 2008); Samantha Besson, 'Democratic Representation within International Organizations: From International Good Governance to International Good Government' (2022) 19(4) *International Organizations Law Review* 489; Rebecca Mignot-Mahdavi, *Drones and International Law: A Techno-Legal Machinery* (Cambridge University Press, 2023).

[41] James G. Devaney, 'A Coherence Framework for Fact-finding before the International Court of Justice' (2023) 36 *Leiden Journal of International Law* 1073; Gleider Hernandez, 'The Responsibility of the International Legal Academic: Situating the Grammarian within the "Invisible College"', in Jean d'Aspremont, Tarcisio Gazzini, André Nollkaemper, and Wouter Werner (eds.), *International Law as a Profession* (Cambridge University Press, 2017) p. 177.

[42] Robert Jennings, 'What Is International Law and How Do We Tell It When We See It?' (1981) 37 *Schweizerisches Jahrbuch für Internationales Recht* 59; Robert Jennings, 'The Identification of International Law', in Bin Cheng (ed.), *International Law: Teaching and Practice* (Stevens & Sons, Ltd, 1982) p. 3; Jean d'Aspremont, *Formalism and the Sources of International Law: A Theory of the Ascertainment of Legal Rules* (Oxford University Press, 2011); Bruno Simma and Philip Alston, 'The Sources of Human Rights Law: Custom, Jus Cogens and General Principles' (1988–1989) 12 *Australian Yearbook of International Law* 82; Vladimir-Djuro Degan, *Sources of International Law* (Kluwer Law International, 1997); Anthony D'Amato, 'What "Counts" as Law?', in Nicholas G. Onuf (ed.), *Law-Making in the Global Community* (Carolina Academic Press, 1982) pp. 83–107; Gerald Fitzmaurice, 'Some Problems Regarding the Formal Sources of International Law', in *Symbolae Verzijl* (Martinus Nijhoff, 1958); Alan E. Boyle and Christine Chinkin, *The Making of International Law* (Oxford University Press, 2007); Hernandez, 'The Responsibility of the International Legal Academic' p. 176.

distinction[43] and the limitations thereof,[44] the middle ground between opposite positions,[45] what makes a valid international legal argument,[46] the interactions between international law and social realities,[47] the extent of the need for change and reform of international law,[48] affects,

[43] Anthea E. Roberts, 'Traditional and Modern Approaches to Customary International Law: A Reconciliation' (2001) 95 *American Journal of International Law* 757; Van Hoof, *Rethinking the Sources of International Law*; P. Weil, 'Towards Relative Normativity in International Law' (1983) 77 *American Journal of International Law* 413; Kenneth W. Abott and Duncan Snidal, 'Hard and Soft Law in International Governance' (2000) 54 *International Organization* 421; Hans Kelsen, 'Theorie du droit international public' (1953-III) 84 *Collected Courses* 1 at 136; Jacqué, *Elements pour une théorie de l'acte juridique en Droit international public* pp. 47–56; Kal Raustiala, 'Form and Substance in International Agreements' (2005) 99 *American Journal of International Law* 581; René-Jean Dupuy, 'Declaratory Law and Programmatory Law: From Revolutionary Custom to "Soft Law"', in Robert J. Akkerman, Peter J. van Krieken, and Charles O. Pannenborg (eds.), *Declarations on Principles: A Quest for Universal Peace. Liber Amicorum discipulorumque Prof. Dr. Bert. V.A. Röling* (Sijthoff, 1977) p. 247.

[44] For some famous support to the idea of normative continuum, see Richard R. Baxter, 'International Law and Her Infinite Variety' (1980) 29 *International and Comparative Law Quarterly* 549 at 563; Oscar Schachter, 'The Twilight Existence of Non binding International Agreements' (1977) 71 *American Journal of International Law* 296; Alan Boyle, 'Some Reflections on the Relationship of Treaties and Soft Law' (1999) 48 *International Law and Comparative Law Quarterly* 901 at 913; Christine Chinkin, 'The Challenge of Soft Law: Development and Change in International Law' (1989) 38 *International Law and Comparative Quarterly* 850 at 866; Alain Pellet, 'Complementarity of International Treaty Law, Customary Law and Non-Contractual Law-Making', in Rüdiger Wolfrum and Volker Röben (eds.), *Developments of International Law in Treaty Making* (Springer, 2005) p. 415; Jutta Brunnée and Stephen J. Toope, 'International Law and Constructivism, Elements of an International Theory of International Law' (2000–2001) 39 *Columbia Journal of Transnational law* 19; Rosalyn Higgins, *Problems and Process: International Law and How We Use It* (Oxford University Press, 1995) pp. 8–10.

[45] Alain Pellet, 'Cours général: Le droit international entre souveraineté et communauté internationale' (2007/II) *Anuário Brasileiro de Direito Internacional* 12; Klabbers, *The Concept of Treaty in International Law* p. 12.

[46] Tanja Aalberts and Ingo Venzke, 'Moving Beyond Interdisciplinary Turf Wars: Towards an Understanding of International Law as Practice', in Jean d'Aspremont, Tarcisio Gazzini, André Nollkaemper, and Wouter Werner (eds.), *International Law as a Profession* (Cambridge University Press, 2017) pp. 289–292; Fuad Zarbiyev 'The "Cash Value' of the Rules of Treaty Interpretation' (2019) 32 *Leiden Journal of International Law* 33.

[47] Hernandez, 'The Responsibility of the International Legal Academic' p. 178.

[48] Hernandez, 'The Responsibility of the International Legal Academic' pp. 178–181; see also some of the contributions to Ingo Venzke and Kevin Jon Heller, *Contingency in International Law: On the Possibility of Different Legal Histories* (Oxford University Press, 2021).

desires, ambitions, and passions that drive international legal thought and practice,[49] certain methodological vogues,[50] etc.

It has also been claimed that the hidden that international legal scholars ought to locate and find is 'the doctrinal structure, role and societal affects of the language of international law within this globalized environment'[51] as well as 'where international legal norms come from, how they are doctrinally constructed, how they shape perceptions, foster particular references and how existing international legal rules interact with other rules in international legal practice'.[52] Even when elucidating or challenging the principles of interpretation, scholars are seeking to say something about what is hidden in hermeneutical practices.[53]

[49] Anne Saab, 'Emotions and International Law' (2021) 10/3 *ESIL Reflections* 1; Andrea Bianchi and Anne Saab 'Fear and International Law-making: An Exploratory Inquiry' (2019) 32 *Leiden Journal of International Law* 351; Andrea Bianchi, 'Fear's Legal Dimension: Counterterrorism and Human Rights', in Laurence Boisson de Chazournes and Marcelo Kohen (eds.), *International Law and the Quest for Its Implementation – Le droit international et la quête de sa mise en oeuvre: Liber Amicorum Vera Gowlland-Debbas* (Brill, 2010) pp. 175–192; Gerry Simpson, *The Sentimental Life of International Law: Literature, Language, and Longing in World Politics* (Oxford University Press, 2021); Emily Kidd White, 'Images of Reach, Range, and Recognition: Thinking about Emotions in the Study of International Law', in Susan A. Bandes, Jody Lynee Madeira, Kathryn Temple, and Emily Kidd White (eds.), *Research Handbook on Law and Emotion* (Edward Elgar, 2021) pp. 492–512; Rebecca Sutton, 'How the Emotions and Perceptual Judgments of Frontline Actors Shape the Practice of International Humanitarian Law', in Susan A. Bandes, Jody Lynee Madeira, Kathryn Temple, and Emily Kidd White (eds.), *Research Handbook on Law and Emotion* (Edward Elgar, 2021) pp. 477–491; Rebecca Sutton and Emily Paddon Rhoads, 'Empathy in Frontline Humanitarian Negotiations: A Relational Approach to Engagement' (2022) 7 *International Journal of Humanitarian Action* 23; Rebecca Sutton, 'Read the Room: Legal and Emotional Literacy in Frontline Humanitarian Negotiations' (2021) 24 *Yearbook of International Humanitarian Law* 103. I have myself attempted to sketch the rudiments of a theory of emotions in relation to international organizations, see Jean d'Aspremont, *The Experiences of International Organizations: A Phenomenological Approach to International Institutional Law* (Edward Elgar, 2023); see also Jean d'Aspremont, 'The Love for International Organizations' (2023) 20 *International Organizations Law Review* 111; David Kennedy, 'The Disciplines of International Law and Policy' (1999) 12 *Leiden Journal of International Law* 9 at 84–87.

[50] Greg Shaffer and Tom Ginsburg, 'The Empirical Turn in International Legal Scholarship' (2012) 106 *American Journal of International Law* 1.

[51] Jochen von Bernstorff, 'The Relationship between Theory and Practice in International Law: Affirmative versus Reflexive Distance', in Jean d'Aspremont, Tarcisio Gazzini, André Nollkaemper, and Wouter Werner (eds.), *International Law as a Profession* (Cambridge University Press, 2017) p. 224.

[52] von Bernstorff, 'The Relationship between Theory and Practice in International Law. Affirmative versus Reflexive Distance' pp. 224 and 243.

[53] See Bianchi and Zarbiyev, *Demystifying Treaty Interpretation*; Corten, *Sociologies du droit* pp. 153–206; Hersch Lauterpacht, 'Restrictive Interpretation and the Principle of

In those scholarly works less concerned with the actual content of legal rules, legal regimes, and legal practices, but which explicitly focus on what international law hides and conceals, there is also a wide range of contents that are posited as being hidden and in need of being made known. Indeed, such works commonly hunt for hidden patterns of thoughts and sensibilities,[54] for hidden ideologies behind certain legal constructions and practices,[55] for hidden 'international law's dark and

Effectiveness in The Interpretation of Treaties'(1949) 26 *British Yearbook of International Law* (1949) 48; Georg Schwarzenberger, 'Myths and Realities in Treaty Interpretation' (1968) 9 *Virginia Journal of International Law* 1; Serge Sur, *L'interprétation en droit international public* (LGDJ, 1974); see also Jean-Marc Sorel, 'Article 31', in Klein and Corten, *Les Conventions de Vienne sur le Droit des Traités* pp. 1289–1338; Alexander Orakhelashvili, *The Interpretation of Acts and Rules in Public International Law* (Oxford University Press, 2008); Gleider Hernandez, 'Interpretation', in Jörg Kammerhofer and Jean d'Aspremont (eds.), *International Legal Positivism in a Postmodern World* (Cambridge University Press, 2014) pp. 317–348; Andrea Bianchi, Daniel Peat, and Matthew R. Windsor (eds.), *Interpretation in International Law* (Oxford University Press, 2015); I. Ingo Venzke, *How the Practice of Interpretation Makes International Law: On Semantic Change and Normative Twists* (Oxford University Press, 2012); Andrea Bianchi, 'Textual Interpretation and (International) Law Reading: The Myth of (In)determinacy and the Genealogy of Meaning', in Pieter H. F. Bekker (ed.) *Making Transnational Law Work in the Global Economy – Essays in Honour of Detlev Vagts* (Cambridge University Press, 2010) p. 35; Isabelle Van Damme, *Treaty Interpretation by the WTO Appellate Body* (Oxford University Press, 2009). For a more recent work focused on the microprocess of communication at work in international legal argumentation, see Ian Johnstone and Steven R. Ratner, 'International Legal Argumentation: Practice in Need of a Theory', in Ian Johnstone and Steven R. Ratner (eds.), *Talking International Law: Legal Argumentation Outside the Courtroom* (Oxford University Press, 2021) pp. 3–24.

54 Martii Koskenniemi, *The Gentle Civilizer of Nations: The Rise and Fall of International Law 1870–1960* (Cambridge University Press, 2002) p. 2.

55 See Bhupinder S. Chimni, *International Law and World Order: A Critique of Contemporary Approaches*, 2nd edn (Cambridge University Press, 2017); Emmanuelle Tourme Jouannet, *Le droit international, le capitalisme et la terre. Histoire des accaparements de terres d'hier à aujourd'hui* (Bruylant, 2021); China Miéville, *Between Equal Rights: A Marxist Theory of International Law* (Haymarket Books, 2006); Ntina Tzouvala, *Capitalism as Civilisation: A History of International Law* (Cambridge University Press, 2020); Rose Parfitt, *The Process of International Legal Reproduction. Inequality, Historiography, Resistance* (Cambridge University Press, 2019); Liliana Obregon, 'Empire, Racial Capitalism and International Law: The Case of Manumitted Haiti and the Recognition Debt' (2018) 31 *Leiden Journal of International Law* 597. For some observations on ideology critique in international law, see Walter Rech, 'Ideology', in Jean d'Aspremont and Sahib Singh (eds.), *Concepts for International Law: Contributions to Disciplinary Thought* (Edward Elgar, 2019) pp. 393–412. See also gen. the remarks of Anne Peters, 'International Legal Scholarship under Challenge', in Jean d'Aspremont, Tarcisio Gazzini, André Nollkaemper, and Wouter Werner (eds.), *International Law as a Profession* (Cambridge University Press, 2017) p. 117. On Marxism and international law,

bright sides,[56] for hidden dirty chapters of the history of international law,[57] for hidden 'structural biases',[58] for hidden 'agendas' or 'politics' behind certain legal concepts, for hidden argumentative practices and certain narratives,[59] for hidden

see gen. the remarks of Akbar Rasulov, 'A Marxism for International Law: A New Agenda' (2018) 29 *European Journal of International Law* 631.

[56] Martti Koskenniemi, 'Politics of International Law, 20 Years later' (2009) 20 *European Journal of Internatioal Law* 7 at 8.

[57] Antony Anghie 'Francisco De Vitoria and the Colonial Origins of International Law' (1996) 5 *Social and Legal Studies* 321; Antony Anghie, *Imperialism, Sovereignty and the Making of International Law* (Cambridge University Press, 2004) p. 14. Luigi Nuzzo, 'The Birth of an Imperial Location: Comparative Perspectives on Western Colonialism in China' (2018) 31 *Leiden Journal of International Law* 569; Lauren Benton, 'Made in Empire: Finding the History of International Law in Imperial Locations' (2018) 31 *Leiden Journal of International Law* 473; Nathaniel Berman, 'In the Wake of Empire' (1999) 14 *American University International Law Review* 1515; José-Manuel Barreto, 'Cerberus: Rethinking Grotius and the Westphalian System', in Martti Koskenniemi, Walter Rech, and Manuel Jimenez Fonseca (eds.), *International Law and Empire* (Oxford University Press, 2017) p. 158; Martti Koskenniemi 'Introduction: International Law and Empire – Aspects and Approaches', in Martti Koskenniemi, Walter Rech, and Manuel Jimenez Fonseca (eds.), *International Law and Empire* (Oxford University Press, 2017) p. 4; Benjamin Straumann, '"Ancient Caesarean Lawyers" in a State of Nature: Roman Tradition and Natural Rights in Hugo Grotius's "De iure praedae"' (2006) 34 *Political Theory* 328; Renee Jeffery, *Hugo Grotius in International Thought* (Palgrave Macmillan, 2006) pp. 6–7; Tarik Kochi, *The Other's War: Recognition and the Violence of Ethics* (Birkbeck Law Press, 2009) pp. 59–60; Martti Koskenniemi, 'International Law and the Emergence of Mercantile Capitalism: Grotius To Smith', in Pierre-Marie Dupuy and Vincent Chetail (eds.), *The Roots of International Law. Liber Amicorum Peter Haggenmacher* (Martinus Nijhoff, 2014) p. 3; Obregon, 'Empire, Racial Capitalism and International Law'; Emmanuelle Tourme-Jouannet, 'Des Origines Coloniales du Droit International: A Propos du Droit des Gens Moderne au 18ème Siècle', in Pierre-Marie Dupuy and Vincent Chetail (eds.), *The Roots of International Law. Liber Amicorum Peter Haggenmacher* (Martinus Nijhoff, 2014) p. 648; Mohammad Shahabuddin, 'The "Standard of Civilization' in International Law: Intellectual Perspectives from Pre-war Japan' (2019) 32 *Leiden Journal of International Law* 13; Guy Fiti Sinclair, *To Reform the World: International Organizations and the Making of Modern States* (Oxford University Press, 2017).

[58] Koskenniemi, 'Politics of International Law, 20 Years later' p. 9; see also the remarks of Zarbiyev 'The "Cash Value" of the rules of treaty interpretation'.

[59] David Kennedy, *Of War and Law* (Princeton University Press, 2006); Sinclair, *To Reform the World*; Jan Klabbers, 'The Relative Autonomy of International Law and The Forgotten Politics of Interdisciplinarity' (2004) 1 *Journal of International Law and International Relations* 35; Andrea Bianchi, 'The International Regulation of the Use of Force: The Politics of Interpretive Method' (2009) 22 *Leiden Journal of International Law* 665; Jean d'Aspremont, 'The Politics of Deformalization in International Law' (2011) 3 *Göttingen Journal of International Law* 503; Jean d'Aspremont, 'Wording in International Law' (2012) 25 *Leiden Journal of International Law* 575; d'Aspremont, 'Softness in

mindsets permeating international legal thought and practice,[60] for hidden paradoxes and ironies,[61] for hidden contingencies,[62] for hidden spatialities,[63] for hidden exercises of re-definition by certain categories of legal experts, for hidden imperialist,[64]

International Law; Jean d'Aspremont, *Epistemic Forces in International Law* (Edward Elgar, 2015); Koskenniemi, 'Politics of International Law, 20 Years later' p. 9; Martti Koskenniemi, 'Constitutionalism as Mindset: Reflections on Kantian Themes about International Law and Globalization' (2006) 8 *Theoretical Inquiries in Law* 9; Nikolas Rajkovic, 'Rules, Lawyering, and the Politics of Legality: Critical Sociology and International Law's Rule' (2014) 27 *Leiden Journal of International Law* 331; Koskenniemi, 'Politics of International Law, 20 Years later'; Wouter Werner, 'The Never-ending Closure: Constitutionalism and International Law', in Nicholas Tsagourias (ed.), *Transnational Constitutionalism: International and European Perspectives* (Cambridge University Press, 2007) p. 329; Anne Orford, *Reading Humanitarian Intervention: Human Rights and the Use of Force in International Law* (Cambridge Univeristy Press, 2003) pp. 158–185; Matthias Goldmann, 'The Ambiguity of Colonial International Law: Three Approaches to the Namibian Genocide' (2024) 37 *Leiden Journal of International Law* 1.

60 Koskenniemi, *The Gentle Civilizer of Nations* pp. 500–508; Koskenniemi, 'Constitutionalism as Mindset'; Martti Koskenniemi, 'Letter to the Editors of the Symposium' (1999) 93 *American Journal of International Law* 351; d'Aspremont, 'Wording in International Law'; Bianchi and Zarbiyev, *Demystifying Treaty Interpretation*; Jean d'Aspremont, *The Discourse on Customary International Law* (Oxford University Press, 2021); David Bederman, *The Spirit of International Law* (University of Georgia Press, 2002); Eyal Benvenisti, 'Comments on the Systemic Vision of National Courts as Part of an International Rule of Law' (2012) 4 *Jerusalem Review of Legal Studies* 42; Parfitt, The *Process of International Legal Reproduction* p. 21; Tzouvala, *Capitalism as Civilisation* pp. 38–40; Fuad Zarbiyev, *Le Discours interprétatif en droit international* (Bruylant, 2015) pp. 109–118.

61 Emmanuelle Jouannet, 'Universalism and Imperialism: The True-False Paradox of International Law?' (2007) 18 *European Journal of International Law* 379; Chin L. Lim and Olufemi Elias, *The Paradox of Consensualism in International Law* (Kluwer, 1998); Jan Klabbers, 'The Paradox of International Institutional Law' (2008) 5 *International Organizations Law Review* 151; Jean d'Aspremont, 'The International Court of Justice and the Irony of System-Design' (2017) 8 *Journal of International Dispute Settlement* 366; Kennedy, 'The Disciplines of International Law and Policy'.

62 See the contributions in Venzke and Heller, *Contingency in International Law*.

63 See Gail Lythgoe, *The Rebirth of Territory* (Cambridge University Press, 2024).

64 See, e.g., Antony Anghie, 'Rethinking International Law: A TWAIL Retrospective' (2023) 34 *European Journal of International Law* 7; Anghie, *Imperialism, Sovereignty and the Making of International Law*; Sundya Pahuja, *Decolonising International Law: Development, Economic Growth and the Politics of Universality* (Cambridge University Press, 2011); Sundya Pahuja, 'The Postcoloniality of International Law' (2005) 46 *Harvard International Law Journal* 459; Berman, 'In the Wake of Empire'; Makau Mutua, 'What Is TWAIL?' (2000) 94 *American Society of International Law Proceedings* 31; Antony Anghie, 'The Evolution of International Law: Colonial and Postcolonial Realities' (2006) 27 *Third World Quarterly* 740; Bhupinder S. Chimni, 'Third World Approaches to International Law: A Manifesto' (2006) 8 *International*

phallocentric[65] and capitalist[66] world-making performances of international law,[67] for international law's hidden effects on bodies and societies,[68] for hidden roles of international lawyers in the making of the vocabularies of global governance,[69] for hidden strategical uses of crisis-discourses,[70] for hidden emotions that drive legal thought and practice,[71]

Community Law Review 18; Makau Mutua, 'Savages, Victims and Saviors: The Metaphor of Human Rights' (2001) 42 *Harvard International Law Journal* 201. On the narrative structure of the contemporary discourse on imperialism in international law, see Akbar Rasulov, 'Imperialism', in Jean d'Aspremont and Sahib Singh (eds.), *Concepts for International Law: Contributions to Disciplinary Thought* (Edward Elgar, 2019) p. 422; Goldmann, 'The Ambiguity of Colonial International Law' (.

65 See gen. Karen Engle, Vasuki Nesiah, and Dianne Otto, 'Feminist Approaches to International Law', in Jeffrey L. Dunoff and Mark A. Pollack (eds.), *International Legal Theory. Foundations and Frontiers* (Cambridge University Press, 2022) pp. 174–196; Hilary Charlesworth, Christine Chinkin, and Shelley Wright, 'Feminist Approaches to International Law' (1991) 85 *American Journal of International Law* 613; Charlesworth, and Chinkin, *The Boundaries of International Law*; Hilary Charlesworth, 'Feminist Ambivalence about International Law (2005) 11 *International Legal Theory* 1; Hilary Charlesworth, 'Prefiguring Feminist Judgment in International Law', in Troy Lavers and Loveday Hodson (eds.), *Feminist Judgments in International Law* (Hart, 2019); Hilary Charlesworth, 'The Sex of the State in International Law', in Ngaire Naffine and Rosemary J. Owens (eds.), *Sexing the Subject of Law* (LBC Information Services, 1997); Karen Knop, 'Borders of the Imagination: The State in Feminist International Law', in *Proceedings of the Annual Meeting (American Society of International Law), The Transformation of Sovereignty (April 6–9, 1994)*, vol 88 (1994) pp. 14–18; Dianne Otto, 'Resisting the Heteronormative Imaginary of the Nation-state: Rethinking Kinship and Border Protection', in Dianne Otto (ed.), *Queering International Law: Possibilities, Alliances, Complicities, Risks* (Routledge Research in International Law, 2018), pp. 236–257.

66 See Tourme Jouannet, *Le droit international, le capitalisme et la terre*; Chimni, *International Law and World Order*; Tzouvala, *Capitalism as Civilisation*; Parfitt, *The Process of International Legal Reproduction*; Miéville, *Between Equal Rights*; Obregon, 'Empire, Racial Capitalism and International Law'. On the turn to political economy in general, see John Haskell and Akbar Rasulov, 'International Law and the Turn to Political Economy' (2018) 31 *Leiden Journal of International Law* 243.

67 David Kennedy, *A World of Struggle: How Power, Law, and Expertise Shape Global Political Economy* (Princeton University Press, 2016); Martti Koskenniemi, 'The Politics of International Law – 20 Years Later' (2009) 20 *European Journal of International Law* 7.

68 Mignot-Mahdavi, *Drones and International Law*.

69 Kennedy, *Of War and Law*.

70 See the contributions in Makane Moïse Mbengue and Jean d'Aspremont (eds.), *Crisis Narratives in International Law* (Brill, 2022).

71 See Saab, 'Emotions and International Law'; Bianchi and Saab 'Fear and International Law-making'; Bianchi, 'Fear's Legal Dimension' pp. 175–192; Simpson, *The Sentimental Life of International Law*; White, 'Images of Reach, Range, and Recognition' pp. 49–512; Sutton, 'How the Emotions and Perceptual Judgments of Frontline Actors Shape the

for hidden self-referential dialectics at work in forms' system of differences and the material conditions of their productions,[72] for hidden loss of the critical attitude,[73] etc. Those works, which are often found on the more critical side of the scholarly spectrum, are not less postulating the presence of hidden, unknown, invisible content.

The foregoing should suffice to demonstrate the extent and the variety of the hidden universe that international legal scholars, across the whole international legal literature, deem to be possibly located and found in the texts, practices, actors, effects, representations, past, etc. of international law. Yet, as will be discussed below,[74] the diversity of hidden, unknown, invisible contents that international legal scholars posit and hunt remain very nominal, for there are only so many contents that can possibly be deemed hidden in international legal thought and practice.

4.2 A Necessary Act of Revelation

The following paragraphs show that international courts and tribunals (Section 4.2.1) and international legal scholars (Section 4.2.2.) all experience the necessity to perform an act of revelation of all that lies hidden in the texts, practices, actors, effects, representations, past, etc. of international law with which they are confronted. It particularly demonstrates that international courts and tribunals can be understood as functioning as *revelatory apparatuses* and that international legal scholars behave as *scribes of the invisible.* Here too, the sample of judicial practice is restricted to the practice of the International Court of Justice, which is seen as sufficiently illustrative of the extent to which international courts

Practice of International Humanitarian Law'; Sutton and Rhoads, 'Empathy in Frontline Humanitarian Negotiations'; Sutton, 'Read the Room'; d'Aspremont, 'The Love for International Organizations'.

72 See Wouter Werner, *Repetition and International Law* (Cambridge University Press, 2022); see also d'Aspremont, *International Law as a Belief System*; Jean d'Aspremont, 'Three International Lawyers in a Hall of Mirrors' (2019) 32 *Leiden Journal of International Law* 367.

73 See Orford, 'International Law and the Limits of History' pp. 301–306; Orford, 'On International Legal Method' pp. 170–177. See also the remarks of Matthew Craven, 'Introduction: International Law and Its Histories', in Matthew Craven, Malgosia Fitzmaurice, and Maria Vogiatzi (eds.), *Time, History and International Law* (Brill, 2007) pp. 12–13; Jean d'Aspremont, 'Critical Histories of International Law and the Repression of Disciplinary Imagination' (2019) 7 *London Review of International Law* 89; d'Aspremont, 'Martti Koskenniemi, the Mainstream and Self-Reflectivity'.

74 See infra Section 4.3.

and tribunals are caught in the necessity of revelation composing the epistemology of the secret of international law.

4.2.1 *The International Court of Justice as a Revelatory Apparatus*

Before foregrounding the revelatory functioning of the International Court of Justice, this section starts with a general observation on international courts and tribunals as a whole and their relation with the epistemology of the secret discussed in this book. From the perspective of latter, it should not be too difficult to appreciate the extent to which international courts and tribunals constitute bureaucratic mechanisms[75] geared towards the revelation of a content that is hidden to the parties making use of such mechanisms. From such vantage point, it is argued here that international courts and tribunals can be construed as *revelatory apparatuses*. In fact, most of the time, parties seize international courts and tribunals – and, when applicable, bear the cost thereof – as they seek to have a hidden, unknown, invisible content on a specific question revealed to them and, incidentally, to third parties. In particular, the revelation to the parties of the legal standards or prescriptions applicable to a given situation – to so-called applicable law – is the rationale of most seizures of international courts and tribunals. It is further submitted here that the functioning of international courts and tribunals as revelatory apparatuses is exacerbated by some of the main patterns of thought that govern international dispute settlement. For instance, it is common for international lawyers to assume that there necessarily and always is some applicable law in any case submitted to a court, thereby presupposing that the latter can always find and reveal something. The presumption of the permanent presence of a legal standard to be revealed by international courts and tribunals is itself ensured by a variety of mechanisms,[76] like the presupposition of the

[75] On the idea of international courts and tribunals as bureaucratic mechanisms, see Jean d'Aspremont 'The Control over Knowledge by International Courts and Arbitral Tribunals', in Thomas Schultz and Federico Ortino (eds.), *The Oxford Handbook of International Arbitration* (Oxford University Press, 2020) pp. 331–333.

[76] On the various mechanisms that can prevent a declaration that there is no applicable law, see Alain Pellet, 'Article 38', in Zimmermann, Tams, Oellers-Frahm, and Tomuschat, *The Statute of the International Court of Justice* p. 705 (Refering to adjudication ex æquo et bono, progressive interpretation and customary law). Mechanisms to ensure that judges always find and reveal the applicable law are known in other legal systems, see the famous Article 4 of the French Civil Code.

completeness of the international legal order[77] or the inclusion of general principles of law among the sources that courts and tribunals can resort to.[78] The functioning of international courts and tribunals as revelatory apparatuses is even sometimes formalized through the postulation of a prohibition for courts and tribunals from finding that there is no applicable law – this is the prohibition of the so-called *non liquet*[79] – and the

[77] See Hersch Lauterpacht, *The Function of Law in the International Community* (Clarendon Press, 1933) pp. 53–55; Hersch Lauterpacht, 'Some Observations on the Prohibition of "Non Liquet" and the Completeness of the Law', in *Symbolae Verzijl* (Martinus Nijhoff, 1958) p. 224. See the remarks of Iain Scobbie, 'The Theorist as Judge: Hersch Lauterpacht's Concept of the International Judicial Function' (1997) 8 *European Journal of International Law* 264 at 274–276. See the famous claim by the Permanent Court of International Justice in the Lotus case that everything that is not prohibited by international law is allowed in The Case of SS Lotus (France v Turkey) (1927) PCIJ Ser A No 10. For some famous contentions that contemporary international law has allegedly moved away from the principle established in the Lotus, see the declaration of Judge Bedjaoui and the opinion of Judge Shahabuddeen appended to the advisory opinion on the *Legality of the Threat or Use of Nuclear Weapons*, ICJ Rep 1996, p. 268 et s. and p. 394–396. More recently, see the declaration of Judge Simma appended to the advisory opinion on the *Accordance with International Law of the Unilateral Declaration of Independence in Respect of Kosovo* 22 July 2010, pp. 1–3. See also Alain Pellet, 'Lotus que de sottises on profère en ton nom! Remarques sur le concept de souveraineté dans la jurisprudence de la Cour mondiale', in Edwige Belliard (ed.), *Mélanges en l'honneur de Jean-Pierre Puissochet: L'État souverain dans le monde d'aujourd'hui* (Pedone, 2008) pp. 215–230; see gen. the remarks of Devika Hovell, 'The Elements of International Legal Positivism' (2022) 75 *Current Legal Problems* 71 at 105–108; Scobbie, 'The Theorist as Judge' pp. 292–297; An Hertogen, 'Letting Lotus Bloom' (2015) 26 *European Journal of International Law* 901.

[78] See the proposition of draft Article 38 submitted by Baron Descamps to the Advisory Committee of Jurists in 1920 in Permanent Court of International Justice, Advisory Committee of Jurists, Procès-Verbaux of the Proceedings of the Committee, 16 June–24 July 1920, The Hague, 1920, pp. 322–325. On this debate, see Maarten Bos, *A Methodology of International Law* (T.M.C Asser Instituut, 1984) pp. 68–75; Alain Pellet, 'Article 38' pp. 685–689. See also the separate opinion of Judge Cançado Trindade in the case pertaining to the *Pulp Mills* (Argentina v. Uruguay) before the International Court of Justice, 20 April 2010, ICJ Rep. 2010, 3–6. See generally the remarks of Jean d'Aspremont, 'What Was Not Meant to Be: General Principles of Law as a Source of International Law', in Ricardo Pisillo Mazzeschi and Pasquale De Sena (eds.), *Global Justice, Human Rights, and the Modernization of International Law* (Brill, 2018). It should be noted that general principles of law did not prevent the ICJ from making a finding of non-liquet in advisory proceedings, see Legality of the Threat or Use of Nuclear Weapons, ICJ Reports (1996), pp. 226, 263 (para. 97). See also Reparations for Injuries in the Service of the United Nations, ICJ Reports (1949), pp. 174, 185 ('in such case, there is no rule of law which assigns priority to one or to the other, or which compels either the state or the Organization from bringing an international claim').

[79] Lauterpacht, 'Some Observations on the Prohibition of "Non Liquet" and the Completeness of the Law' p. 205; see also Hersch Lauterpacht, *The Function of Law in the International Community* (Clarendon Press, 1933) p. 67. On the invention of general principles of law to

claim that they accordingly have a permanent obligation to reveal an applicable legal standard.

To demonstrate the extent to which international courts and tribunals function as revelatory apparatuses, it suffices, as was already said, to look at the practice of the International Court of Justice (hereafter the Court). Indeed, the Court is systematically 'requested' to perform a variety of tasks of revelation, including the revelation of the existence or content of a right or an obligation under international law,[80] of the existence of a breach of international law,[81] of the content of customary

prevent the finding of a *non liquet*, see Permanent Court of International Justice, Advisory Committee of Jurists, Procès-Verbaux of the Proceedings of the Committee, 16 June–24 July 1920, The Hague, 1920, pp. 322–325. On this debate, see Bos, *A Methodology of International Law* pp. 68–75; Pellet, 'Article 38' pp. 685–689. This did not prevent the ICJ from making a finding of *non liquet* in advisory proceedings – see ICJ, Legality of the Threat or Use of Nuclear Weapons, Advisory Opinion of 8 July 1996, ICJ Reports 1996, para. 97; see also the Dissenting Opinion of Judge Higgins, ICJ Reports (1996) 583, paras. 36–38; See also ICJ, Reparations for Injuries in the Service of the United Nations, Advisory Opinion of 11 April 1949, ICJ Reports 1949, pp. 174, 185: 'in such case, there is no rule of law which assigns priority to one or to the other, or which compels either the state or the Organization from bringing an international claim'.

[80] See, e.g., Dispute over the Status and Use of the Waters of the Silala (Chile v. Bolivia), Judgment of 1 December 2022; Alleged Violations of Sovereign Rights and Maritime Spaces in the Caribbean Sea (Nicaragua v. Colombia), 21 April 2022; Obligation to Negotiate Access to the Pacific Ocean (Bolivia v. Chile), Judgment of 1 October 2018, para. 176.

[81] As most cases pertain to the declaration of a behaviour or an act being contrary to international law, only a few examples can be provided here. See, e.g., Alleged Violations of Sovereign Rights and Maritime Spaces in the Caribbean Sea (Nicaragua v. Colombia), 21 April 2022; Immunities and Criminal Proceedings (Equatorial Guinea v. France), Judgement of 11 December 2020; Jadhav (India v. Pakistan), Judgment of 17 July 2019; Certain Activities Carried Out by Nicaragua in the Border Area (Costa Rica v. Nicaragua), Judgment of 16 December 2015; Obligations concerning Negotiations relating to Cessation of the Nuclear Arms Race and to Nuclear Disarmament (Marshall Islands v. Pakistan), Judgment of 5 October 2016; Obligations concerning Negotiations relating to Cessation of the Nuclear Arms Race and to Nuclear Disarmament (Marshall Islands v. United Kingdom), Judgement of 5 October 2016; Obligations concerning Negotiations relating to Cessation of the Nuclear Arms Race and to Nuclear Disarmament (Marshall Islands v. India), Judgment of 5 October 2016; Application of the Convention on the Prevention and Punishment of the Crime of Genocide (Croatia v. Serbia), Judgment of 3 February 2015; Whaling in the Antarctic (Australia v. Japan: New Zealand intervening), Judgement of 31 March 2014; Questions relating to the Obligation to Prosecute or Extradite (Belgium v. Senegal), Judgment of 20 July 2012; Jurisdictional Immunities of the State (Germany v. Italy: Greece intervening), Judgment of 3 February 2012; Application of the Convention on the Prevention and Punishment of the Crime of Genocide (Bosnia and Herzegovina v. Serbia and Montenegro), Judgment of 26 February 2007; East Timor (Portugal v. Australia), Judgment of 30 June 1995.

international law,[82] of the existence and contours of a legal dispute,[83] of the criteria for a boundary or maritime delimitation,[84] of the status of a river,[85] of the legality of a declaration by a non-state actor,[86] of the legality of the use of a certain type of weapon,[87] of the legality of a certain infrastructure,[88] of the situation that would have existed had the wrongful incident concerned not occurred,[89] of the financial value of the loss of human life, natural resources, property damage, or any harm due a result of a breach of international law,[90] of the ground for its

[82] See, e.g., Dispute over the Status and Use of the Waters of the Silala (Chile v. Bolivia), Judgment of 1 December 2022; See, e.g., Question of the Delimitation of the Continental Shelf between Nicaragua and Colombia beyond 200 nautical miles from the Nicaraguan Coast (Nicaragua v. Colombia), Judgement of 13 July 2023.

[83] See, e.g., Dispute over the Status and Use of the Waters of the Silala (Chile v. Bolivia), Judgment of 1 December 2022; Application of the International Convention on the Elimination of All Forms of Racial Discrimination (Qatar v. United Arab Emirates), Judgement of 4 February 2021.

[84] See, e.g., Question of the Delimitation of the Continental Shelf between Nicaragua and Colombia beyond 200 nautical miles from the Nicaraguan Coast (Nicaragua v. Colombia), Judgement of 13 July 2023; Maritime Delimitation in the Indian Ocean (Somalia v. Kenya), Judgement of 12 October 2021; Land Boundary in the Northern Part of Isla Portillos (Costa Rica v. Nicaragua), Judgment of 2 February 2018; Maritime Delimitation in the Caribbean Sea and the Pacific Ocean (Costa Rica v. Nicaragua), 2 February 2018; Certain Activities Carried Out by Nicaragua in the Border Area (Costa Rica v. Nicaragua), Judgment of 16 December 2015; Maritime Dispute (Peru v. Chile), Judgment of 27 January 2014; Frontier Dispute (Burkina Faso/Niger), Judgment of 16 April 2013; Territorial and Maritime Dispute (Nicaragua v. Colombia), Judgement of 13 December 2007; North Sea Continental Shelf (Federal Republic of Germany/ Netherlands), Judgment of 20 February 1969.

[85] See, e.g., Dispute over the Status and Use of the Waters of the Silala (Chile v. Bolivia), Judgment of 1 December 2022; Certain Activities Carried Out by Nicaragua in the Border Area (Costa Rica v. Nicaragua), Judgment of 16 December 2015.

[86] Accordance with international law of the unilateral declaration of independence in respect of Kosovo, Advisory Opinion of 22 July 2010; Certain Activities Carried Out by Nicaragua in the Border Area (Costa Rica v. Nicaragua), Judgment of 16 December 2015; Pulp Mills on the River Uruguay (Argentina v. Uruguay), Judgment of 20 April 2010.

[87] Legality of the Threat or Use of Nuclear Weapons, Advisory Opinion of 8 July 1996.

[88] Legal Consequences of the Construction of a Wall in the Occupied Palestinian Territory, Advisory Opinion of 9 July 2004.

[89] Alleged Violations of Sovereign Rights and Maritime Spaces in the Caribbean Sea (Nicaragua v. Colombia), 21 April 2022.

[90] Armed Activities on the Territory of the Congo (Democratic Republic of the Congo v. Uganda), Judgement of 9 February 2022; Application of the International Convention on the Elimination of All Forms of Racial Discrimination (Qatar v. United Arab Emirates), Judgement of 4 February 2021; Certain Activities Carried Out by Nicaragua in the Border Area (Costa Rica v. Nicaragua), Judgment of 16 December 2015; Application of the Convention on the Prevention and Punishment of the Crime of

jurisdiction,[91] etc. In all such cases and advisory proceedings, the Court is always approached and reacting as a revelatory apparatus for a great diversity of acts of revelation. It is argued here that no other international court or tribunal illustrates better than the International Court of Justice the institutionalization of the necessity of a revelation characteristic of the epistemology of the secret of international law.

4.2.2 *International Legal Scholars as Scribes of the Invisible*

It is argued here that international legal scholars commonly understand their role as that of scribes of the invisible.[92] Indeed, those international lawyers that devote most of their professional activities to teaching and research are, like international judges, absorbed by the experience of the necessity of a revelation typical of the epistemology of the secrets of international law as it is understood here. Although the bureaucratic and managerial decaying of the contemporary university has dramatically worsened the conditions in which such professionals conduct their research,[93] and even if it may be that the contemporary university has ceased to be an intellectual place,[94] the role of international legal scholars remains construed, represented, and practiced as geared towards an act of revelation. It is true that, since the consolidation of international law as a profession and as a discipline,[95] the role of the international legal

Genocide (Croatia v. Serbia), Judgment of 3 February 2015; Ahmadou Sadio Diallo (Republic of Guinea v. Democratic Republic of the Congo), Judgment of 19 June 2012.

91 This is the case of any proceedings.

92 The expression comes from Régis Debray, see Régis Debray, *Le Scribe* (Editions Grasset et Fasquelle, 1980).

93 On the idea that it is the quietude of the life of a bourgeois that allow some people to take care of marginal thoughts, practices, behaviours, texts, representations, etc., see Michel Foucault, *Dits et écrits, I (1954–1975)* (Gallimard, 2001) p. 685.

94 On the idea that all human beings are potentially intellectuals in the sense of having an intellect and using it but not all are intellectuals by social function and that non-intellectuals do not exist, see Antonio Gramsci, *Selections from the Prison Notebooks*, trans. and ed. Quintin Hoare and Geoffrey Nowell Smith (Lawrence and Wishart, 2003) p. 9; see also Louis Althusser, *Initiation à la Philosophie pour les Non-Philosophes* (Presses Universitaires de France, 2014) pp. 55–57.

95 Stephen C. Neff reports that an early professorship in the subject was established at the University of Turin in 1851, see Neff, *Justice among Nations*. The Chichele Chair of International Law and Diplomacy was established in 1859 at Oxford University. The Whewell Chair in International Law at Cambridge University was created in 1867. See also the remarks of Ignacio de la Rasilia del Moral, 'The Ambivalent Shadow of the Pre-Wilsonian Rise of International Law' (2014) 7 *European Law Review* 2 (he argues that in the wake of the independence of the American Republics from Spain, the university

scholar has moved from that of a generalist in the humanities to that of an expert in a specific body of law, area of legal practice, attitude, or method,[96] thereby mirroring a phenomenon witnessed with intellectuals in general.[97] Yet, such alteration has not recast the necessity of revelation that commands what is socially expected from international legal scholars and informs how the latter construe their profession. In fact, international legal scholars understand their role as making visible what is counted as invisible and especially disclosing hidden actualities, universalities, memories, necessities. The following paragraphs highlight some of the most common (self-)representations of international legal scholars according to which their role is that of revealers of hidden, unknown, invisible actualities, universalities, memories, or necessities.

As a first illustration, it is worth referring to the common depictions of the role of international legal scholars that explicitly acknowledge the

teaching of international law emerged comparatively earlier in the US than in Europe, maybe with the exception of Spain. The first courses of international law in the United States were taught in 1846 at Yale by Theodore Woolsey and Francis Lieber later on). For some general remarks on the professionalization of international law, see Jean d'Aspremont, 'The Professionalization of International Law', in Jean d'Aspremont, Tarcisio Gazzini, André Nollkaemper, and Wouter Werner (eds.), *International Law as a Profession* (Cambridge University Press, 2017); Anne Orford, 'Scientific Reason and the Discipline of International Law' (2014) 25 *European Journal of International Law* 369 at 373; Benjamin Allen Coates, *Legalist Empire: International Law and American Foreign Relations in the Early Twentieth Century* (Oxford University Press, 2016) pp. 18–21 and 61–68. For a discussion of some of the manifestations of the professionalization of international law in Latin America and Asia, see, e.g., Arnulf Becker Lorca, *Mestizo International Law: A Global Intellectual History 1842–1933* (Cambridge University Press, 2014); see also Arnulf Becker Lorca, 'Universal International Law: Nineteenth-Century Histories of Imposition and Appropriation' (2010) 51 *Harvard International Law Journal* 475.

96 The idea of 'managerialism' in international legal thought was coined by Martti Koskenniemi, see Martti Koskenniemi, 'Constitutionalism, Managerialism and the Ethos of Legal Education' (2007) 1 *European Journal of Legal Studies* 1; Koskenniemi, 'The Politics of International Law - 20 Years Later'; see also the remarks of Martti Koskenniemi who sees Lauterpacht's 1933 *The Function of Law in the Inter-national Community* as a treatise of managerialism for international lawyers who want to rule the world, see the introduction of Martti Koskenniemi, in Lauterpacht, *The Function of law in the International Community* p. xlvii; Kennedy, *A World of Struggle*. On governance through knowledge by international courts and tribunals, see d'Aspremont 'The Control over Knowledge by International Courts and Arbitral Tribunals' pp. 328–353.

97 Michel Foucault, *Dits et écrits, II* (Gallimard, 2001) pp. 111 and 154. Such parallel is possibly not a coincidence, for the figure of the lawyer has always informed the contours of the figure of the intellectual (and of the representations thereof), see Noam Chomsky and Michel Foucault, *The Chomsky-Foucault Debate on Human Nature* (The New Press, 2006) p. 165; Foucault, *Dits et écrits, II* p. 111.

necessity of a revelation. In that regard, one cannot help being struck by the widespread use in the international legal literature of analogies with priests' and theologians' activities when describing international legal scholars' engagements with international legal thought and practice.[98] The use of the metaphors of archaeology or excavation to depict the role of scholars similarly bespeaks the necessity of an act of revelation of what lies hidden.[99] Likewise, the claims that scholarship is geared towards "new discoveries"[100] or towards the disclosure of the "mysteries"[101] of international legal thought and practice also intimate a necessity to reveal what is hidden in the texts, practices, actors, effects, representations, past, etc. of international law.

The same necessity of revelation permeates ordinary claims that international legal scholars speak truth to power and show errors of others[102] as well as their typical portrayals as a grammarians[103] whose responsibility the international legal scholar is to reveal the systematicity of legal practices and of the structure of international legal argumentation.[104] The same necessity of revelation informs widespread accounts according to which the problem of international legal academics is to solve the

[98] International lawyers themselves have relished using such theological analogy for analytical and descriptive purposes, see, e.g., James Crawford, 'International Law as Discipline and Profession' (2012) 106 *ASIL Proceedings* 471; Jason Beckett, 'The Politics of International Law - Twenty Years Later: A Reply', in EJIL:TALK!, 19 May 2009, www.ejiltalk.org/the-politics-of-international-law-twenty-years-later-a-reply/; Martti Koskenniemi, 'The Fate of Public International Law: Between Technique and Politics' (1997) *The Modern Law Review* 1 at 30; Anthony Carty, *Post-Modern Law: Enlightement, Revolution and the Death of Man* (Edinburgh University Press, 1990); Martti Koskenniemi, 'Miserable Comforters: International Relations as New Nature Law' (2009) 15 *European Journal of International Relations* 395 at 396; David Kennedy, 'When Renewal Repeats: Thinking against the Box' (1999–2000) 32 *New York University Journal of International Law and Politics* 335 at 375.

[99] Charlesworth and Chinkin, *The Boundaries of International Law* p. 18.

[100] See the remarks of Peters, 'International Legal Scholarship under Challenge' p. 139.

[101] Martti Koskenniemi, 'The Mystery of Legal Obligation' (2011) 3 *International Theory* 319.

[102] Martti Koskenniemi, 'Between Commitment and Cynicism: Outline for a Theory of International Law as Practice', in Jean d'Aspremont, Tarcisio Gazzini, André Nollkaemper, and Wouter Werner (eds.), *International Law as a Profession* (Cambridge University Press, 2017) p. 64.

[103] Dupuy, 'L'unité de l'ordre juridique international' p. 205; see also Martti Koskenniemi, *From Apology to Utopia: The Structure of International Legal Argument* (Cambridge University Press, 2005) pp. 563–573; Hernandez, 'The Responsibility of the International Legal Academic' p. 161.

[104] On the idea that scholars create systematized material, Hernandez, 'The Responsibility of the International Legal Academic' p. 177.

problems about the content of international legal rules and how such contents are (or ought to be) applied in practice.[105] The same goes for the very common assertions that scholarly theories and frameworks' main function is to produce new knowledge about law, legal practices, the world, and the structures of knowledge itself.[106]

Unsurprisingly,[107] the necessity of a revelation is even more tangible in the scientifically minded streams of the international legal scholarship that came to emerge at the end of the nineteenth century.[108] In fact, the scientific study of international law has amounted to a commitment to produce knowledge about the hidden realities of international law.[109] Such scientistic ambition is premised on the idea that international law is an actuality grounded in the real and deployed or invoked to intervene in the real. From such perspective, a statement about international law, its origin, its effects, its functioning, etc. must amount to a truth-claim by being grounded in the real that has been properly revealed. It is true that, in recent decades, the representation of the study of international law as

[105] Hernandez, 'The Responsibility of the International Legal Academic' p. 160; see also Martti Koskenniemi, 'Law, Teleology and International Relations: An Essay in Counter disciplinarity' (2011) 26 *International Relations* 3 at 20.

[106] Peters, 'International Legal Scholarship under Challenge' pp. 140–142.

[107] On the resemblance and possible kinship between modern thought and the epistemology of the secret of international law, see supra Section 2.3.

[108] For a classical example, see, e.g., Lassa Oppenheim, 'The Science of International Law: Its Task and Method' (1908) 2 *American Journal of International Law* 313. On the rise of the scientistic project in international law, see Monica Garcia-Salmones Rovira, *The Project of Positivism in International Law* (Oxford University Press, 2013); Orford, 'Scientific Reason and the Discipline of International Law' p. 93; Aalberts and Venzke, 'Moving Beyond Interdisciplinary Turf Wars' pp. 297–298; see also Jean d'Aspremont, 'International Legal Positivism and the European Quest for Scientificity', in Anne van Aaken, Pierre d'Argent, Lauri Mälksoo and Johann Justus Vasel (eds.), *Oxford Handbook of International Law in Europe* (Oxford University Press, 2025), pp. 253–272.

[109] It is no surprise that those studying international law have sought to represent themselves as social scientists. In fact, in the nineteenth and twentieth century, many existing disciplines came to revamp their methods and self-representations with a view to securing the venerated status of discipline about the real. Such quest for the venerated status of discipline about the real find its roots in eithteenth-century discursive hierarchies that came to dominate the eighteenth and nineteenth centuries and whereby the real trumps the narrative, the factual eclipses the literary, and the physical overwrites the metaphysical. As a result, disciplines that produce necessities through realities and facts have enjoyed primacy over those that do not, the latter being marred with suspicion. On the modern and scientific ambitions of this type of international legal scholarship, see also Jean d'Aspremont, 'International Law and the Rage against Scienticism' (2022) 33 *European Journal of International Law* 679.

belonging to social sciences have retreated.[110] Yet, it is argued here that the abovementioned scientistic spirit has continued to inhabit a great deal of scholarly engagements with international law until today, notwithstanding the fall from grace of the idea of legal science. Indeed, an important part of the international legal scholarship, although less explicitly committed to the idea that legal scholarship is a social science, has continued to be articulated around scientistic aspirations, such scientistic aspiration being nothing more and nothing less than a revelatory ambition.[111] For these legal scientists in all but name, scholarship is about 'cognizing, structuring, and apprehending legal materials',[112] assuming that the international legal scholars 'can penetrate appearance to perceive a reality that remains "hidden" from those who advocate governmental or political causes'.[113] It could even be said that discussions about international legal methods, which can be read as a remnant of the idea of an international legal science,[114] still harbour revelatory ambitions.[115] Likewise, the so-called New Haven School can be interpreted as yet another attempt to reveal the actual functioning of international law.[116] Studies on the legitimacy of international law witnessed in the 1990s[117] similarly sought to better reveal compliance dynamics.[118] In recent decades, the promotion of a new legal realism in international law,[119]

110 On some traditional criticisms of scientifically minded scholarship as hiding its own politics, see Hernandez, 'The Responsibility of the International Legal Academic' pp. 160–173.

111 See recently Daniel Abebe, Adam Chilton, and Tom Ginsburg, 'The Social Science Approach to International Law' (2021) 22 *Chicago Journal of International Law* 1.

112 Hernandez, 'The Responsibility of the International Legal Academic' p. 162.

113 Koskenniemi, 'Between Commitment and Cynicism' pp. 38–64.

114 Orford, 'Scientific Reason and the Discipline of International Law' p. 94.

115 For similar observations, see Koskenniemi, 'Letter to the Editors of the Symposium'.

116 See gen. W. Michael Reisman, 'The View from the New Haven School of International Law' (1992) 86 *ASIL Proceedings* 118; W. Michael Reisman, Siegfried Wiessner, and Andrew Willard, 'The New Haven School: A Brief Introduction,' (2007) 32 *Yale Journal of International Law* 576. For a similar reading of the New Haven approach, see Orford, 'Scientific Reason and the Discipline of International Law' pp. 381–382. On New Haven's scientific ambitions, see Peters, 'International Legal Scholarship under Challenge' p. 138.

117 See Thomas Franck, *Fairness in International Law and Institutions* (Clarendon Press 1995) p. 6. On the turn to legitimacy, see the remarks of Corten, *Sociologies du droit* pp. 435–482.

118 On this aspect of the turn to legitimacy, see Bederman, *The Spirit of International Law* p. 3.

119 See gen. Gregory Shaffer, 'A New Legal Realism: Method in International Economic Law Scholarship', in Colin B. Picker, Isabella Bunn, and Douglas Arner (eds.), *International Economic Law – The State and Future of the Discipline* (Hart, 2008) pp. 29–42; Howard

or the vindication, under the banner of a 'new empirical turn', of a more organized and systematized use of empirical data to study the practical conditions under which international law is formed and has effects[120] have constituted scholarly enterprises that are similarly articulated around an act of revelation. In studies of the history of international law, a whole range of scholars, often teaming up with historians interested in international law, have come to advocate a return to scientific methods to apprehend the hidden reality of the past of international legal thought and practice that they ought to reveal.[121] All such scientifically minded endeavours indicate that, notwithstanding some compelling contestations, the necessity of a revelation about the hidden realities of international law continue to enjoy some substantial support in international legal thought and practice.[122]

The necessity of revelation yet expresses itself in other ways, for instance, when scholarship seeks to invent or propose new frameworks and concepts.[123] It is true that these frameworks or concepts are not approached as hidden, unknown, invisible content that is out there and

Erlanger, Bryant Garth, Jane Larson, Elizabeth Mertz, Victoria Nourse, and David Wilkins, 'New Legal Realism Symposium: Is It Time for a New Legal Realism?' (2005) 2 *Wisconsin Law Review* 335; Stewart Macaulay, 'The New versus the Old Legal Realism: Things Ain't What They Used to Be' (2005) 2 *Wisconsin Law Review* 365 at 375; Victoria Nourse and Gregory Shaffer, 'Varieties of New Legal Realism: Can a New World Order Prompt a New Legal Theory' (2006) 95 *Cornell Law Review* 61.

120 See, e.g., Shaffer and Ginsburg, 'The Empirical Turn in International Legal Scholarship'. For an illustration, see Pierre-Hugues Verdier and Erik Voeten, 'How Does Customary International Law Change? The Case of State Immunity' (2015) 59 *International Studies Quarterly* (2015) 209; see also Jakob V. H. Holtermann and Mikael Rask Madsen, 'Toleration, Synthesis or Replacement? The "Empirical Turn" and Its Consequences for the Science of International Law' (2016) 29 *Leiden Journal of International Law* 1001. For a claim about the virtuosity of empirical sensitivity, see Jorge E. Vinuales, 'On Legal Inquiry', in Denis Alland, Vincent Chetail, Olivier de Frouville, and Jorge Vinuales (eds.), *Unity and Diversity of International Law: Essays in Honour of Professor Pierre-Marie Dupuy* (Martinus Nijhoff, 2014) pp. 72–75.

121 See the account of such return to scientific methods in the study of the history of international law provided by Anne Orford, *International Law and the Politics of History* (Cambridge University Press, 2021), especially chapters 3 and 4. See also d'Aspremont, 'International Law and the Rage against Scienticism'.

122 For some general and critical remarks on the traditional depiction of international legal scholarship as being divided between those who see it as legal science and those critical legal scholars that do meta-theory and are very theoretical, see Besson, 'International Legal Theory Qua Practice of International Law' pp. 272–273.

123 Devaney, 'A Coherence Framework for Fact-finding before the International Court of Justice'; Hernandez, 'The Responsibility of the International Legal Academic' pp. 164 and 177.

revealed but as content that is explicitly created. Yet, what is relevant for the account of the manifestations of the epistemology of the secret provided in the present chapter is that such frameworks and concepts created by legal scholars are most of the time designed and put forward with a view to locating the hidden limits of current international legal thought and practice.[124] Likewise, the avenues of re-imagination of world politics at work in international law[125] or the potential for change in international law[126] that are produced through new frameworks and concepts invented by legal scholars remain something that is held to be hidden had they not been revealed through application of such new frameworks or concepts. By the same token, when defining or projecting a new area of legal regulation (a so-called law of) international legal scholars not only invent a field but they also claim to mobilize a new lens that makes a hidden actuality of legal thought and practice visible.[127] In short, the new frameworks and the new concepts that regularly emerge in the international legal literature are devices meant to be revelatory of a content held to be otherwise hidden, unknown, and invisible.

When one turns to the more critical side of the scholarly spectrum, not much difference is witnessed, for the same necessity of a revelation governs what international legal scholars do. Indeed, those scholarly works that mobilize tools from structuralism[128] and popularize findings

[124] Benedict Kingsbury, Nico Krisch, and Richard B. Steward, 'The Emergence of Global Administrative Law' (2005) 68 *Law and Contemporary Problems* 15; Nico Krisch, *Beyond Constitutionalism: The Pluralist Structure of Postnational Law* (Oxford University Press, 2010); Charlesworth and Chinkin, *The Boundaries of International Law* pp. 1 and 23; Klabbers, *The Concept of Treaty in International Law* p. 13; Mattias Kumm, 'The Legitimacy of International Law: A Constitutionalist Framework of Analysis' (2004) 15 *European Journal of International Law* 917; C. Brölmann, *The Institutional Veil in Public International Law: International Organisations and the Law of Treaties* (Hart, 2007).

[125] Anne Orford, *International Law and Its Others* (Cambridge University Press, 2006); Orford, *Reading Humanitarian Intervention* pp. 82–125.

[126] Carty, *The Philosophy of International Law.*

[127] Nigel White, *The Law of International Organizations* (Manchester University Press, 2005); Eyal Benvenisti, *The International Law of Occupation*, 2nd edn (Oxford University Press, 2012); Raič, *Statehood and the Law of Self-Determination*; Samantha Besson, 'The "Human Right to Science" qua Right to Participate in Science and Enjoy Its Benefits: The Participatory Good of Science and Its Human Rights Implications' (2023) *International Journal of Human Rights* 1.

[128] On the structuralist foundations of Martti Koskenniemi's account of international legal argumentation, see supra note xxx.

already made in the 1970s[129] and early 1980s[130] in literary and linguistic studies – which once called themselves 'new streams'[131] or 'new approaches'[132] but now prefer not to be identified this way[133] – are not at variance with the rest of the legal scholarship when it comes to a commitment to an act of revelation of hidden, unknown, invisible content. When seeking to shed light on what certain institutional, argumentative, and social practices – and especially the constant mediation between the world that is perceived (concreteness) and the world that is wanted (normativity)[134] – do to the world and to people, they perform an act of revelation.[135] Such scholarly engagements with international law are about divulging oscillations or dialectics between opposites in international legal thought and practice as well as the politics behind it.[136] When giving expression to some forgotten or invisibilized

[129] George Steiner, *After Babel: Aspects of Language and Translation* (Oxford University Press, 1975).

[130] Robert Cover, 'The Supreme Court, 1982 Term – Foreword: Nomos and Narrative' (1983–1984) 97 *Harvard Law Review* 4 at 9.

[131] Jeffrey Dunoff and Mark A. Pollack, 'Introduction to International Legal Theory: Taking Stock, Looking Ahead', in Jeffrey L. Dunoff and Mark A. Pollack (eds.), *International Legal Theory. Foundations and Frontiers* (Cambridge University Press, 2022) p. 19; Deborah Z. Cass, 'Navigating the Newstream: Recent Critical Scholarship in International Law' (1996) 65 *Nordic Journal of International Law* 341; David W. Kennedy, 'A New Stream of International Law Scholarship' (1988) 7 *Wisconsin International Law Journal* 1.

[132] Bhupinder S. Chimni, 'New Approaches to International Law: The Critical Scholarship of David Kennedy and Martti Koskenniemi', in Bhupinder S. Chimni (ed.), *International Law and World Order: A Critique of Contemporary Approaches*, 2nd edn (Cambridge Univeristy Press, 2017) pp. 246–357; José María Beneyto and David Kennedy, *New Approaches to International Law: The European and the American Experiences* (Springer, 2013); Ntina Tzouvala, 'New Approaches to International Law: The History of a Project' (2016) 27/1 *European Journal of International Law* 215.

[133] Fleur Johns, 'Critical International Legal Theory', in Jeffrey L. Dunoff and Mark A. Pollack (eds.), *International Legal Theory. Foundations and Frontiers* (Cambridge University Press, 2022) pp. 133–152.

[134] David Kennedy, *International Legal Structures* (Nomos, 1987); Koskenniemi, *From Apology to Utopia*; Koskenniemi, 'The Fate of International Public Law'.

[135] In the same vein, see Michelle Staggs Kelsall, 'Disordering International Law' (2022) 33 *European Journal of International Law* 729 at 735 (she argues that the primary goal of critique remains to expose what is wrong or lacking in the current legal order).

[136] Koskenniemi, *From Apology to Utopia*; Koskenniemi, 'The Fate of Public International Law'; Koskenniemi, 'Between Commitment and Cynicism' pp. 495–523; Kennedy, 'When Renewal Repeats'; Jean d'Aspremont, 'The Law of International Organizations and the Art of Reconciliation: From Dichotomies to Dialectics' (2014) 11 *International Organizations Law Review* 428; Martti Koskenniemi, 'Theory: Implications for the Practitioner', in Philip Allott, Tony Carty, Martti Koskenniemi. and Colin Warbrick,

voices,[137] they made visible marginalization, ostracization, and invisibilization of certain people or groups.[138] Whilst widely acknowledging the indeterminacy of rules and legal practices,[139] those scholars continue to construe their role as revealing the truth, whether the latter is a truth about indeterminacy or what is done to the world behind and through such indeterminacy.[140] It is submitted that all such critical works are animated by a spirit of revelation.[141]

Mention must finally be made of a – rather marginal – body of international legal scholarship that contemplates and experiments modes of misreading of international legal texts, understood as modes of slow, meticulous, metonymizing, and surprise-inducing reading that stop short

Theory and International Law: An Introduction (The British Institute of International and Comparative Law and International Law Group, Society of Public Teachers of Law, 1991) pp. 3–45, esp. pp. 19–20; Klabbers, 'Two Contending Approaches to the Law of International Organizations' pp. 3–30; see also Klabbers, 'Two Concepts of International Organization'.

137 Mohammad Shahabuddin, *Minorities and the Making of Postcolonial States in International Law* (Cambridge University Press, 2021); Charlesworth, Chinkin, and Wright, 'Feminist Approaches to International Law'; Charlesworth and Chinkin, *The Boundaries of Iinternational Law* p. 1.

138 Charlesworth and Chinkin, *The Boundaries of International Law* p. 19.

139 On the idea that such discussions of the indeterminacy of rules remain very meaning-centric and grounded in the postulation that law has meaning albeit indeterminate, see Jean d'Aspremont, *After Meaning: The Sovereignty of Forms in International Law* (Edward Elgar, 2021) pp. 13 and 24.

140 Koskenniemi, 'Between Commitment and Cynicism' p. 64.

141 Koskenniemi, 'The Politics of International Law – 20 Years Later'; Ingo Venzke, *How Interpretation Makes International Law: On Semantic Change and Normative Twists* (Oxford University Press, 2012); Sundhya Pahuja, 'Decolonization and the Eventness of International Law', in Fleur Johns, Richard Joyce, and Sundhya Pahuja (eds.), *Events: The Force of International Law* (Routledge, 2011), pp. 91–105. See also the success of the so-called constructivist approaches to world-making, see Jutta Brunnée and Stephen Toope, 'Constructivism and International Law', in Jeffrey L. Dunoff and Mark A. Pollack (eds.), *Interdisciplinary Perspectives on International Law and International Relations: The State of the Art* (Cambridge University Press, 2012) pp. 119–145; Jutta Brunnée and Stephen Toope, 'International Law and Constructivism: Elements of an International Theory of International Law' (2000) 39 *Columbia Journal of Transnational Law* 19; Nicholas G. Onuf, *World of Our Making: Rules and Rules in Social Theory and International Relations* (University of South Carolina Press, 1989); Nicholas G. Onuf, 'The Constitution of International Society' (1994) 5 *European Journal of International Law* 1 at 6. For compilation of the concepts at work in world-making by international law, see Jean d'Aspremont and Sahib Singh (eds.), *Concepts for International Law: Contributions to Disciplinary Thought* (Edward Elgar, 2019); see also the general observations of Andrea Bianchi, see Andrea Bianchi, *International Law Theories. An Inquiry into Different Ways of Thinking* (Oxford University Press, 2016) pp. 16–19.

of revealing any hidden, unknown, invisible content.[142] These are modes of readings that belong to poetics rather than hermeneutics[143] in that they seek to overinterpret and test the possibilities of signification of international legal texts rather than revealing something that those texts hide to the readers.[144] Because they are not pursuing any disclosure of some content hidden by international legal texts but explore the semantic possibilities of texts,[145] such works of legal poetics do not espouse any necessity of hidden, unknown, invisible content as well as any necessity of revelation characteristic of the epistemology of the secret of international law. They thus stand out as works of scholars who do not construe their role as that of scribes of the invisible. And yet, these works still ought to be mentioned here, for they are not devoid of revelatory ambitions. In fact, although not in a quest for a hidden, unknown, invisible content that ought to be revealed, such works of legal poetics

[142] Orford, *Reading Humanitarian Intervention* pp. 38–81; d'Aspremont, *After Meaning*; Jean d'Aspremont, 'Two Attitudes towards Textuality in International Law: The Battle for Dualism' (2022) 42 *Oxford Journal of Legal Studies* 963.

[143] On the distinction between a tradition based on hermeneutics and one based on poetics, see Jonathan Culler, *Structuralist Poetics: Structuralism, Linguistics, and the Study of Literature* (Routledge, 2002) pp. vii–viii. It is interesting to note that Edward Morgan (who similarly questions the very notions of meaning) speaks of aesthetics rather than poetics, see Edward Morgan, *The Aesthetics of International Law* (University of Toronto Press, 2007). See also d'Aspremont, 'Two Attitudes towards Textuality in International Law'.

[144] Comp. with Roland Barthes who speaks of 'manhandling' (malmener) the text, see Roland Barthes, *S/Z* (Editions du Seuil, 1970) p. 15. See also Edward Said, *The World, the Text, and the Critic* (Harvard Universiy Press, 1983) p. 39. On misreading in relation to international legal studies, see also Orford, *Reading Humanitarian Intervention* pp. 38–40.

[145] Such works are fundamentally distinct from those works that promote oppositional reading. This observation is important because oppositional reading is a move that is sometimes observed in the international legal literature and that remains entirely committed toward the necessity of secret content and the necessity of revelation. For a promotion of oppositional reading in international legal studies, see Tzouvala, *Capitalism as Civilisation* pp. 9–10 (drawing on I. Bennett Capers, 'Reading Back, Reading Black' (2006) 35 *Hofstra Law Review* 9; see also Juan M. Amaya-Castro and Hassan El Menyawi, 'Moving Away From Moving Away: A Conversation About Jacques Derrida and Legal Scholarship' (2005) 6 *German Law Journal* 101 at 109–110. In fact, if reading seeks to generate the opposite, this presupposes the necessary presence of an original content that it will seeks to reveal and reverse. For some similar reservations towards the methodological unpicking of binary oppositions in texts, see Simon Critchley, 'Derrida's Influence on Philosophy . . . and on My Work' (2005) 6 *German Law Journal* 25 at 26.

are still animated by a revelatory spirit, that of revealing the semantic possibilities of international legal texts.

4.3 Ordering through Mass Production and Suppression

The two samples of international legal discourse examined in the previous sections, namely judicial decisions by the International Court of Justice and international legal scholarship, suffice to expose the extent to which international lawyers, in their various capacities, are caught by the necessity of secret content and the necessity of revelation composing the epistemology of the secret of international law. Simultaneously, the previous sections illustrate the everlasting outpouring of judicial decisions and scholarly works in international legal thought and practice spawned by the epistemology of the secret of international law. This outpouring is constitutive of the *discursive stuffing*, which was mentioned earlier and which is characteristic of what the epistemology of the secret of international law does.[146] It must be acknowledged that this phenomenon is surely not new and that the epistemology of the secret of international law has not been working alone in that respect. Such mass production of speech materials has been exacerbated by the dramatic upsurge of university degrees and positions in international legal studies since the end of the nineteenth century[147] as well as the proliferation of international courts and tribunals[148] in the twentieth century, bringing

[146] See supra Section 1.2.2.

[147] On the consolidation of international law as an academic discipline, see d'Aspremont, 'The Professionalization of International Law' pp. 19–37; Orford, 'Scientific Reason and the Discipline of International Law' p. 373; Coates, *Legalist Empire* pp. 18–21 and 61–68. I have examined elsewhere some of the consequences of the mass production of scholarly materials, see, e.g., d'Aspremont, 'Wording in International Law'; see also d'Aspremont, 'Softness in International Law'.

[148] Thomas Buergenthal, 'Proliferation of International Courts and Tribunals: Is It Good or Bad?' (2001) 14 *Leiden Journal of International Law* 267; Roger P. Alford, 'The Proliferation of International Courts and Tribunals: International Adjudication in Ascendance' (2000) 94 *ASIL Proceedings* 160; Lucy Reed and Andrew Jacovides, 'Great Expectations: Where Does the Proliferation of International Dispute Resolution Leave International Law' (2002) 96 *ASIL Proceedings* 219; Benedict Kingsbury, 'Is the Proliferation of International Courts and Tribunals a Systemic Problem?' (1999) 31 *New York University Journal of International Law and Politics* 679; Hugh Thirlway, 'The Proliferation of International Judicial Organs and the Formation of International Law', in Wybo P. Heere (ed.), *International Law and The Hague's 750th Anniversary* (T.M.C Asser, 1999) pp. 251–278; Mohamed Bennouna, 'How to Cope with the Proliferation of International Courts and Coordinate Their Action', in Antonio Cassese (ed.), *Realizing*

the production of judicial and scholarly speech materials to an 'industrial' level.[149]

It is submitted here that the mass production of speech materials by international judges and international legal scholar to which the two necessities composing the epistemology of the secret of international law have been conducive does warrant further evidencing. It will most likely be very manifest to any possible reader of the present book whilst having been extensively discussed[150] – and bemoaned[151] – elsewhere. Not to mention that such massive production of speech materials has already been extensively referenced in the preceding sections. This is why the rest of this section concentrates on the consequences of the outpouring of speech materials induced by the epistemology of the secret of international law. It is specifically argued in this section that the mass production of speech materials by international judges and international legal scholars, like in any epistemology of the secret,[152] is instrumental in the ordering of what can possibly be said, thought, perceived, and actioned through international law. It is through the mass production of speech materials about international law through judicial decisions and legal literature – as a result of the necessity of secret content and the necessity of revelation, that the epistemology of the secret of international law proves to be an ordering epistemology,[153] one that determines what can be, and cannot be, said, thought, perceived, and actioned through international law

Utopia: The Future of International Law (Oxford University Press, 2012) pp. 287–294; Chester Brown, 'The Proliferation of International Courts and Tribunals: Finding Your Way Through the Maze' (2002) 21 *Melbourne Journal of International Law* 453.

149 On the idea of academic industry, see Jan Klabbers, 'The Ethics of Inter-disciplinarity and the Academic Industry' (on file with the author).

150 See gen. Sandra Acker and Carmen Armenti, 'Sleepless in Academia' (2004) 16 *Gender and Education* 3; Browyn Davies and Peter Bansel, 'The Time of Their Lives? Academic Workers in Neoliberal Time(s)' (2005) 14 *Health Sociology Review* 47; Eugenie Samier, 'The Evolution of the Modern University: From Scholarship to Disenchanted Economic Handmaiden' (2010) 8 *Policy Futures in Education* 238.

151 On the push for slow scholarship, see gen. Yvonne Hartman and Sandy Darab, 'A Call for Slow Scholarship: A Case Study on the Intensification of Academic Life and Its Implications for Pedagogy' (2021) 34 *Review of Education, Pedagogy, and Cultural Studies* 49; Alison Mountz, Anne Bonds, Becky Mansfield, Jenna Loyd, and others, 'For Slow Scholarship: A Feminist Politics of Resistance through Collective Action in the Neoliberal University' (2015) 14 *An International Journal for Critical Geographies* 1235; M. Merje Kuus 'For Slow Research' (2015) 39 *International Journal of Urban and Regional Research* 838.

152 See supra Chapter 2.

153 See supra Section 1.2.

The first consideration that can possibly arises in that respect is whether there is a specific type of order that is sought and instigated by international law through its epistemology of the secret. Indeed, claiming that the epistemology of the secret of international law is conducive to discursive ordering inevitably raises the question of the kind of order, and thus the kind of sayings, thoughts, perceptions, and actions, that are pursued by international law and its epistemology of the secret. Broadly speaking, this is the normative question – rather popular in international legal literature these days[154] – of which agenda, which organization of the world, which geographies, which ideology, which hierarchy, which centre, which geography, which (in)justice, etc. is vindicated and promoted by international law though its epistemology of the secret and the mass production of speech materials enabled by the latter.

The above mentioned question (what type of order?) is undoubtedly pivotal. Yet, it is submitted here that it has no answer. It cannot have one. Indeed, it is impossible to identify the very type of order sought by the epistemology of the secret of international law for at least three reasons. First, whilst it is uncontested that international law is more often than not at the service of a nationalist, Western-centric, racist, phallocentric, virilist, masculinist, capitalist, and bourgeois organization of the world, one cannot identify any single agenda, any single organization of the world, any single centre, any single geography, any single ideology, any single hierarchy, etc. possibly pursued by the epistemology of the secret of international law.[155] The latter is at the service of a multiplicity of normative projects – each of them interpreted, experienced, and actioned differently by anyone mobilizing international law – and cannot be seen as working for any of them in particular.[156] Second, the causal relationship between the various (fluid) projects vested in international law and the ordering pursued by the epistemology of the secret is bound to remain unascertainable.[157] Pretending to draw causal relationships

[154] See supra Section 4.1.2.

[155] Foucault, *Dits et écrits, II* p. 379.

[156] For sure, the epistemology of the secret specific to international law that is discussed here has contributed to the instrumentality of international law in the development of national and world capitalist societies. On how regimes of truth have been instrumental in the construction of the capitalist system, see Foucault, *Dits et écrits, II* p. 160.

[157] On the very slipperiness of questions of causality, see Foucault, *Dits et écrits, I (1954–1975)* p. 879 (arguing that causalities are often magical). See also Foucault, *Dits et écrits, I (1954–1975)* p. 729; Michel Foucault, *L'archéologie du savoir* (Gallimard, 1969) p. 34. On the idea of history as a hotchpotch of superposed discontinuities, see

between any of the many nationalist, Western-centric, racist, phallocentric, virilist, masculinist, capitalist, bourgeois, etc. organizations of the world that are nested in international law condemns one to fall into a caricature.[158] Third, and possibly most importantly, the epistemology of the secret of international law, albeit enabling ordering, has not been consciously built by certain people or group of people at certain times and in certain places to serve certain agendas.[159] The epistemology of the secret, as this book argues, is the very condition of the international legal discourse and of what this discourse does to the world. To put it simply, ordering is what the international legal discourse, as any discourse built on an epistemology of the secret,[160] does, irrespective of what it does it for.

As has just been argued, it is not possible to trace and pinpoint all the types of order(s) for which the epistemology of the secret of international law works, other than providing a few generalities on its complicity with a nationalist, Western-centric, racist, phallocentric, virilist, masculinist, capitalist, and bourgeois organizations of the world. It should be emphasized, however, that the notebook appended to this book will return to how the epistemology of the secret of international law has supported and continue to serve a (neo-)colonial organization of the world.[161]

Irrespective of the specific organizations of the world that benefits from the epistemology of the secret of international, it remains relevant to provide some illustrations of how the mass production of speech materials on international law, as a result of the latter's epistemology of the secret, comes to generate ordering. I must acknowledge that, in a number of other works of mine that will be referenced here, I already had the opportunity to extensively elaborate on the ordering that anyone engaging with international law is subjected to. Although, back then, I did not directly ascribe such ordering to the epistemology of the secret of international law – which I had not theorized yet, I deem it

Foucault, *Dits et écrits, I (1954–1975)* p. 1147. On the precarity of any historical causality, see Paul Ricoeur, *Histoire et vérité* (Editions du Seuil, 1955) pp. 33–34.

[158] See however the compelling exploration of how the ideology of race operates within legal discourse by Justin Desautels-Stein, see Justin Desautels-Stein, *The Right to Exclude: A Critical Race Approach to Sovereignty, Borders, and International Law* (Oxford University Press, 2023).

[159] On the idea that the technology of governance put in place by the bourgeoisie did not originate in a conscious decision of the bourgeoisie, see supra Section 1.2.1.2.

[160] See supra Chapter 2.

[161] See infra the Notebook appended to this book.

unnecessary to reproduce here the abundant speech materials I myself rolled out on that occasion. Yet, because I claim here that such specific constraints on the sayable, thinkable, perceivable, and actionable I have explored then amount to a manifestation of the epistemology of the secret of international law, I feel it is warranted to summarize below some of those earlier inquiries into the ordering of international legal thought and practice. In the following paragraphs, I will accordingly provide examples of the determination of the (un)sayable, (un)thinkable, (un)perceivable, un(actionable) in relation to the ascertainment of international law and the doctrine of sources (Section 4.3.1), the law of international organizations (Section 4.3.2), the histories of international law (Section 4.3.3), and the exercise of comparison (Section 4.3.4). A few observations are also formulated on the constraints on the sayable, thinkable, perceivable, and actionable explicitly envisioned in the speech materials produced about the modes of interpretation of international law (Section 4.3.5).

4.3.1 Mass Production, Suppression, and the Sources of International Law

The epistemology of the secret of international law brings about a huge amount of scholarly and judicial discussions about the ascertainment of international law. Indeed, the sources of international law are continuously approached as having not revealed all their secrets, which international lawyers, including judges, spend much effort extracting and making known. It is submitted here that such mass production of speech materials related to the sources of international law puts in place very extensive constraints on what can be said, thought, perceived, and actioned in relation to international law. In fact, the luxuriant discussions of the modes of ascertainment of international law, commonly systematized and mobilized under the banner of the sources of international law, generate what is the most elementary but also most constraining mode of thinking about international law, namely a division of the world between the 'legally binding' and 'the rest', the former belonging to the world of what can possibly said, thought, perceived, and actioned and the latter belong to the world of what cannot be said, thought, perceived, and actioned. Said differently, by virtue of the so-called sources of international law, the world of the 'legally binding' is the only world that international lawyers can think of and should pose demand on. It is only once validated (and thus anchored in the world of the 'legally binding') by virtue of the sources of international law that a text, a standard, a rule, a concept, an idea, and all the hidden, unknown, invisible content extracted from it come to constitute material eligible for international lawyers' sayings, thoughts, perceptions, and actions, conversely leaving all the other texts, standards, rules, concepts, ideas in a state of irrelevance for international lawyers' sayings, thoughts, perceptions, and actions. What is more, the constraints generated and nurtured by the speech materials on the modes of ascertainment of international law also include a prescription to envisage everything in terms of rules. Indeed, it universalizes a 'ruleness' of thought, which also comes to define for international lawyers what can be said, thought, perceived, and actioned through international law in a very narrow way.

Needless to say that the modes of ascertainment of international law have been the object of contestations and reformist interventions. In fact, the constraints on the sayable, thinkable, perceivable, and actionable regularly bring about unease, leading, for instance, for calls for greater embrace of questions of authority and legitimacy. Yet, it is interesting that such attempts to take some liberty with the sources of international law and the modes of thinking they put in place have reproduced similar constraints on the sayable, thinkable, perceivable, and actionable, simply replacing the distinction between the 'legally binding' and the 'legally non-binding' by similar binary and dichotomic structures, that is, the legitimate and the illegitimate, the authoritative and the non-authoritative, the liquid and the solid, etc. In sum, the outpouring of speech materials related to the sources of international law and the modes of law-ascertainment they put in place, which is induced by the epistemology of the secret of international law, determines the very first register of the sayable, thinkable, perceivable, and actionable for international lawyers, their constraining dimension being second to none.[162]

[162] I have examined such ordering in Jean d'Aspremont, 'Bindingness', in Jean d'Aspremont and Sahib Singh (eds.), *Concepts for International Law, Contribution to Disciplinary Thought* (Edward Elgar, 2019) pp. 67–82; see also d'Aspremont, *International Law as a Belief System*; d'Aspremont, 'The Idea of "Rules" in the Sources of International Law' p. 103; d'Aspremont, 'Three International Lawyers in a Hall of Mirrors'; Jean d'Aspremont, 'The International Court of Justice as the Master of the Sources', in Carlos Espósito, Kate Parlett (eds.), *The Cambridge Companion to the International Court of Justice* (Cambridge University Press, 2023) pp. 165–186.

4.3.2 Mass Production, Suppression, and the Law of International Organizations

The epistemology of the secret of international law, and the two necessities that compose it, have turned the law of international organizations, also commonly referred to as international institutional law, into a very rich area of judicial and scholarly discussion. In fact, international lawyers continue to assume that international organizations and their alleged common rules governing their the status, rights, duties, responsibility, relations, functioning, normative outputs, failures, and falls have yet to reveal their secrets. It is submitted here that the ensuing mass production of speech materials about international organizations have also restricted the sayable, the thinkable, the perceivable, the actionable to a few key patterns of thoughts. Among such constraining patterns of thought, mention must be made of the affection for international organizations, the need for insulation of international law, the possibility of edification of knowledge about international organization, the need for a restriction of the powers and competences of international organizations, and the quest for a reconciliation of the various theorizations of international organizations. It is argued here that these five patterns of thought inform, which have consolidated in the prolific speech materials about international organizations brought about by the epistemology of the secret of international law, and shape most legal claims about the status, rights, duties, responsibility, relations, functioning, normative outputs, failures, and falls of international organizations. Even the most critical engagements with the law of international organizations are constrained by the ideas of affection, insulation, edification, restriction, and reconciliation.

Given the highly constraining character of these patterns of thought on what can be said, thought, perceived, and actioned in relation to the law of international organizations, each of them is sketched out here. *Affection* is what justifies that international organizations have been elevated into a very central phenomenon in international legal thought and practice and that international law can hardly be thought of short of any reference to international organizations. It refers to the great attachment to international organizations that international lawyers, notwithstanding compelling criticisms of international organizations in recent decades, come to feel in a great variety of ways. The idea of affection is commonly nurtured by specific (mis-)representations of international organizations, namely the latter's taking care of people, their showing where to look for power, their knowing so much, their romanticizing history, their providing a common standard of experience, their textualizing the universe, their providing and organizing space for discontent, their expanding international lawyers' field of study, and their holding many secrets. *Insulation* is a way to construe international organizations as independent actors insulated from other actors as well as from constraints of the community to which they are deemed to belong. It entails that international lawyers approach international organizations as self-contained units in terms of agency and self-sufficiency. Insulation is what permits that international organizations be approached, discussed, and thought of as a cognizable and self-contained units. It leads international lawyers to think of international organizations as self-sufficient agents with a distinct will, distinct modes and means of action, distinct features, distinct rules, distinct relations with other actors, distinct constraints, etc. *Edification* refers to international lawyers' confidence that they accumulate knowledge about international organizations thanks to their continuous study of the latter's falls and failures. It makes international lawyers feel they can learn from mistakes, collapses, foundering, debacles of – once promising – international organizations. A very common example of where this pattern of thought is seen thriving is provided by the luxuriant and abundant international legal literature on the League of Nations. *Restriction* enables the thought that international organizations, although in need of insulation from communitarian constraints and other actors, notwithstanding their common presupposition that international organizations take care of people, must be subjected to a series of constraints. By virtue of this pattern of thought, international lawyers come to feel a need for carefully restricting some of the exercises of power by international organizations, such thoughts being inflated by contemporary contestations of some of the activities of international organizations. Finally, *reconciliation* is the systematic inclination of international lawyers to reconcile all the contradictions and tensions that they perceive in their own engagements with international organizations. By virtue of reconciliation, international lawyers engaging with international organizations come to perceive a score of contradictions and tensions between the concepts they mobilize whilst simultaneously feeling the need to quell or lessen them through reconciliatory mechanisms or constructions. Surely there are other patterns of thoughts that determine the sayable, thinkable, perceivable, and actionable in terms of the law of international organizations. Yet, the foregoing should already suffice to show how the perpetuation of these five key patterns of thought through the mass production of speech materials on the law of international organizations engendered by the epistemology of the secret of international law heavily bears upon what can be said, thought, perceived, and actioned in relation to international organizations.[163]

4.3.3 *Mass Production, Suppression, and the Histories of International Law*

Over the last three decades, and especially after what has been called the 'turn to history', critical engagements with the history of international law have proliferated and flooded the international legal literature. Indeed, as a result of the postulation of the necessary presence of hidden, unknown, invisible histories that have yet to be revealed, mass speech materials have been produced with the ambition to repudiate, among others, the Enlightenment narratives of progress informing common disciplinary histories, the narrative of universality that has accompanied mainstream linear disciplinary histories, and some of the fundamental markers of the discipline – for instance, the fatherhood of Grotius, the canonical status of his work, and the cosmopolitan project associated therewith. Interestingly, this abundant literature suspicious of mainstream histories of international law has remained articulated around the very same markers, periodization, and causal sequencing of the narratives they seek to disrupt, thereby showing the weight of the dominant patterns of thought related to the history of international law on the determination of the sayable, thinkable, perceivable, and actionable. Indeed, by confining themselves to the very same terms, categories, and vocabularies of the linear disciplinary histories at which they take aim, these new critical histories still uphold more than they disrupt or displace. Even if they provide some significant nuances, the critical histories that have flourished after the 'historical turn' in international legal scholarship have fallen short of renewing the markers, periodization, and causal sequencing around which they have been built.[164] Such historical critique has merely been a matter of 'applying' differently the

[163] These five patterns of thoughts have been examined in further details in d'Aspremont, *The Experiences of International Organizations*; see also d'Aspremont, 'The Love for International Organizations'.

[164] As a result, historiographical imagination of international lawyers continues to revolve around the same genealogical inquiries, namely whether Gentili, Vitoria, Grotius, Vattel, Lauterpacht etc. are the spearheads, the heroes, the founding 'fathers', the (re-)inventers, or the heirs of the Western Enlightenment and (pre- or post-)modern international law.

very categories around which mainstream historical narratives are articulated, critical histories often being reduced to a variant of the linear disciplinary histories with which they are engaged. In that sense, the disruptive ambitions of such critical historical works have been turned on their head and have perpetuated the constraints on the sayable, the thinkable, the perceivable, and the actionable provided by the mainstream histories that had populated international legal thought and practice since the end of the nineteenth century.[165] The prolific scholarly engagements with the history of international law in the last three decades, and their quest for a rewriting of the histories of international law by virtue of the discovery of new (dirty) secrets, have, notwithstanding very welcome disruptive ambitions and compelling post-colonial counter-narratives, remained a site where the traditional markers, periodization, and causal sequencing of the dominant histories of international law continue to discipline historical story-telling and determining the sayable, thinkable, perceivable, and actionable in terms of history of international law.

4.3.4 *Mass Production, Suppression, and Comparison in International Law*

Another illustration of the ordering enabled by the mass production of speech materials spurred by the epistemology of the secret of

It could even be argued that the critical discussions of these 'founding fathers' may well have contributed to their further canonisation. In the same vein, it is conspicuous that historiographical debates in international legal scholarship are restricted to the same periodical controversies articulated around the scholastic, the pre-modern, Westphalia, the Enlightenment, the modern, colonisation, the nineteenth century, the interwar period, the post–League of Nations, the post–second-world war period, decolonisation, the Cold War, the post–Cold War period etc. It could be contended that even the agendas debated in such historiographical literature are identical: humanism, cosmopolitanism, modernism, state-centrism, voluntarism, colonialism, hegemony, capitalism etc., those works that seek to emphasise non-European perspectives, for they too re-centre non-Western locations and perspectives within a very Eurocentric history and through European markers, periods, and causal sequencing. In such works, non-Western contexts and practices remain 'peripheral', accounted for as a response to (or an encounter with) European or Western international law.

165 I have examined the constraints of critical histories of international law on disciplinary imagination in d'Aspremont, 'Critical Histories of International Law and the Repression of Disciplinary Imagination'; see also Jean d'Aspremont, *The Critical Attitude and the History of International Law* (Brill, 2019) and Jean d'Aspremont, 'Turntablism in the History of International Law' (2020) 22 *Journal of the History of International Law* 472.

international law is found in the vast amount of thought and practice centred on the exercise of comparison. Given the strong affinity of international legal reasoning with comparison – which in itself is the result of some ordering of the legal discourse – comparison seems to be one of those intellectual operations that international lawyers must be capable of undertaking when they seek to make international law less obscure and to reveal its secrets. Comparison is a very common tool for international lawyers, one they commonly use to reveal the hidden, the unknown, the invisible and thus to enact the necessities composing the epistemology of the secret of international law. Calls have even been made to generalize the use of comparison in international law and make it one of the main – and allegedly pluralist – modes of engagement with international law, and thus one of the main tools to reveal international law's secrets. Whilst a common mode of reasoning, comparison has been exercised by international lawyers, be they judges or scholars, with a total disregard for all the pitfalls that critical comparative lawyers had warned against. Indeed, in the comparative law literature, there has been a lot of insistence on the extent to which claims of difference and resemblance are always 'self-confirming' in that they confirm the very terms with which the comparison is premised on and conducted through. Comparative lawyers have always insisted that nothing is fully or purely autochthonous or foreign and that the 'foreign' is always construed as 'like or unlike home'. It has similarly been shown in international comparative law studies that claims of difference and resemblance are always made within an already-understood world marked in advance by representations and historically constituted categories. Some of these critical comparative lawyers have even gone so far as to emphasize the resilience of neo-colonial definitions of difference and the perpetuation of a Western-centric and imperialist conception of the world through the exercise of comparison. Having turned a blind eye to the warnings of critical comparative lawyers, international lawyers, be they judges or scholars, have done just that, that is, entering the exercise of comparison from their home – often located in imperial locations – and constructing 'the compared other' according to thought categories of their own. In other words, international lawyers' disregard critical comparative lawyers' caution for ethnocentrism and self-confirming thinking have made the omnipresent exercise of comparison, a forceful reproducer of all the constraints on the sayable, thinkable, perceivable, and actionable that already inhabit the imperial home of comparativist international lawyers. Comparativist international lawyers thus always end up producing the very differences and similarities they anticipate, thereby perpetuating the already-in-place sayable, thinkable, perceivable, and actionable. At the same time, by deploying an already-made 'prediscursive' to apprehend alterity, the mass speech materials that are sites of the exercise of comparison come to prohibit alternative discourses on difference and resemblance. In that sense, comparison, because it is so carelessly wielded by international lawyers, amplifies all the ordering already at work in international legal thought and practice.[166] Comparison, when used to reveal the hidden, the unknown, the invisible, and thus to enact the necessities composing the epistemology of the secret of international law, proves a formidable ordering device.

4.3.5 *Mass Production, Suppression, and the Interpretation of International Law*

Finally, a few observations on the numerous speech materials produced on the practice of interpretation of international law that international lawyers continue to approach as being replete with hidden, unknown, and invisible dimensions. Actually, there is hardly a more secret-hunting debate than that pertaining to the modes of interpretation of international law, be it in judicial and scholarly circles. The mass production of speech materials on how to interpret international law, being nurtured by the necessity of secret content and the necessity of revelation, is second to none. Like for other areas where the epistemology of the secret of international law has been instrumental in the mass production of speech materials, one could expect that, supported by the necessity of secret content and the necessity of revelation, the abundant speech materials on interpretation would carry the same ordering effects as those briefly examined in the previous paragraphs.

Debates on the interpretation of international law also warrant attention because they point to a huge paradox. Albeit possibly constituting the most massive production of speech materials witnessed in relation to international law, the very modes of interpretation traditionally discussed and practiced by international lawyers barely constrain the sayable, thinkable, perceivable, and actionable. Contrary to the rest of the practice and literature, that devoted to interpretation is not a site where the

[166] Jean d'Aspremont, 'Comparativism and Colonizing Thinking in International Law' (2020) 57 *Canadian Yearbook of International Law* 89; d'Aspremont, *After Meaning* pp. 105–111.

epistemology of the secret of international law, notwithstanding generating a lot of discursive stuffing like on other questions of international law, deploys its ordering with full thrust. This paradox can be explained as follows. Questions of interpretation of international law, commonly construed as questions of restrictions on what can possibly be said about international legal texts are better construed as enablers of an infinity of deferral of meanings between texts and thus enablers of a huge intertextual universe of signification. Once conceived to constrain the hidden, unknown, invisible content that can possibly be extracted from international legal texts, the doctrine of interpretation, itself the object of infinite interpretations, always multiplies semantic possibilities rather than restricts them. From such perspective, the prolific debates on the modes of interpretation of international law can be read as continuously stretching the sayable, the thinkable, the perceivable, and the actionable available to international lawyers.[167] Surely, the prolific debates on questions of interpretation constitute speech materials where other types of constraints on the sayable, thinkable, perceivable, and actionable will surface, for interpretation is always discussed in relation to other legal questions. Yet, the debates on the very modes of determination of the content of international law are themselves very open textual spaces where little ordering is possible given the emptiness of such content-determination modes. Hence the paradox according to which the practice and literature related to the interpretation of international law may prove to be that part of the discourse where the ordering of the epistemology of the secret of international law is least potent. This however is a rare exception to an otherwise gigantic amount of speech materials bred by the epistemology of the secret of international law where the latter deploys its fierce ordering on what can be said, thought, perceived, and actioned through international law.

[167] I have looked at the enabling dimension of the doctrine of interpretation and its lack of constraining character in d'Aspremont, *After Meaning*, section 4.1; d'Aspremont, 'Two Attitudes towards Textuality in International Law'; Jean d'Aspremont, 'The Multidimensional Process of Interpretation: Content-Determination and Law-Ascertainment Distinguished', in Andrea Bianchi, Daniel Peat, and Matthew Windsor (eds.), *Interpretation in International Law* (Oxford University Press, 2015) pp. 111–129.

5

Resistance to the Epistemology of the Secret of International Law

This chapter explores the question of whether the epistemology of the secret of international law and the necessities it puts in place can be resisted. No definite answer to that question is sought here and only tentative reflections on the possibility of resisting the epistemology of the secret are provided in the following paragraphs. This chapter proceeds as follows. Although the consequences of the ordering enabled by the epistemology of the secret of international law have already been broached earlier in this book,[1] this chapter starts by elaborating on why it matters to spare no effort to resist the epistemology of the secret and rein in its consequences (Section 5.1). The chapter then recalls that a mere termination or discontinuation of the epistemology of the secret, of its necessities, and of all the literary, hermeneutical, critical, economic, and ideological attitudes it entails is an impossibility (Section 5.2). Resistance, it is subsequently argued, can only take the form of an act of *obnubilation* (Section 5.3), a notion whose concrete implications for international legal thought and practice are subsequently spelled out (Section 5.4).

5.1 Why Resisting?

The previous chapters have shown the extent to which the epistemology of the secret of international law, like other epistemologies of the secret in other places and other times, performs an ordering function. Articulated around the fundamental distinction between the hidden, the unknown, the invisible, on the one hand, and the revealed, the known, and the visible on the other, the epistemology of the secret of international law organizes the enabling and disabling of certain sayings, thoughts, perceptions, and actions by virtue of a mass

[1] See supra Section 1.2 and Section 4.3.

production of speech materials as well as the suppression of all that has not been made an invisible-instantly-made-visible.[2] Indeed, the mass production of speech materials about the invisible-instantly-made-visible and the simultaneous suppression of all that has not been made an invisible-instantly-made-visible, the epistemology of the secret determines, on the one hand, the sayable, the thinkable, the perceivable, and the actionable through international law – which is all that has been made an invisible-instantly-made-visible – and, on the other hand, defines the unsayable, the unthinkable, the unperceivable, and the unactionable through international law – which is all that has not been made an invisible-instantly-made-visible. Examples have been provided to illustrate how such epistemology enables and disables sayings, thoughts, perceptions, and actions and, in doing so, enables and disables what international law can do to the world.[3]

Establishing both the sayable, the thinkable, the perceivable, and the actionable, on the one hand, and the unsayable, the unthinkable, the unperceivable, and the unactionable, on the other, does not suffice to justify that one resists the epistemology of the secret of international law. After all, the epistemology of the secret of international law is not alone in ordering what can be said, thought, perceived, and actioned through international law. Any discourse, system of thought, language, profession, ideology, etc. has a disciplinary dimension and contributes to enable and disable sayings, thoughts, perceptions, and actions.[4] One could even argue that dismantling discourses, systems of thoughts, languages, professions, and ideologies would annihilate the very possibility of thinking, saying, percepting, and doing.

It is argued here that, although ordering constitutes a property of any discourse, system of thought, language, profession. or ideology, there are important reasons to resist the epistemology of the secret of international

[2] See supra Section 1.2.

[3] See supra Section 4.3.

[4] On the idea that critique does not simply cut off, estrange, or isolate but also collects, composes, gathers together, creates imagined or real communities around a sensibility, ethos, and practice of reading, see Rita Felski, *The Limits of Critique* (University of Chicago Press, 2015) p. 49. On the idea that any society orders and is articulated on relations of power, see Michel Foucault, *Dits et écrits, II* (Gallimard, 2001) pp. 158, 483, and 1058; see gen. Cornelius Castoriadis, *L'Imaginaire comme tel* (Hermann Editeurs, 2007) p. 52. On the idea that any discipline is built on restrictions on thoughts, see Hayden White, *Tropics of Discourses: Essays in Cultural Criticism* (Johns Hopkins University Press, 1978) p. 126.

law, its two necessities, and all the literary, hermeneutical, critical, economic, and ideological practices such epistemology brings about. First, it can be said that, even if they saturate human thoughts, ordering devices ought to be permanently scrutinized and resisted. The epistemology of the secret of international law should be no exception to such permanent quest for scrutiny and resistance. Second, the epistemology of the secret of international law hampers a reinvention of the latter and the possibility to fix all that is wrong with it. In fact, international law's epistemology of the secret restricts the questions that can be asked to the former and limits the problems that can be solved by it. Only those questions and those problems that arise within the realm of the sayable, the thinkable, the perceivable, and the actionable as determined by the epistemology of the secret of international law can come into the purview of international lawyers.[5] Third, by creating an invisible-instantly-made-visible,[6] and thus by claiming to be revealing something that was held to be hidden, rather than making it clear that the invisible does not precede the visible and that the invisible and the visible are always simultaneously produced, the epistemology of the secret of international law always cheats.[7] I can see no reason for international lawyers to leave unchallenged an epistemology that lies to them. Fourth, the epistemology of the secret of international law, even if it was not designed consciously and purportedly by a dominant class to consolidate the centre position of the latter in the world,[8] is at the service of ideologies that deserve the greatest wariness. Indeed, the sayings, thoughts, perceptions, and actions that the epistemology of the secret of international law enables and disables are infused with capitalism, colonialism, racism, bourgeois ideology, phallocentrism, virilism, and masculinism, which all operate through (and thanks to) the epistemology of the secret of international law in which they find extremely efficacious modes of ordering.[9] Actually, this argument could

5 On the idea that modernity does not raise and consider the issues it cannot resolve, see the remarks of Régis Debray, *Le Scribe* (Editions Grasset et Fasquelle, 1980) p. 177.

6 See supra Section 1.1.3.2.

7 Comp. with the idea that critique always stacks the card and win, see Felski, *The Limits of Critique* p. 150. On the modes of representation that makes modernity is invincible, see Bruno Latour, *Nous n'avons jamais été modernes. Essai d'anthropologie symétrique* (La Découverte, 1997) pp. 56–59.

8 See Section 1.2.1.2.

9 On the idea that the colonial discourse employs a system of representation that is structurally similar to realism and produces a colonized as a social reality that is at once an 'other and yet entirely knowable and visible', see Homi K. Bhabba, *The Location of Culture* (Routledge, 1994) p. 101. On the colonial dimension of knowledge and the idea

even be pushed further. Not only does the epistemology of the secret of international law allow capitalism, colonialism, racism, bourgeois ideology, phallocentrism, virilism and masculinism to inform international legal thought and practice, it also serves as a distraction that allows such ideologies to thrive unnoticed and unchallenged. Indeed, it is whilst international lawyers work hard and relentlessly at searching for hidden, unknown, invisible content for the sake of revealing it, thereby spending their days and nights producing massive textual materials about international law, that people die, starve, are exploited, are discriminated, are thrown at sea, are colonized, are bombarded, are exterminated, are forcefully transferred, see their environment contaminated, etc.[10] In that sense, the price of the epistemology of the secret of international law in terms of dehumanization and inequality is exorbitant and can accordingly not be left unquestioned. Finally, it is submitted that the hermeneutics of suspicion and the paranoid reading with which the epistemology of the secret bears resemblance[11] are no commendable attitudes and certainly not a way of life that international lawyers should resign themselves to.[12]

As the foregoing indicates, there are many reasons to loathe the epistemology of the secret of international law and not to endorse the roles of secret-hunter, archaeologist, speleologist, or porn-producer – to use some of the metaphors that have been mobilized in the previous chapters – which such epistemology condemns international lawyers to.

5.2 There Is No Way Out of the Epistemology of the Secret

To appreciate the scope of what resisting the epistemology of the secret of international law can possibly entail, a few remarks are warranted on the idea of a termination or discontinuation thereof. In that regard, it is better to be forthright: *there is no way out of the epistemology of the secret*

that European human sciences are the depository of knowledge about humanity, indigenous people, and traditional societies whose secret it has pierced, see Mohamed Amer Meziane, *Au bord des mondes: Vers une anthropologie métaphysique* (Vues de l'Esprit, 2023) p. 30.

10 This is a criticism raised against the Renaissance, see Debray, *Le Scribe* p. 242.

11 See supra Section 1.1.1.3.

12 In the same sense, see Felski, *The Limits of Critique* pp. 6 and 45; see also Eve Kosofsky Sedgwick, 'Paranoid Reading and Reparative Reading; or, You're So Paranoid, You Probably Think This Introduction Is about You', in Eve Kosofsky Sedgwick (ed.), *Novel Gazing: Queer Readings in Fiction* (Duke University Press, 1997) pp. 1–38.

of international law. Such epistemology being embedded in an enduring intellectual tradition as was demonstrated above,[13] it is difficult to see how contemporary international lawyers, especially as long as they remain caught in a Western modern episteme,[14] can fully emancipate themselves from the necessity of secret content, the necessity of revelation as well as from the literary, hermeneutical, critical, economic, and ideological practices the epistemology of the secret of international law brings about.

The best example of such parochial inextricability is the present book. Although taking a hard look at the necessity of secret content and the necessity of revelation composing the epistemology of the secret of international law, this very book is itself postulating the presence of a hidden epistemology, that is, the epistemology of the secret of international law, whose revelation it works for through the composition and publication of the present manuscript. In that sense, this book can hardly be external to the epistemology of the secret of international law that it discusses, as it remains confined to such epistemology's two main necessities as well as the literary, hermeneutical, critical, economic, and ideological practices that accompany it.[15]

That there is no way out of the epistemology of the secret of international law, of its main necessities as well as all its accompanying literary, hermeneutical, critical, economic, and ideological practices is

[13] See supra Chapter 2.

[14] See Bhabba, *The Location of Culture* pp. 6, 347, and 354. See also the remarks of Michel Foucault, *Dits et écrits, I (1954–1975)* (Gallimard, 2001) p. 1284. See also Jean d'Aspremont, 'International Law, Universality, and the Dream of Disrupting from the Centre' (2018) 7/7 *ESIL Reflections*.

[15] Such posture is sometimes met with the objection that it rests on a performative contradiction. See, e.g., Jürgen Habermas, *The Philosophical Discourse of Modernity. Twelve Lectures*, trans. Frederik Lawrence (Polity Press, 1987) pp. 185–186 and 279; see also Alasdair MacIntyre, *Three Rival Version of Moral Inquiry: Encyclopaedia, Genealogy, and Tradition* (University of Notre Dame Press, 1990) pp. 55–56. In my view, such objection is futile, if not non-sensical. Indeed, such objection is based on the belief in the possibility of a meta scientific vantage point, and thus the possibility of a critique that is fully external to its object. On the rebuttal of that objection, see White, *Tropics of Discourse* pp. 142–143 and 252–253; Paul Ricoeur, *La mémoire, l'histoire, l'oubli* (Editions du Seuil, 2000) p. 399; Jean-François Lyotard, *La Condition Postmoderne* (Editions de Minuit, 1979) p. 107; Jacques Derrida, *L'écriture et la différence* (Editions du Seuil, 1967) p. 46; Edward Said, *The World, the Text, and the Critic* (Harvard University Press, 1983) p. 26; Michel Foucault, *Les mots et les choses* (Gallimard, 1966) p. 12 ; Michel Foucault, *Naissance de la biopolitique. Cours au Collège de France (1978–1979)* (Gallimard/Seuil, 2004) p. 37.

nothing controversial. The impossibility of a critique that is meta or external as well as the confinement of critique to the values, norms, standards of normality, presuppositions, frameworks of intelligibility, vocabularies, and patterns of thoughts of its object have long been acknowledged in the literature. For instance, the inevitable degree of conservatism of any critical move is what Barthes famously identified as the 'tragedy' of writing.[16] Homi K. Bhabba puts it even stronger when he claims that postmodernism, as long as it is about fragmenting grand post-enlightenment narratives is a profoundly parochial enterprise.[17] In the same vein, Rita Felski has convincingly claimed that critical scholars cannot pride themselves on being very different from the texts that they subject to scrutiny and that critique can never be external and non-complicit.[18] Louis Althusser said even more explicitly that there is no meta or external critique, for a critique is always embedded in its object.[19] It is also because of the impossibility of a natural autonomous own language that Edouard Glissant construed resistance as counter poetics (*contre-poétique ou poétique forcée*), understood as a strategy of both resistance and accommodation that contests the language from within.[20] By the same token, Michel Foucault famously said that the critique of order necessarily belongs to that order and that power and resistance always go hand in hand with one another.[21] Jacques Derrida similarly showed how much subversion is bound to be internal and how deconstruction is condemned to be limited by its own object,[22] also making a similar argument about the inescapability of logocentrism with which he took issue.[23] Edward Said has also argued that any critical

[16] Roland Barthes, *Le degré zéro de l'écriture* (Editions du Seuil, 1972) pp. 6–67.

[17] Bhabba, *The Location of Culture* p. 6.

[18] Felski, *The Limits of Critique* pp. 116 and 146–147.

[19] Louis Althusser, *Être Marxiste en Philosophie* (Presses Universitaires de France, 2015) p. 308.

[20] Édouard Glissant, *Le discours antillais* (Editions du Seuil, 1981) pp. 237 and 402–402. See the remarks as well as the translation of that concept by Celia M. Britton, *Edouard Glissant and Postcolonial Theory: Strategies of Language and Resistance* (University Press of Virginia, 1999) pp. 31–34.

[21] Foucault, *Les mots et les choses* p. 12; Michel Foucault, *Histoire de la Sexualité 1. La volonté de savoir* (Gallimard, 1976) pp. 126–127. On this aspect of Foucault's work, see the remarks of Edward Said, *Reflections on Exile and Other Literary and Cultural Essays* (Granta, 2001) pp. 187–197.

[22] Jacques Derrida, *De la grammatologie* (Editions de Minuit, 1976) p. 38; see also Derrida, *L'écriture et la différence* p. 47.

[23] Jacques Derrida, *Positions* (Editions de Minuit, 1972) pp. 21, 35, and 56; see also Derrida, *L'écriture et la différence* p. 46. On the idea that recuperative powers of logocentrism in

consciousness is bound to be part of its actual social world and of a certain literal body.[24] In the same vein, Judith Butler has convincingly made the point that the performativity of any critical performance in the present is always dependent on the mobilisation of a certain past and of a normative heritage.[25] In another context, Frantz Fanon, discussing the endeavours of African intellectuals in newly independent States to create an African culture, showed the extent to which such cultures were fabricated with the tools, the categories, the historical markers, and the geographies of the former colonizers.[26]

The impossibility for any critical engagement not to be bound by the terms of its object and thus to be external to it is no different in international legal thought and practice. Reversing and abolishing the values, norms, standards of normality, presuppositions, frameworks of intelligibility, vocabularies, and patterns of thoughts that are the object of a critical scrutiny has never been an immediate possibility, certainly not one that is provided by critique itself. Even the type of critical scholarship that was once referred to as a 'new stream' or as part of the 'new approaches'[27] is not spared by such conservatism.[28] Such critical works, like the rest of the international legal scholarship, are bound to remain confined to the values, norms, standards of normality, presuppositions, frameworks of intelligibility, vocabularies, patterns of thoughts, temporalities, etc. of the very object that they scrutinize. Such conservatism of critique has been widely documented in the international legal literature itself, especially in relation to critical historical narratives,[29] to the modern and structuralist temporalities informing critical histories,[30] to

legal studies must not be underestimated, see Pierre Schlag, '"Le Hors de Texte, C'est Moi": The Politics of Form and the Domestication of Deconstruction' (1990) 11 *Cardozo Law Review* 1631 at 1649.

[24] Said, *The World, the Text, and the Critic* p. 16.

[25] Judith Butler, 'Critically Queer' (1993) 1 *GLQ: A Journal of Lesbian and Gay Studies* 17 at 24.

[26] See Frantz Fanon, *The Wretched of the Earth*, trans. Richard Philcox (Grove Press, 2004) chapter 4.

[27] See supra Section 4.4.2.2.

[28] See gen. Schlag '"Le Hors de Texte, C'est Moi"' p. 1631.

[29] Jean d'Aspremont, 'Critical Histories of International Law and the Repression of Disciplinary Imagination' (2019) 7 *London Review of International Law* 89; Martti Koskenniemi, 'Histories of International Law: Significance and Problems for a Critical View' (2013) 27 *Temple International and Comparative Law Journal* 215 at 216.

[30] On the idea that critical histories have remained loyal to a very modern and structuralist understanding of time, see David M. Scott, 'History as Deconstruction, History as

the liberal description of the international legal order,[31] to the meaning-centrism and formalism of critical works about international law,[32] the empiricist and contextualist genre at work in such critical works,[33] to modern and colonial geographies,[34] etc. Such critical strands of international legal scholarship, just like any other scholarly engagement with international law, are always caught in a very traditional and modern idea of critique that perpetuates its own object and is not external to it.[35] In that context, it is even less a surprise that such critical strands of international legal thought, as was already highlighted earlier,[36] have proved to be most loyal to the epistemology of the secret of international law exposed in this book. In fact, postulating the necessary presence of hidden, unknown, invisible content and experiencing the necessity to reveal it has been very central to the genre, practices, hermeneutics, raison d'être, and even the identity of such critical works on international law.[37] It is fair to say that the epistemology of the secret of international law has been, possibly even more than for more traditional international legal scholarship, the linchpin of most critical engagements with international law.[38]

Reconstruction: Time and Structure in Critical International Law' (2022) 35 *Hague Yearbook of International Law* 109.

31 Michelle Staggs Kelsall, 'Disordering International Law' (2022) 33 *European Journal of International Law* 729 at 730–731.

32 Jean d'Aspremont, *After Meaning: The Sovereignty of Forms in International Law* (Edward Elgar, 2021).

33 Jean d'Aspremont, 'International Law and the Rage against Scienticism' (2022) 33 *European Journal of International Law* 679.

34 This is an argument made, at a more general level, by Arjun Appadurai, *Modernity at Large: Cultural Dimensions of Globalization* (University of Minnesota Press, 1996) pp. 158–159.

35 On the modernity of critique in international legal thought, see Jean d'Aspremont, 'International Law and Its Critical Misrepresentations' (2024) 2 *Journal du Droit Transnational.* More generally, see Reinhart Koselleck, *Kritik und Krise* (Verlag Karl Albert, 1959); see also Terry Eagleton, *The Function of Criticism* (Verso, 2005) and Laurent de Sutter, *Superfaible. Penser aux XXIe siècle* (Climats, 2023).

36 See Section 4.4.2.2.

37 Some of them have explicitly claimed to espouse 'the hermeneutics of suspicion', see, e.g., Anne Orford, *International Law and the Politics of History* (Cambridge University Press, 2021) pp. 5–6.

38 It is interesting to note the extent to which what is called here the epistemology of the secret is present in the ten moves of critique identified by Jorge Esquirol, see Jorge Esquirol, 'Making the Critical Moves: A Top Ten in Progressive Legal Scholarship' (2021) 92 *University of Colorado Law Review* 1089.

The foregoing explains why a meta or external critique of the epistemology of the secret, one that would be emancipated from it and that would not be caught in a necessity of secret content and a necessity of revelation is beyond the bounds of possibility. Even the most robust discussion of the epistemology of the secret of international law, as the one this book seeks to offer, is condemned to espouse the necessities composing it as well as many of the literary, hermeneutical, critical, economic, and ideological practices that come with such epistemology. This is why, as is argued in Section 5.3, resistance to the epistemology of the secret must go down a route that is not mere opposition, contradiction, discontinuation, or termination of the epistemology of the secret of international law but that follows what is called here a practice of obnubilation.

5.3 Resistance as a Practice of Obnubilation

Given that abolishing or eliminating the epistemology of the secret is no option, resistance must be envisaged, as is submitted in this section, as an attitude of transgression, of cracking, of displacement.[39] In other words, rather than emancipating oneself from the epistemology of the secret of international law, one should seek, for the sake of resisting it, to outmanoeuvre such epistemology and its necessities.[40] Outmanoeuvring the epistemology of the secret of international law for the sake of resisting it is what is more specifically called here the practice of *obnubilation*.

The choice of the term 'obnubilation' to metaphorically represent[41] the practice of resistance to the epistemology of the secret is directly informed by its common association, in mainstream British English,[42] with the practice of obscuring, darkening, or covering with a cloud. Indeed, obnubilation refers here to a new form of engagement with

[39] Roland Barthes, *Le grain de la voix. Entretiens 1962–1980* (Editions du Seuil, 1981) pp. 34, 53–54, 139, 156, and 175. See more generally Roland Barthes, *Critique et vérité* (Editions du Seuil, 1999). See also Foucault, *Dits et écrits, II* p. 253.

[40] Comp. with the idea of Gilles Deleuze, when referring to Proust, of inventing a foreign language in one's native language, see Gilles Deleuze, *Critique et Clinique* (Editions de Minuit, 1993) p. 9.

[41] On the idea that the language is always metaphoric, see White, *Tropics of Discourse* p. 252; see also Steven L. Winter. *A Clearing in the Forest: Law, Life and Mind* (University of Chicago Press, 2001) p. 65.

[42] It is interesting to note that in other languages, obnubilate enjoys a greater polysemy. For instance, in French, the term refers not only to the practice of obscuring but also to that of being obsessed. In that language, obnubilation thus also evokes an obsession.

international law, one that resists the epistemology of the secret by throwing the texts, practices, actors, effects, representations, past, etc. of international law in obscurity.[43] From the perspective of the practice of obnubilation promoted here, resistance amounts to *refusing the clarity* of international law and of the world to which it is applied that is served by the epistemology of the secret.

Once thrown in obscurity by the practice of obnubilation, everything that is at work in international legal thought and practice comes to be neither visible nor invisible but is simply *nebulous*. As a result, the practice of obnubilation, as it obscures the texts, practices, actors, effects, representations, past, etc. of international law, does away with the distinction between the hidden, the unknown, the invisible, on the one hand, and the revealed, the known, and the visible, on the other. Said differently, obnubilation does not annihilate the epistemology of the secret of international law – because it cannot[44] – but outmanoeuvres it by refusing to uphold the distinction between the hidden, the unknown, the invisible, on the one hand, and the revealed, the known, and the visible, on the other. From the perspective of the practice of obnubilation, the entirety of international legal thought and practice is reduced to a huge semiotic cloud where one cannot distinguish what is covered and uncovered.[45]

The practice of obnubilation advocated here as a practice of resistance foregrounds the idea that the hidden, the unknown, the invisible are always produced through the making of the visible, the known, and the hidden. Obnubilation accordingly contests the very pretence, at the heart of the epistemology of international law,[46] of an invisible-instantly-made-visible and does away with the idea that there is a hidden, an unknown, an invisible that precedes its visible-making revelation. For the sake of the practice of obnubilation, the invisible and the visible being always simultaneously produced, it is not possible to distinguish between the invisible and the visible. It is a practice that seeks to make the

[43] Comp. with Homi Bhabba's attempt to write the Western nation as an obscure and ubiquitous form of living the locality of culture. See Bhabba, *The Location of Culture* p. 200.

[44] See supra Section 5.2.

[45] Comp. with the very interesting notion of disordering sensibility promoted by Michelle Staggs Kelsall whereby she seeks to attempts to break down the binary relationships central to liberal understandings of legal order (self/other, public/private, rights/ obligations, domestic/international, masculine/feminine), see Kelsall, 'Disordering International Law'.

[46] See supra Section 1.1.3.2.

distinction between the hidden, the unknown, the invisible, on the one hand, and the revealed, the known, and the visible, on the other, collapse.

For readers of postcolonial critical literature, the practices of obnubilation, understood here as a practice of obscuring international law, are surely reminiscent of Edouard Glissant's famous concept of opacity (*opacité*). Opacity is construed by Glissant as a right *not to be understood*, that is, a right not to be subjected to the necessarily reductive intelligibility frameworks and paradigms of differences applied by the (Western) discoverers.[47] Opacity is thus, for Glissant, a principle of nonunderstanding according to the dominant categories of the discourse for the sake of protecting oneself against the oppression of that discourse and of those mobilizing such a discourse. So construed, opacity shares with the practice of obnubilation promoted here both as an ambition to obscure its object as well as a commitment to resisting the universal truths imposed by an oppressive discoverer through nonunderstanding. Both similarly seek to escape the invisible-instantly-made-visible produced by the discoverer. Glissant's opacity and the practice of obnubilation envisaged in this section thus have much in common. For that reason, as a mode of resistance to the epistemology of the secret of international law, the practice of obnubilation, even if it is not meant to be a right not to be essentialized or a strategy of protection for those agents caught in the necessity of secret content and the necessity of revelation, must acknowledge its prestigious and very compelling postcolonial pedigree.

In the same vein, it must be acknowledged that the practice of obnubilation put forward here, and its emphasis on the need to obscure the texts, practices, actors, effects, representations, past, etc. of international law, is not without echoing the idea of *post-critique*, which one encounters sometimes in the humanities. The idea of a post-critique is not new. As early as 1958, Michael Polanyi promoted the idea of a move away from the idea of an observed reality external to us, which can be revealed without the mobilization of prior commitments.[48] Although not using the very concept of post-critique, Roland Barthes had, in the 1970s, already played with the idea of an constant attitude of transgression, of

[47] See Glissant, *Le discours antillais* p. 356; Édouard Glissant, *Poétique de la relation* (Gallimard, 1990) pp. 204–205. See the remarks of Celia M. Britton, see Britton, *Edouard Glissant and Postcolonial Theory* pp. 18–25; see also Alain Murdoch, 'Edouard Glissant's Creolized World-Vision: From Resistance and Relation to Opacité' (2013) 26 *Callaloo* 875.

[48] Michael Polanyi, *Personal Knowledge: Towards a Post-Critical Philosophy* (University of Chicago Press, 1958) pp. 295 and 311.

cracking, of outmanoeuvring, of displacement of the modern discourse in place, an attitude that cannot be a mere reversal, opposition, or rejection of that discourse.[49] Likewise, Gilles Deleuze called for a move away from critique by invoking the idea of clinic – which he opposed to that of critique[50] – as well as the necessity to speak one's native language as foreign.[51] Jacques Derrida, in seeking to reinvent the linear and logocentric format of inscriptions provided by books could be read as having toyed with the idea of post-scriptural critique.[52] Bruno Latour, for his part, after lamenting the troubling similar structures between the critique of the modern naturalization and objectification of facts and contemporary populism and conspiracism, invited us to redefine its targets from matters of facts to 'matters of concern'.[53] More recently, in her famous *The Limits of Critique*, Rita Felski defended the embrace of a post-critique whereby interpretation becomes a coproduction between actors that brings new things to light rather than an endless rumination on a text's hidden meaning or representational failures.[54] For her, such post-critique is a way to turn reading into an act of composition, of creative remaking, that binds text and reader in ongoing struggles, translations, and negotiations.[55] In an even more recent book, Laurent de Sutter has similarly advocated a post-critical attitude whereby weakness – rather than strength – is valued and promoted.[56] For him, a post-critique is an anti-foundational and non-originist mode of thinking whereby one does not systematically put the world, oneself, others, the latter's sayings and findings on trial to determine the right and the wrong.[57] Post-critique is a type of engagement that is not premised on values, norms, standards of

[49] Barthes, *Le grain de la voix* pp. 34, 53–54, 139, 156, and 175; see more generally Barthes, *Critique et vérité*.

[50] Gilles Deleuze, *Clinique et Critique* (Editions de Minuit, 1999).

[51] Gilles Deleuze and Felix Guattari, *Qu'est-ce que la philosophie?* (Editions de Minuit, 2019).

[52] For an attempt to escape the logocentrism of the book through disruptive typographies, see Jacques Derrida, *Glas* (Galilée, 1974); Jacques Derrida, *La carte postale. De Socrate à Freud et au-delà* (Flammarion, 1980). Comp. with the attempt to escape the logocentrism of the law article by Juan M. Amaya-Castro and Hassan El Menyawi, 'Moving Away from Moving Away: A Conversation about Jacques Derrida and Legal Scholarship' (2005) 6 *German Law Journal* 101.

[53] Bruno Latour, 'Why Has Critique Run out of Steam? From Matters of Facts to Matters of Concern' (2004) 30 *Critical Inquiry* 225.

[54] Felski, *The Limits of Critique* p. 174.

[55] Felski, *The Limits of Critique* p. 182.

[56] de Sutter, *Superfaible* pp. 22–24.

[57] de Sutter, *Superfaible* pp. 20 and 342.

normality, presuppositions, frameworks of intelligibility, vocabularies, patterns of thoughts, of those narratives and system of thoughts it seeks to reveal, question, or unravel because it seeks to think about the disorder, the impossible, the unknown, and the obscure.[58]

Surely, there are important common denominators between the resistance to the epistemology of the secret of international law in the form of obnubilation, as is promoted here, and some of the abovementioned articulations of the idea of a post-critique. It is submitted here, however, that the practice of obnubilation advocated here, although it is overtly inspired by some of the post-critical ventures mentioned in the previous paragraph, ought not to be construed as a type of post-critique for several reasons. First, just like all critical engagements with international law, the practice of obnubilation called for in this book remains caught in the epistemology of the secret outside which it is incapable of manifesting itself. In that sense, there cannot be a post-epistemology of the secret.[59] Second, obnubilation, as is construed here, ought not to be approached, let alone described, as a type of critique. Critique, as I have argued elsewhere,[60] also building on some of the abovementioned authors, is no distinct attitude in international legal thought and practice. The very idea of critique was born with modern thought,[61] which has always defined itself by its critical questioning of the necessities that govern action, perception, experience, and discourses[62] and a contestation of those necessities that are unacknowledged and unconsented to.[63] The same goes with the international legal scholars who constantly portray their own works and themselves as being critical. Anything that has to do with the study of international law affirms and claims critical credentials. In international legal thought, saying one is critical does not say much, such descriptive category having lost much of its relevance in my view. This is why it would be futile to qualify the resistance to the epistemology of the secret of international law in the form of a practice of obnubilation

[58] de Sutter, *Superfaible* pp. 144, 209, and 320.

[59] See however the claim of Homi Bhabha that the 'post' is neither a new horizon, nor a leaving behind of the past, see Bhabba, *The Location of Culture* pp. 1–2.

[60] d'Aspremont, 'The Idea of Critique in International Law'.

[61] This is one of the main theses defended by Reinhart Koselleck in Koselleck, *Kritik und Krise*; see also Eagleton, *The Function of Criticism*; de Sutter, *Superfaible*.

[62] Eagleton, *The Function of Criticism*; White, *Tropics of Discourse* p. 1.

[63] See the famous essay of Immanuel Kant, see Immanuel Kant, 'What Is Enlightenment?', in Friedrich Gedike and Johann Erich Biester (eds.), *Berlinische Monatsschrift* (December 1784).

as being post-critical. It is not less or more critical than a practice that is loyal to the epistemology of the secret of international law. For all these reasons, it is preferred not to describe the practice of obnubilation promoted here as a post-critical one.

Two final observations are in order before this chapter moves on to unpacking the concrete implications of the mode of resistance to the epistemology of the secret advocated here. First, it must be emphasized that the practice of obnubilation promoted here should certainly not be conflated with a practice of obscurantism.[64] Indeed, obnubilation, contrary to obscurantism, is not about preventing some existing knowable content from becoming known but about navigating the texts, practices, actors, effects, representations, past, etc. of international law without ascertaining what is hidden and revealed, what is known and unknown, or what is visible and invisible. In contrast to obnubilation, obscurantism is an attitude that continues to distinguish between the hidden, the unknown, the invisible, on the one hand, and the revealed, the known, and the visible, on the other. Obscurantism is also an attitude that continues to abide by the first necessity of the epistemology of the secret, namely the necessity of hidden, unknown, invisible content but whilst dispensing with the second necessity of the epistemology of the secret, namely the necessity of revelation. In that sense, obscurantism postulates and identifies hidden, unknown, invisible content but strives to keep it hidden, unknown, invisible. The practice of obnubilation pushed forward here thus departs from obscurantism in that it does away, not only with the distinction between the hidden, the unknown, the invisible, on the one hand, and the revealed, the known, and the visible, on the other, but also with the necessity of secret content all together. For the sake of the practice of obnubilation promoted here, there simply is no content that is hidden, unknown, invisible. There only is the obscurity of the texts, practices, actors, effects, representations, past, etc. of international law that one ought to navigate and embrace.

Second, the practice of obnubilation and the way it is construed here as a way to outmanoeuvre the epistemology of the secret of international law may remind some readers of the idea of a culture of formalism that had famously been coined and promoted by Martti Koskenniemi two

[64] See contra de Sutter, *Superfaible* pp. 344–345. On obscurantism as a common charge raised against poststructuralist thinkers, see the remarks of Johann Chapoutot, *Le Grand Récit. Introduction à l'histoire de notre temps* (Presses Universitaires de France, 2021) pp. 265–270.

decades ago.[65] This chapter on the resistance to the epistemology of the secret of international law is not the place to attempt an – always dubious –[66] comparative exercise between these two modes of resistance.[67] They are undoubtedly points of convergence between the abovementioned culture of formalism and the practice of obnubilation advocated here, if only because they share the unattainable ambition to resist the universality and the hegemony of the revealed, the known, and the visible.[68] Yet, the ways in which these two practices of resistance are theorized,[69] including their respective approaches to textuality and

[65] See, e.g., Martti Koskenniemi, *The Gentle Civilizer of Nations: The Rise and Fall of International Law 1870–1960* (Cambridge University Press, 2002) pp. 502–509; Martti Koskenniemi, 'What Is International Law For?', in Malcolm Evans (ed.), *International Law*, 2nd edn (Oxford University Press, 2006) pp. 69–70; see also Martti Koskenniemi and Carl Schmitt, 'Hans Morgenthau and the Image of Law in International Relations', in Michael Byers (ed.) *The Role of Law in International Politics: Essays in International Relations and International Law* (Oxford University Press, 2000) pp. 32–33.

[66] Gunter Frankenberg, 'Critical Comparisons: Re-thinking Comparative Law' (1985) 26 *Harvard International Law Journal* 411 at 412 and 422–423; Pierre Legrand, 'Comparative Legal Studies and the Matter of Authenticity' (2006) 1 *Journal of Comparative Law* 365 at 422; Pierre Legrand, 'The Same and the Different', in Pierre Legrand and Roderick Munday (eds.), *Comparative Legal Studies: Traditions and Transitions* (Cambridge University Press, 2003) pp. 255, 261, 287, 300, and 307–308; Michael Werner and Bénédicte Zimmermann, 'Beyond Comparison: Histoire Croisée and the Challenge of Reflexivity' (2006) 45 *History and Theory* 30 at 34; Horatia Muir Watt, 'Globalization and Comparative Law', in Mathias Reimann and Reinhard Zimmermann (eds.), *The Oxford Handbook of Comparative Law* (Oxford University Press, 2007) pp. 596 and 603; Upendra Baxi, 'The Colonialist Heritage', in Pierre Legrand and Roderick Munday (eds.), *Comparative Legal Studies: Traditions and Transitions* (Cambridge University Press, 2003) pp. 46–51; William Twining, 'Social Science and Diffusion of Law' (2005) 32 *Journal of Law and Society* 203 at 207 and 239; Pier G. Monateri, 'Black Gaius: A Quest for Multicultural Origins of the "Western Legal Tradition"' (2000) 51 *Hastings Law Journal* 479.

[67] For an earlier engagement with the culture of formalism, see Jean d'Aspremont, *Formalism and the Sources of International Law: A Theory of the Ascertainment of Legal Rules* (Oxford University Press, 2011) pp. 27–29.

[68] Martti Koskenniemi claims that the culture of formalism amounts to a 'culture of resistance to power, a social practice of accountability, openness and equality whose status cannot be reduced to the political positions of any one of the parties whose claims are treated within it', see Koskenniemi, *The Gentle Civilizer of Nations* p. 500.

[69] It should be noted that Martti Koskenniemi has always remained rather terse and concise when it comes to the specifics of the idea of the culture of formalism, unsurprisingly and possibly conveniently provoking an enormous amount of scholarly glossing on that notion. Among others, see Emmanuelle Jouannet, 'Présentation critique', in Martti Koskenniemi, *La Politique du Droit International* (Pedone, 2007) pp. 32–33; see also Ignacio de la Rasilla del Moral, 'Martti Koskenniemi and The Spirit of the Beehive in International Law' (2010) 10 *Global Jurist* 1; Jochen von Bernstorff, 'Sisyphus Was an

structures,[70] denote too much incommensurability for any serious insights to be drawn from any possible convergence or divergence between these two modes of resistance.

5.4 Concrete Implications of the Practice of Obnubilation

This section sketches out some of the most salient consequences of a practice of obnubilation understood here as an engagement with international law that resists the epistemology of the secret of international law by putting an end to the distinction between the hidden, the unknown, the invisible, on the one hand, and the revealed, the known, and the visible, on the other, and obscuring the texts, practices, actors, effects, representations, past, etc. of international law. In other words, this section examines what it entails for international legal thought and practice to be serious about the claim that the hidden and the revealed are simultaneously produced and cannot be distinguished whilst also holding that all of the texts, practices, actors, effects, representations, past, etc. of international law are nebulous.

Before doing so, a quick preliminary remark is needed. The following implications of the practice of obnubilation advocated here for the sake of resisting the epistemology of the secret of international law echo some of the repercussions of my earlier engagements with the meaning-centrism of international legal thought and practice.[71] Such resemblance is especially tangible when it comes to the consequences of the practice of obnubilation for the way international lawyers practice and theorize interpretation as well as the centrality of narration as a mode of engagement with international law. This is no coincidence given how much the epistemology of the secret of international law draws on meaning-

International Lawyer: On Martti Koskenniemi's "From Apologia to Utopia" and the Place of Law in International Politics' (2006) 7 *German Law Journal* 1015 at 1029–1031; Jason A. Beckett, 'Rebel without a Cause' Martti Koskenniemi and the Critical Legal Project' (2006) 7 *German Law Review* 1045; see also the book review of Martti Koskenniemi, '*The Gentle Civilizer of Nations: The Rise and Fall of International Law 1870–1960* by Nicholas Tsagourias' (2003) 16 *Leiden Journal of International Law* 397 at 398–399.

[70] On the idea that critical legal scholarship has remained wedded to structuralist thought and has never seriously embraced the poststructuralist revolution, see Jean d'Aspremont, *After Meaning* p. 9.

[71] See Jean d'Aspremont, 'Two Attitudes towards Textuality in International Law: The Battle for Dualism' (2022) 42 *Oxford Journal of Legal Studies* 963; see d'Aspremont, *After Meaning* esp. chapter 4.

centrism.[72] The extent of such convergences does however not obviate the need for spelling out what the practice of obnubilation means to international legal thought and practice, if only because challenging and rethinking our dominant patterns of thought can always go down several routes, take different expressions, use distinct conceptual apparatuses and be narrated in a novel way.

5.4.1 *Killing Your Secret Darlings*

As could be anticipated, the very first implication of the practice of obnubilation – which in turn bears upon all the other consequences thereof – is the embrace of a new type of engagement with international law, one that is alien to any quest for the hidden, the unknown, and the invisible as well as any quest to reveal something and making it known and visible. This obviously entails a total repudiation, in the international legal scholarship, of the common heroic role of the courageous archaeologist and whistle-blower, which the international legal scholar usually bestows upon herself. As she practices obnubilation, the international legal scholar comes to terms with the fact there is not anything that the texts, practices, actors, effects, representations, past, etc. of international law are hiding from her and that she must go on revealing at the alleged price of telling an (in)convenient truth.[73] Although the epistemology of the secret of international law has come with all kinds of literary, hermeneutical, critical, economic, and ideological practices that may inextricably continue to inform the main genre of the international legal literature, the practice of obnubilation first calls for a radical change of the mindset of the international legal scholar, one whereby there is nothing hidden, unknown, invisible that ought to be revealed, made known, and made visible.

5.4.2 *Nebulous Words in a Nebulous World*

Second, a serious embrace of the practice of obnubilation entails a complete upheaval of the international lawyer's relationship with the world and especially of her understanding of what is held as being real, actual, and material. In fact, the practice of obnubilation leads the international lawyer to interact with reality, actuality, and materiality irrespective of the latter's

[72] See supra Section 1.1.2.1.

[73] Comp. with the call of Laurent de Sutter to forsake the critical mind's obsession with the need to always dig out little dirty secrets, see de Sutter, *Superfaible* p. 319.

visibility or indivisibility. By virtue of the practice of obnubilation, the world is construed as nebulous and no longer a trove of hidden secrets, let alone a trove external to international law. Facts are neither there to be ascertained and discovered, nor to be seized and governed by international law. Facts are not in-the-world but are part of the nebulosity formed by the texts, practices, actors, effects, representations, past, etc. of international law.[74] The international lawyer's wordy interventions in the world are nothing more than textual wanders in a worldly nebulosity that is not distinct from the nebulous texts, practices, actors, effects, representations, past, etc. of international law. In that sense, the practice of obnubilation means undoing one of the main paradigms of modern thought, namely the determination of the real through the visible.[75] It also entails doing away with those crude (but so typical) cartesian beliefs in a reality-in-itself that is allegedly observable and cognizable through the visible,[76] which is no minor apostasy for international lawyers.[77]

5.4.3 *Interpretation: From Hermeneutics to Poetics (bis)*

The third – and equally dramatic – consequence of the attitude of obnubilation advocated here pertains to interpretation.[78] The

[74] Comp. Jacques Derrida's famous claim that there is nothing outside the text in Derrida, *De la Grammatologie* pp. 225–226. See also the remarks of Geoffrey Bennington, *Jacques Derrida* (Editions du Seuil, 1991) p. 83; Peter Salmon, *An Event Perhaps* (Verso, 2020) p. 143. With an emphasis on legal studies, see the remarks of Pierre Legrand, 'Foreign Law: Understanding Understanding' (2011) 6 *Journal of Comparative Law* 67 at 80.

[75] On this main paradigm of modern epistemology, see Michel de Certeau, *L'invention du quotidien. 1. Arts de faire* (Gallimard, 1990) p. 272.

[76] For a similar rejection of the association of reality with what is made visible, see Roland Barthes, *Mythologies* (Editions du Seuil, 1957) p. 254; Jacques Rancière, *L'inconscient esthétique* (Galilée, 2001) p. 22; Jacques Rancière, *Le partage du sensible. Esthétique et politique* (La fabrique éditions, 2000) p. 62; Michel Foucault, *L'archéologie du savoir* (Gallimard, 1969) p. 205; Michel Foucault, *Naissance de la clinique* (Presses Universitaires de France, 1963) pp. 165 and 270; Régis Debray, *Vie et mort de l'image* (Gallimard, 1992) p. 499. See also the idea that empiricism is always bound to be a myth by Louis Althusser, *Initiation à la Philosophie pour les Non-Philosophes* (Presses Universitaires de France, 2019) p. 129.

[77] See my remarks in Jean d'Aspremont, 'A Worldly Law in a Legal World', in Andrea Bianchi and Moshe Hirsch (eds.), *International Law's Invisible Frames* (Oxford University Press, 2021) pp. 110–123; see also Jean d'Aspremont, 'The Chivalric Pursuit of Coherence in International Law' (2024) 37 *Leiden Journal of International Law* 191. Comp. with the disordering sensibility promoted by Kelsall, 'Disordering International Law'.

[78] On the kinship between secrets and a certain type of hermeneutics, see Barthes, *Le grain de la voix* p. 182.

international lawyer practicing obnubilation and obscuring the texts, practices, actors, effects, representations, past, etc. of international law can no longer approach interpretation as a meaning-centric hermeneutical activity whereby a text can mechanically and methodically be interpreted as to make it deliver its original and pre-existing meaningful content that had allegedly been uploaded thereupon. Indeed, the practice of obnubilation is a practice that postulates the nebulosity of the texts, practices, actors, effects, representations, past, etc. of international law, and, in doing so, contradicts outright the dominant approach to interpretation based on *hermeneutics* and the search for an original and pre-existing meaning.[79] Instead, the practice of obnubilation, as a mode of resistance to the epistemology of the secret of international law supports an understanding of interpretation as *poetics*.[80]

The transformation of the activity interpretation from hermeneutics to poetics, as a result of the practice of obnubilation, can be explained as follows. The key is that the practice of obnubilation and the obscuring of international law turn all of the texts, practices, actors, effects, representations, past, etc. of international law into a nebulous space[81] where

[79] Literary theory and twentieth-century philosophy have long distinguished between these two attitudes towards interpretation. For instance, Barthes claimed that there are two ways in which one can engage with a piece of literary work: one that seeks to map and catalogue all its distinct meanings and one that seeks to pick just one meaning, see Barthes, *Critique et vérité* p. 60. In the same vein, Deleuze, speaking about the act of writing about texts, distinguished between those who territorialise themselves within the territory of a state of things that they deem established and those who write to become alien to writing, see Gilles Deleuze and Claire Parnet, *Dialogues* (Champs essais, 1996), p. 89. Derrida similarly drew a distinction between two types of interpretations of texts: one that dreams of deciphering a truth and that experiences the necessity of interpretation as a banishment and another that is informed by an attempt to go beyond man and humanism, see Derrida, *L'écriture et la différence* p. 427.

[80] On the distinction between a tradition based on hermeneutics and one based on poetics, see Jonathan Culler, *Structuralist Poetics: Structuralism, Linguistics, and the Study of Literature* (Routledge, 2002) pp. vii–viii. It is important to emphasize that the understanding of poetics advocated here is different from that of Culler. For the latter, poetics ought to remain structuralist and seek to account for the rules, the conventions, and the procedures whereby texts do what they do. As the following paragraphs should make clear, the poetics advocated here shares neither the 'scientific' and explanatory ambitions of Culler's structuralist poetics nor the latter's attempt to formulate general and universal laws about the literary experience generated by the reading of international legal texts.

[81] See Roland Barthes, *L'aventure sémiologique* (Editions du Seuil, 1985) p. 13; see also Roland Barthes, *Le bruissement de la langue. Essais critiques IV* (Editions du Seuil, 1984) p. 56; Roland Barthes, *S/Z* (Editions du Seuil, 1970) pp. 10–11.

something is permanently happening[82] once the international lawyer steps in. Indeed, once obnubilated, international law comes to be experienced as *site of infinite passage*[83] – or a wandering space[84] – with thousands of entries and exits.[85] Such nebulous space is also a space of indefinite possibilities of connections between the texts, practices, actors, effects, representations, past, etc. of international law.[86] This is why interpretation, when following the practice of obnubilation, becomes poetics: interpretation boils down to appreciating and making use of international legal texts, practices, actors, effects, representations, past, etc.'s infinite nebulous possibilities in terms of saying, thinking, perceiving, and doing.[87]

It should be made clear, however, that an obnubilating interpretation, as has just been depicted in the previous paragraphs, does not entail that everything goes and that anything can be said, thought, perceived, or actioned through international law.[88] The activity of interpretation and the use of international legal texts, practices, actors, effects, representations, past, etc.'s infinite nebulous possibilities always remain informed by the forms, experiences, sensibilities, histories, temporalities, geographies, etc. that are available to the interpreter by virtue of all the discourses, systems of thought, languages, professions, experiences, ideologies in which she is caught, including the epistemology of the secret of

[82] On the idea of text as an event, see Legrand, 'The Same and the Different' p. 244. See also Pierre Legrand, '"Il n'y a pas de hors-texte": Intimations of Jacques Derrida as Comparatist-at-Law', in Peter Goodrich, Florian Hoffmann, Michel Rosenfeld and Cornelia Vismann (eds.), *Derrida and Legal Philosophy* (MacMillan, 2008) p. 143.

[83] On the idea of passage in the text, see Barthes, *Le bruissement de la langue* p. 75. On the idea that the text is a volume of traces and deferrals, see Barthes, *L'aventure sémiologique* p. 13.

[84] On the idea of wandering, see Peter Goodrich, 'Europe in America: Grammatology, Legal Studies, and the Politics of Transmission' (2001) 101 *Columbia Law Review* 2033 at 2063. Pierre Legrand speaking of tracing as meandering, see Legrand, 'Foreign Law' p. 154.

[85] Barthes, *S/Z* p. 17.

[86] Comp. with the idea of intertextuality as understood by Barthes, *S/Z* p. 11; Barthes, *Le grain de la voix* p. 56; see also Paul Ricoeur, *Temps et récit, Volume 1, L'intrigue et le récit historique* (Editions du Seuil, 1983), p. 151.

[87] Barthes, *S/Z* pp. 11 and 20. In the same vein, see Legrand, '"Il n'y a pas de hors-texte"' p. 131.

[88] Derrida, *L'Écriture et la différence* p. 427; Jonathan Culler, *On Deconstruction: Theory and Criticism after Structuralism* (Routledge, 2008), p. 132. See also the remarks of Jack M. Balkin, 'Deconstructive Practice and Legal Theory' (1987) 96 *Yale Law Journal* 743 at 776–777 and 785; Jack M. Balkin, 'Deconstruction's Legal Career' (2005) 27 *Cardozo Law Review* 719 at 719.

international law.[89] Said differently, there is always so much the interpreting international lawyer can do in the nebulous space composed of the texts, practices, actors, effects, representations, past, etc. of international law. This point is important, for it indicates that the practice of obnubilation does not amount to a replacement of the problems of hermeneutics by the pleasure of infinite creation[90] as well as a glorification of the aleatory.[91]

5.4.4 Theoractice

The practice of obnubilation that is called for here with a view to resisting the epistemology of the secret of international law also bears upon this time-honoured distinction between theory and practice that systematically punctuates international legal thought and practice. By virtue of such a distinction, international lawyers are trained to think that theory and practice are distinct activities, each of them mobilizing different resources, requiring different skills, and serving different goals. From this perspective, if one is a theorist, one is not practitioner, and vice-versa. The distinction informs career trajectories, self-profiling practices by members of the field, the identity of scholarly journals, the curriculum of international law degrees, etc. Even the collective imagination of the discipline is articulated around this distinction, the ability to move between these internal conditions often being construed as a heroic achievement.[92]

It is noteworthy that the distinction between theory and practice is itself very enmeshed in the distinction between the hidden, the unknown, the invisible, on the one hand, and the revealed, the known, and the visible, on the other, at the heart of the epistemology of the secret of international

[89] This is different from claims that vest the determination of meaning in the community of interpreters that continues to be meaning-centric and rests on a type of deliverability thinking (comp. Stanley Fish, *Is There a Text in This Class?* [Harvard University Press, 1980] p. 147). See also supra Section 1.1.2.1 and Section 1.1.2.5.

[90] This is a charge made by Jonathan Culler, see Culler, *Structuralist Poetics* p. 289.

[91] Culler, *Structuralist Poetics* p. 295. Comp. with the notion of disordering sensibility of Kelsall, 'Disordering International Law' (she argues that adopting a disordering sensibility is not to succumb to chaos and illiberalism).

[92] On the move away from practice by scholars like Philip Allott, David Kennedy, or Martti Koskenniemi, see Akbar Rasulov, 'What Is Critique? Towards a Sociology of Disciplinary Heterodoxy in Contemporary International Law', in Jean d'Aspremont, Tarcisio Gazzini, André Nollkaemper, and Wouter Werner (eds.), *International Law as a Profession* (Cambridge Univerisity Press, 2017) pp. 189–220.

law. In fact, the distinction between theory and practice reserves a very specific fate to practice. According to such distinction, practice has a visible side. It is what is out-there in the world and that can be made visible (and thus revealed) by virtue of a mere act of observation. Practice simultaneously has an invisible side, which is deemed intolerable and which makes the act of observation even more necessary. The international lawyer, by virtue of the distinction between theory and practice, is expected to carry out a constant observation of practice, one that will lead her to rely on or act upon the visible practice as well as to reveal the practice that was, until it was observed, invisible and that, once made visible by the act of observation, must be acted upon. Clearly, such a fate is not shared by theory, which is commonly considered to have no visible side and which is not a thing-in-the-world that can be made visible. Theory is commonly considered as unmaterial, unactual, intangible and ... nebulous. Theory is not in-the-world. There is nothing to be made visible or invisible about it. Holding theory as being nebulous, that is, outside the dichotomy between the visible and the invisible, is the way in which the distinction between theory and practice organizes a hierarchy between the two, giving primacy to the latter. Yet, once one approaches international law and the world in which the former is mobilized as a nebulous space, there is no longer any practice out there that can be made visible and revealed by a mere act of observation. By virtue of obnubilation, practice joins theory in the nebulous space where the latter had been parked.[93] It is *theoractice* all the way.

In challenging the distinction between theory and practice, obnubilation has the potential to dramatically reshuffle the distribution of social capital in the disciplinary field of international law. Indeed, because the production of practice has always been given an existential and ontological function, that is, that of providing the main object to which international law applies and in which it is rooted,[94] those international lawyers associated with such existential production are given much higher social capital,[95] and, in contrast, those involved in the production

[93] In the same vein, see Althusser, *Initiation à la Philosophie pour les Non-Philosophes* pp. 112–113 and 137. See also Gaston Bachelard, *Le nouvel esprit scientifique* (Presses Universitaires de France, 1934) pp. 9–10; Jacques Derrida, *Théorie et pratique. Cours de l'ENS-Ulm 1975–1976* (Galilée, 2017).

[94] See d'Aspremont, 'A Worldly Law in a Legal World' pp. 110–123.

[95] For some critical remarks, see Mario Prost, *The Concept of Unity in Public International Law* (Hart, 2012) pp. 149–153. See also Jean d'Aspremont, 'If International Judges Say So, It Must Be True: Empiricism or Fetishism?' (2015) 4/9 *ESIL Reflections*.

of theory are given less social capital.[96] In that sense, obscuring the texts, practices, actors, effects, representations, past, etc. of international law, and doing away with the distinction between theory and practice, would not only overhaul the way the field describes itself and the various roles played by everyone but would also bring about a complete upheaval of the way social capital is apportioned therein.

5.4.5 *Nothing to Be Represented, Everything to Be Narrated*

A fifth implication of the practice of obnubilation contemplated here for the sake of resisting the epistemology of the secret of international law pertains to how writing and making arguments about international law should be construed and theorized. Once the texts, practices, actors, effects, representations, past, etc. of international law are held as nebulous as well as alien to any distinction between the hidden, the unknown, the invisible, on the one hand, and the revealed, the known, and the visible, on the other, writing and making arguments about them can no longer be approached as a rendition activity. Indeed, writing and making arguments about the nebulosity of international law and of the world to which it is applied cannot amount to a representation, be it of rules, systems, positions, ideas, facts, etc. In the nebulosity of international law and of the world to which it is applied, *there is nothing to be represented and everything to be narrated.* The practice of obnubilation is accordingly synonymous with a practice of narration: engaging with international law is nothing more than narrating what international law did, does, is not doing, or should be doing to the world.[97] It simultaneously means giving up on being right and proving the other wrong as to how international law and the world are represented.[98]

[96] For instance, it has been claimed that theory 'provide[s] no real benefits' and supposedly has the tendency to 'obscure the more interesting questions', see Ian Brownlie, 'International Law at the Fiftieth Anniversary of the United Nations: General Course on Public International Law' (1995) 255 *Collected Courses* 9 at 30. On the anti-theoretical character of the field, see gen. Martti Koskenniemi, 'Repetition as Reform' (1998) 9 *European Journal of International Law* 405 at 406; see also Jan Klabbers, 'Constitutionalism and the Making of International Law' (2008) 5 *NoFo* 84 at 95.

[97] On a distinction between a discourse that narrates and a discourse that narrativizes, see Hayden White, *The Content of the Form: Narrative Discourse and Historical Representation* (John Hopkins University Press, 1987) p. 2.

[98] Comp. with de Sutter, *Superfaible* pp. 20–24; Laurent de Sutter, 'Pour une clinique', in Laurent de Sutter (ed.), *Postcritique* (Presses Universitaires de France, 2019) p. 233. Comp with the idea of failing better by Pierre Legrand, *Negative Comparative Law: A Strong Programme for Weak Thought* (Cambridge University Press, 2022) pp. 1–46.

It should not be necessary to point out that the practice of obnubilation's elevation of the legal discourse into a practice of narration is no demotion of the former. Narration is what governs the world: one does what one does, thinks, perceives, experiences because of what one is told.[99] Said differently, narration is very conducive to the determination of the sayable, which in turns determines the perceivable, thinkable, and actionable.[100] The practice of obnubilation can accordingly be read as a rehabilitation of narration as a type of approaching the world that had been demoted to the non-real, non-scientific, non-rigorous, and non-relevant by modern thought.[101]

Narration is obviously not a neutral discursive activity but always works for certain epistemic, ideological, world-making, moral, etc. choices.[102] Likewise, narration is not indifferent to the social, institutional, and cultural capital one is endowed with. Narration similarly is a very coded mode of approaching the world[103] that always requires what has been called narrative intelligence.[104] Yet, narration promoted by the practice of obnubilation, notwithstanding its being inescapably caught in codes, repertoires of the possible, and the unequal distribution of social as well as cultural capital, has the advantage, compared to the speech materials produced by the epistemology of the secret of international law, of always facilitating non-conformism and possibly innovation. Indeed, by virtue of the narration promoted by the practice of obnubilation, one never knows in advance how one will move in the nebulosity of international law and the world to which it is applied. One cannot predict which direction and route the story will take: the very direction as well as the meandering of the story is never determined from the start.[105] In that sense, it can be said that the narration enabled by the practice of obnubilation facilitates micro-subversion, micro-reinvention, and

[99] Steven L. Winter, *A Clearing in the Forest: Law, Life and Mind* (University of Chicago Press, 2001) p. 128; Paul de Man, *The Resistance to Theory* (University of Minnesota Press, 1986) p. 11; Michel de Certeau, *Histoire et psychanalyse entre science et fiction* (Gallimard, 2016) p. 75; Barthes, *Critique et vérité* p. 35.

[100] See supra note 99.

[101] Lyotard, *La Condition Postmoderne* p. 18; White, *The Content of the Form* p. 57.

[102] White, *The Content of the Form* p. ix.

[103] In the same vein, see de Certeau, *Histoire et psychanalyse entre science et fiction* p. 7; Lyotard, *La Condition Postmoderne* p. 47. See however the remarks of Paul Ricoeur, see Paul Ricoeur, *Temps et récit, Volume 2, La configuration dans le récit de fiction* (Editions du Seuil, 1984) pp. 293–296.

[104] Ricoeur, *Temps et récit, Volume 1* p. 403.

[105] See Foucault, *Dits et écrits, II* pp. 268–269; see de Sutter, *Superfaible* pp. 232 and 333.

micro-appropriation by the users of international law.[106] If *bricolage*, to use a word too much *en vogue*, means anything when describing international legal thought and practice,[107] it is maybe the possibility for each and every one to subvert and reinvent a text, a rule, a practice, a history, a representation, etc. according to one's interest, one's perception of global interest, one's sense of justice, etc.[108] Narration permits one to indulge in one's dreams of indocility[109] towards international law as it is served to us by the epistemology of the secret of international law. Said differently, the narration facilitated by the practice of obnubilation allows the permanent tricking of the sayable, thinkable, perceivable, and actionable as they are determined by the ordering carried out by the epistemology of the secret of international law.[110]

Such permanent tricking of what is commonly deemed sayable, thinkable, perceivable, and actionable is what allows the practice of obnubilation, and its practice of narration, to give rise to a new type of subversive thought, one that is not wedded to modernity, to the distinction between the hidden, the unknown, the invisible, on the one hand, and the revealed, the known, and the visible, on the other, and more generally to the epistemology of the secret of international law. Indeed, obscuring the texts, practices, actors, effects, representations, past, etc. of international law by virtue of the practice of obnubilation advocated here is

[106] Comp. with the notion of reparative reading of Eve Kosofsky Sedgwick. For her, reparative reading refers to a mode of selective scanning and amplification informed by the experience of love and pleasure and geared at being ameliorative by reorganizing the fragments of texts, see Sedgwick, 'Paranoid Reading and Reparative Reading' pp. 1–38.

[107] It is fashionable to refer to the idea of bricolage nowadays, a notion he borrows from French structuralist thought and especially from Claude Lévi-Strauss. See Martti Koskenniemi, *To the Uttermost Parts of the Earth* (Cambridge University Press, 2021) p. 2. In some earlier work, Koskenniemi defined the act of bricolage as 'trying to construct a persuasive argument from the bits and pieces of authoritative language lying about in the appropriate professional context' and as 'grasping other texts and utopias so as to try as best we can to persuade audiences of the authority of what we have to say, provided that there is anything we are able to say', see Martti Koskenniemi, 'Imagining the Rule of Law: Rereading the Grotian "Tradition"' (2019) 30 *European Journal of International Law* 17 at 24 and 28. Comp. with the idea of bricolage by Legrand, 'Foreign Law' pp. 82 and 154.

[108] For such an understanding of bricolage, see de Certeau, *L'invention du quotidien* pp. xxxix and xl.

[109] The expression is from Françoise Vergès, *Un féminisme décolonial* (La fabrique éditions, 2019) p. 127.

[110] Comp. with the idea of ruse of Michel de Certeau, see de Certeau, *L'invention du quotidien.* p. xl; see gen. Paul Feyerabend, *Against Method* (New Left Books, 1975).

a way to attempt to redefine the very modes of enunciation currently practiced by international lawyers, which are all articulated around a hidden, an unknown and an invisible that ought to be revealed, made known, and made visible. Undoubtedly, the practice of obnubilation is not in itself sufficient to transform the site of enunciation of international law and of the world to which it is applied.[111] Yet, the subversion enabled by the practice of obnubilation can be instrumental in re-inscribing the texts, practices, actors, effects, representations, past, etc. of international law in a way that the narrating international lawyer deems fairer, less capitalist, less colonialist, less racist, less bourgeois, less phallocentric, less virilist, less masculinist, etc. Said differently, the practice of obnubilation advances new modes of intervention in the international legal discourse and in the latter's sites of contestation, thereby allowing one to *inhabit a new space of intervention in the here and now.*[112]

The foregoing should suffice to show that nebulosity postulated by the practice of obnubilation should not be construed as the promotion of emptiness but rather as the enabling of a permanent tricking of international law and how the latter is revealed by its own epistemology of the secret.[113] From this perspective, the narrative mode of engagement with international law entailed by the practice of obnubilation dramatically contrasts with the very conformist representations of international law produced by the epistemology of the secret of international law: such representations always are within the sayable, the thinkable, the perceivable, and the actionable defined by the epistemology of the secret of international law[114] and, in that sense, always are prefigured from the start.[115]

By rehabilitating narration as the main mode of engagement with international law, the practice of obnubilation brings about, here too, a disruption of the social hierarchization that regulates the reading of international legal texts. Indeed, in contemporary international legal

111 For such an attempt, see Bhabba, *The Location of Culture* p. 347.
112 I borrow this expression from Bhabba, *The Location of Culture* p. 10.
113 Comp. with the notion of emptiness of Barthes, *Le grain de la voix* pp. 126–127.
114 See Eagleton, *The Function of Criticism* p. 15; see also Barthes, *Critique et vérité* p. 14.
115 On the idea that, in modern thought, the process is always decided from the start, see Theodor Adorno and Max Horkheimer, *Dialectic of Enlightenment* (Verso, 1997) p. 24. On the idea that concepts are deployed as identity checks, see Theodor W. Adorno, *Negative Dialectics* (Continuum, 2007) p. 5. See also Henri Bergson, *La pensée et le mouvant* (Flammarion, 2014) pp. 229 and 240. See also supra Section 1.1.2.5.

thought and practice, the determination of who is right and wrong in the revelation of previously hidden, unknown, invisible content of legal text commonly hinges on institutional hierarchies and affiliations as well as social and cultural capital.[116] Once one holds that the texts, practices, actors, effects, representations, past, etc. of international law are nebulous, one terminates the – especially capitalistic and neo-colonial – intellectual mining industry sustained by the epistemology of the secret of international law, thereby making all such hierarchies and distributions of capital irrelevant.

5.4.6 *The End of Critique?*

Sixth, and not least, the type of subversive thought enabled by the practice of obnubilation, is one, as was alluded to above, that is alien to the common idea of critique that was born with modern thought[117] and which is usually geared towards the questioning of the unacknowledged or unconsented necessities that govern action, perception, experience, and discourses.[118] The type of subversion promoted here in the form of a practice of obnubilation does radically away with the whole range of critical attitudes commonly found in international legal thought and practice and that have not been less modern than traditional modern critique, let alone not less wedded to the epistemology of the secret of international law.[119] In other words, being subversive, by virtue of this new practice of obnubilation, does accordingly not mean being critical as is now commonly understood in international legal thought and practice, if only because subversion is now a mode of narrating the nebulous and is no longer fixated on the postulation of dirty hidden secrets that the 'crit' ought to reveal.

Here too, the practice of obnubilation, by virtue of the new subversive thought it brings about, has the merit of reshuffling the distribution of social and cultural capital in the field in that it democratizes the entitlements and possibilities of making subversive interventions.[120] Indeed,

[116] On the social hierarchizations at work in reading practices, see de Certeau, *L'invention du quotidien* p. 248.
[117] See supra note xxx. See also Section 2.4.
[118] Eagleton, *The Function of Criticism* pp. 9–10; White, *Tropics of Discourse* p. 1.
[119] See supra Section 4.2.2.
[120] On the cultural capital and prestige associated with critical thought, see the remarks of Felski, *The Limits of Critique* p. 138.

because subversion, by virtue of this new practice of obnubilation, can no longer be reduced to the critical attitude as it is socially and institutionally defined in the recognized intellectual hubs of critical thought – and especially in imperial American and European locations,[121] subversion is made more widely available across the world, across institutional networks, across disciplines and across social groups.

[121] On the reminiscent neo-colonial image according to which metatheorizing and critical theory are primarily a European and American activity, see the comments of Bhabba, *The Location of Culture* p. 29.

NOTEBOOK

This notebook contains some of the ideas, ambitions, hopes, anxieties, interrogations, and fears that randomly or expectedly came to punctuate the writing of the previous chapters. This notebook does not, in any way, provide elements of context. I have long ceased to believe that a text and the context of such text can ever be distinguished, for the former always precedes and constitutes the latter, which is, at best, the context *of the text* concerned to which it is necessarily second. This is no different with respect to the following considerations, which, although came to surface in the writing-process of this book, are now bound to be continuations – and thus no preconceptions – of the forms that constitute this book.

In mentioning some of the ideas, ambitions, hopes, anxieties, angers, interrogations, and fears that infused the writing of the previous chapters, this notebook returns to some of the key claims made throughout the previous chapters, sometimes giving them a different twist or verbalizing them in another fashion. It also provides thoughts not yet encountered, some of them relating to horrific as well as ominous developments that came to rock the world as this book was brought to completion. If anything, these considerations should remind the reader that, even if the preceding study of international law's epistemology of the secret can occasionally read abstract and arcane, this remains a book about the world, how it is governed, and how it is sometimes failed by the modes of governance put in place by disciplines, cultures, languages, discourses, systems of thought, and belief systems.

Revelation Then and Now

Epistemologies of the secret have long been with us. And they have always been with us for the same reason: producing truth out of the revelation of the hidden, the unknown, the invisible for the sake of governing us, our sayings, our thoughts, our perceptions, and our actions. Whenever we have tried to outsmart them, epistemologies of the secret have reinvented themselves and continued to make us believe that the truth originates in the hidden, unknown, and invisible being revealed. Even when the moderns blew to pieces the Christian governance of the mind, they happily borrowed the latter's modes of production of truth through the revelation of the hidden, the unknown, the invisible. It is accordingly no surprise that even the most forceful contestations of modern thought hardly eroded the reign of epistemologies of the secret. Even critique, whether in its modern or postmodern variant, has remained centred on the revelation of the hidden, the unknown, the invisible in order to put the world on trial and produce a truth that everyone ought to conform with.

A Simple World: The Sovereignty of the Visible

Epistemologies of the secret are offspring of the primacy awarded to the visible. They rest on the kinship between truth and what is visible and hence hinge on the illusion that the visible is produced by the revelation of a previously invisible truth. Epistemologies of the secret conceal the fact that the invisible does not precede the visible and that the invisible and the visible are always simultaneously produced. In a way, epistemologies of the secret boil down to a very simple epistemology, one that is shared both by the young toddler who discovers the world through her sight and by the dark forces that currently roam our public institutions and our streets who all trumpet together 'if we see it, it must be true'. For them, the world is simple and is nothing more than what we see, can see, and should see.

A Loyal Servant

Under the uninterrupted reign of epistemologies of the secret, international legal thought and practice have proved a very loyal servant. Be it in its premodern expression or in its modern variant, international law has been the site of one of the most successful and uncontested epistemologies of the secret of all. Even the most compelling contestations of international legal thought and practice have perpetuated the necessity of revealing hidden, unknown, invisible content. Actually, looking at international law (and international lawyers), as the previous chapters did, allows one to grasp what epistemologies of the secret do to the human mind and to the world. This is why this book, although zeroed in on international law, tells us a story that goes well beyond international legal thought and practice.

The Dark Side of the Story

The epistemology of the secret of international law has surely allowed the latter to do a lot of good. Postulating the necessary presence of hidden, invisible, unknown content in international law's texts, practices, actors, effects, representations, past, etc. has made it possible to protect, liberate, emancipate, rehabilitate, give a voice, salvage, etc. Indeed, whenever they came to protect the groups, individuals, the environment, equality and ensure some decency when it had been lost, the rules of international law were deemed to have a secret content whose revelation by courts, scholars, activists, counsels, legal advisors, decision-makers, etc. helped deliver on the hopes that had been pinned on the rules concerned. Yet, the epistemology of the secret of international law is also what has enabled violence, oppression, discrimination, repression, silencing, humiliation, cancellation, etc. Among those many calamities, there is no doubt that imperialism (including its most abject form, i.e., colonialism) has thrived thanks to the efficacy of the epistemology of the secret around which international law is articulated. In fact, the necessary presence of a distinction between legal traditions, groups, locations, interpretations, institutions, and the constant revelation of the 'true' and 'natural' superiority of some of them over the others is what has made one of the darkest chapters of human history possible.[1] What is more, thanks to the epistemology of the secret of international law, imperialism, in all its legal materializations, has continuously rested on the postulation that what the empire cannot see in others (including in other traditions, groups, locations, interpretations, institutions) constituted secret content that those working for the empire ought to reveal in order capture it, distinguish it, replace it, dominate it, annihilate it, etc.[2]

[1] Frantz Fanon has cogently demonstrated that, in the aftermath of decolonization, the quest for an African culture has remained informed by a racial delimitation of the world inherited from the colonizer and is nothing more than the reverse thesis of the colonial idea of a-cultural negro, see Frantz Fanon, *The Wretched of the Earth*, trans. Richard Philcox (Grove Press, 2004) chapter 4. Comp. with Jacques Derrida, *Le dernier des Juifs* (Galilée, 2014) pp. 35–37.

[2] Frantz Fanon has compellingly demonstrated how the attempts of the French colonizers to unveil Algerian women were premised on the postulation by the colonizers that behind the veil there was a secret body, a secret culture, a secret tradition that they ought to reveal

But imperialism is not the only beneficiary of the epistemology of the secret of international law. As was alluded to at regular intervals in the preceding chapters, the epistemology of the secret of international law has also been intensively complicit with capitalism, the destruction of the planet, many forms of racism, bourgeois ideology, phallocentrism, virilism, masculinism, etc. There is no doubt that the misery and moral collapse of the world currently witnessed as these pages draw to a close continues to owe much of its own possibility to the epistemology of the secret of international law as has been described in this book.

A Shared Heritage?

Some may think we are all the children of some metaphysical phenomenon or person. What is sure, however, is that we are all the children of European imperialism, and especially of the vilest variant of it, that is, colonialism. In fact, as Edward Said taught us, one of imperialism's paradoxical achievements was to bring the world closer, albeit through an unjust and despicable process of separation.[3] The result is that the historical experience of empire, and all the apparatuses imperialism has mobilized, are now a common heritage shared, albeit in dramatically different ways, by anyone on this planet: no individual, no group, no family, no intellectual tradition, no culture, no space on this globe has been spared and unaffected by imperialism as well as its intellectual and legal machinery. But imperialism is also what taught the villains and bastards that they could get away with the most ignominious forms of inhumanity. In fact, the most horrific crimes of the twentieth and twenty-first centuries, including those presently witnessed as these ultimate lines are written, could not have been committed without the historical, symbolic, intellectual, discursive, legal, scientific, ethnocentric, lethal, and inhumane capital accumulated and generated as a result of European imperialism.[4] As this book draws to a close, it behoves us not

and get access to with a view to subjecting the colonized to the empire, see Frantz Fanon, 'Algeria Unveiled', in Frantz Fanon, *A Dying Colonialism*, trans. Haakon Chevalier (Monthly Review Press, 1965) pp. 35–64.

[3] Edward Said, *Culture and Imperialism* (Vintage books, 1994) pp. xxi–xxii.

[4] As early as 1946, W. E. B. Du Bois wrote that 'there was no Nazi atrocity – concentration camps, wholesale maiming and murder, defilement of women or ghastly blasphemy of childhood – which the Christian civilization of Europe had not long been practicing against colored folk in all parts of the world in the name of and for the defense of a Superior Race born to rule the world', see William E. B. Du Bois, *The World and Africa*

to forget that the epistemologies of the secret examined in this book, including the epistemology of the secret of international law, are inevitably part of the intellectual and legal capital accumulated and generated by imperialism, which it has extensively facilitated and whose mark it will now always bear.

No Shame?

International lawyers may make the claim that they should not be blamed for letting the international legal discourse function around an epistemology of the secret that has not only done good to the world but has also been complicit to the unforgivable. In particular, they may say it is not their fault but that of 'the tradition they have inherited'. From a similar perspective, they may come to argue that international law's epistemology of the secret is an ancestral lofty tradition, which, as an intellectual and cultural artefact, should be respected and upheld. In the same vein, when confronted with the realization of what the epistemology of the secret of international law has done to the world, international lawyers may be tempted to contend that enabling and disabling sayings, thoughts, perceptions, and actions is what disciplines, cultures, languages, discourses, systems of thought, belief systems etc. do. That means, from this vantage point, that being organized around an ordering epistemology is nothing diseased. On the contrary, some international lawyers could go as far as saying, 'it is natural, this is what we have always done'! If this is the case, why couldn't international lawyers go on with their job as secret-hunter, archaeologist, speleologist, and porn-producer, which the epistemology of the secret of international law has bestowed upon them?

Our Sole Hope?

One must acknowledge that when one sees the current cynicism and moral collapse that inform global and domestic governance, it may sometimes feel risky to go after the epistemology of the secret of international law: do we not run the risk of losing the only hopes we have left, leaving the bastards with a blank cheque and no authoritative standards

(Oxford University Press, 2007) p. 15; see also Aimé Césaire, *Discours sur le colonialisme* (Ed. Présence Africaine, 1955) pp. 13–14 and 77–78; Hannah Arendt, *The Origins of Totalitarianism* (World, 1962) pp. 158–220.

whose breach they could be accountable for? Maybe international law is one of the last sources of hope one wants to cling to? So why take such a hard look, as this book does, at an epistemology that has been so central in what international law has been doing since its consolidation? Confronted with such preserving postures, I must concede that I can see why the right to self-determination, to take but one of the examples of what one could still be tempted to cling to these days, has continued to be mobilized in 2024. Whatever the huge problems with the idea of right, the idea of self, and the idea of self-determination may be, and notwithstanding its providing access to a form of political community that was that of the colonizer, I understand why such legal form, among others, can, through an exercise of revelation as the one described in the previous chapters, help us contain some of the ruthless colonialism, mass violence, constant humiliation, and the gravest forms of injustice still witnessed today. That being said, the point I want to make here is distinct. Appreciating how the epistemology of the secret of international law can be reclaimed and turned against those who have been using it to kill, oppress, discriminate, repress, silence, annihilate, humiliate etc. is not exclusive of resisting it through a practice of obnubilation as is has been understood and promoted in this book.

Who Has Ever Spoken of Cancelling Anything?

Let us put it bluntly and explicitly so that it is clear once and for all: the practice of obnubilation promoted here does not cancel the epistemology of the secret of international law, let alone international law as a whole. It simply seeks to outmanoeuvre the epistemology of the secret of international law by refusing to uphold the distinction between the hidden, the unknown, the invisible, on the one hand, and the revealed, the known, and the visible, on the other. It is a practice of non-understanding that seeks to obscure the-invisible-revealed-and-made-visible for the sake of resisting the universal visible truths imposed by an oppressive visibility. Obnubilation allows international law to continue to be a source of hope as well as a tool to fight the bastards and their vile ordering projects. And this simultaneously allows one to recall that those asking for the end of social injustice, of the exploitation of people, of imperialism, of racism, of phallocentrism, of masculinism, of virilism, of the destruction of the planet, etc. are not asking to cancel anything but, on the contrary, that we always teach and recall what such ordering practices do to people and to the world.

A Way of Life

As was shown by this book, epistemologies of the secret hide that the invisible does not precede the visible and that the invisible and the visible are always simultaneously produced. They obfuscate the fact that truth is produced out of simultaneously produced secrets, such obfuscation being the very condition of possibility and functioning of epistemologies of the secret. Thus, epistemologies of the secret always lie. This begs, in my view, the following question: Who would want to live a life where one is permanently tricked? The point I want to make here is that the practice of obnubilation promoted in this book is not only a way to read international law, its texts, its practices, its actors, its effects, its representations, its past, etc. It is also a way of life, one that does not accept to believe in the neat and simplistic the distinction between the hidden, the unknown, the invisible, on the one hand, and the revealed, the known, and the visible, on the other. It simultaneously constitutes an ethical attitude that calls upon the international lawyers to permanently keep disciplines, cultures, languages, discourses, systems of thought, belief systems, epistemologies – and especially their own – under scrutiny for what they do to the mind, to people, and to the world.

Modernity's Self-destruction

Owing much to Western-centrism and imperialism, many of the key epistemologies of the secret that govern the world today, including that around which international law is articulated, have been inherited from the Christian governance of the mind and perpetuated by modern thought. It is noteworthy that it is in mobilizing epistemologies of the secret that modernity left us with science, the critical attitude, the rule of law, the respect for human rights, cosmopolitanism, solidarity mechanisms, etc. Interestingly, and somewhat shockingly, epistemologies of the secret are now the primary discursive weapon that is used by those who pursue the very destruction of those few hallmarks of modern thought that we had hope to uphold. In fact, the dark forces and the conservative traditionalism that came to resurface in the last decade(s) have come to show an unprecedented mastery of epistemologies of the secret in a way that allows them to dismantle, at great speed, and with wide public support, those few modern achievements that we would want to retain. This may not be entirely surprising. After all, epistemologies of the secret function in a way that are very similar to that of the permanent state of suspicion postulated by dark and conservative forces in political settings. Appallingly, science, the critical attitude, the rule of law, the respect for human rights, cosmopolitanism, solidarity mechanisms, etc. are not the only victims of these new dark masters of epistemologies of the secret. All the advances in terms of social justice, non-discrimination, feminism, equality, critical geographies, self-identity, etc. that had been made possible by postmodern humanities are simultaneously being razed to the ground – and with them all the intellectual figures that could support them.[5] Possibly, the destruction of postmodern humanities by those new dark masters of the epistemologies of the secret may be even more alarming than the abovementioned attacks on science, the critical attitude, the rule of law, the respect for human rights, cosmopolitanism, solidarity mechanisms, etc. Indeed, postmodern humanities – including cultural studies, race theory, gender studies, queer theory, postcolonial studies, poststructuralism – remain, in my view, modernity's only hope. Exterminating postmodern humanities through an atomic use of epistemologies of the secret, as we witness it these days, can – somewhat ironically – be construed as modernity's very moment of self-destruction.

Meanwhile in the Global North

Thursday 14 March 2024, somewhere in the heart of Paris. The streets around the campus of a famous university are suddenly filled with heavily armed police forces. Lectures and seminars are suspended and the evacuation of all the university buildings is forced upon students, researchers, and staff. The day before, the head of the government of France had made an unexpected irruption in the meeting of the executive council of that university, actually suspending that university's autonomy, and announcing that, from now on, the contestation of certain current global injustices would be prohibited. Albeit revolting and shocking, such developments did not come as a surprise. Indeed, the very same government had, in October 2022, organized a major conference on the 'deconstruction of deconstruction', denouncing the dangerous 'ideology' composed of gender studies, queer theory, race theories, and postcolonial studies. It is also the same government whose ministry of education had claimed shortly before that Derrida, Deleuze, and Foucault constitute 'viruses' that ought to be wiped out. The country

[5] See gen. Isabelle Alfandary, Anne Emmanuelle Berger and Jacob Rogozinski (eds.), *Qui a peur de la déconstruction?* (Presses Universitaires de France, 2023).

concerned by these events is, of course, only a tiny piece of land somewhere on a large globe. Yet, such events, which echo similar sombre developments in other parts of the Global North over the last years, may be the harbinger of much grimmer times to come. What has this to do with the epistemology of the secret studied in the preceding chapters one may ask? It is simple. As a mode of ordering, epistemologies of the secret will continue to thrive and their efficacy be fully exploited by their new masters, in France and elsewhere, not only to promote simplistic truths about people and the world but also to oppress, discriminate, repress, silence, annihilate, humiliate etc. If international lawyers, be they in the Global North or in the Global South, ever want to remain relevant figures despite what is now looming on the horizon, it is by systematically recalling what their own epistemology of the secret has been doing to the mind, to people, and to the world whilst simultaneously showing their fellow world citizens which modes of resistance they have at their disposal to outmanoeuvre the most cynical uses of epistemologies of the secret.

Meanwhile Along the Mediterranean Sea

On the same day, on a small but densely populated strip of land along the Mediterranean Sea. Only mourning, despair, fear, pain, hunger. Stomachs are empty, bodies are maimed, graveyards are improvised. The children do not even cry anymore when F-35s fly over their tents or their apartment blocks. Tears cost too many calories and, above all, too much hope. Some limited aid is airdropped by a handful of nations, which, at the same time, continue to publicly, proudly, and shamelessly provide the very weapons that cause the sufferance, the mass killings, and the hunger. No one will ever forget. No one should ever forget. And, as far as the readers of this book are concerned, I hope that no one will ever forget that such atrocity is also what epistemologies of the secret facilitate. From the perspective of the active and passive supporters of such tragedy, the state is supposed to have a necessary content and so does its alleged international legal right to self-defence. The mass killing is the moment the state reveals itself, what it stands for, and who warrants its care and who does not. These are epistemologies of the secret at their worst. Throughout the writing of this book, there has not been a single moment where I did not entertain the ambition to convince international lawyers, who have practiced the revelation of the hidden, invisible, and unknown since the inception of international law, that one *cannot* let epistemologies of the secret, and especially that around which international law is articulated, do what they currently do to the mind, to people and to the world along the Mediterranean Sea and elsewhere.

In the End

If there were one lesson from this inquiry into the epistemology of the secret of international law, it could be that one always ought to be on one's guard when truth is produced out of the revelation of simultaneously produced secrets, that is, when ordering is organized around an invisible-instantly-made-visible. As the heirs of an old epistemological tradition whereby truth is produced out of the revelation of an invisible-instantly-made-visible, may international lawyers who can someday read this book always remain alert to what their discursive apparatuses could be used for and, if need be, teach others how the latter ought to be resisted.

BIBLIOGRAPHY

Critical, Literary, and Philosophical Works

Acker, S., and Armenti, C., 'Sleepless in Academia' (2004) 16 *Gender and Education* 3.

Adorno, T., and Horkheimer, M., *Dialectic of Enlightenment* (London: Verso, 1997).

Negative Dialectics (Continuum, 2007).

Agamben, G., *La puissance de la pensée* (Editions Payot & Rivages, 2021).

Alfandary, I., Berger, A. E., and Rogozinski, J. (eds.), *Qui a peur de la déconstruction?* (Presses Universitaires de France, 2023).

Althusser, L., *Initiation à la Philosophie pour les Non-Philosophes* (Presses Universitaires de France, 2014).

Être Marxiste en Philosophie (Presses Universitaires de France, 2015).

Amer Meziane, M., *Au bord des mondes: Vers une anthropologie métaphysique* (Vues de l'Esprit, 2023).

Appadurai, A., *Modernity at Large: Cultural Dimensions of Globalization* (University of Minnesota Press, 1996).

Arendt, H., *The Origins of Totalitarianism* (World, 1962).

Bachelard, G., *Le nouvel esprit scientifique* (Presses Universitaires de France, 1934).

Balibar, E., *Passions du concept. Epistémologie, théologique et politique. Ecrits II* (La découverte, 2020).

Balibar E., and Wallerstein, I., *Race, nation, classe. Des identités ambigües* (La découverte, 2018).

Barthes, R., *Mythologies* (Editions du Seuil, 1957).

S/Z (Editions du Seuil, 1970).

Le degré zéro de l'écriture (Editions du Seuil, 1972).

Leçon (Editions du Seuil, 1978).

Lecture in Inauguration of the Chair of Literary Semiology, Collège de France, January 7, 1977, trans. Richard Howard (Collège de France, 1979).

Le grain de la voix. Entretiens 1962–1980 (Editions du Seuil, 1981).

Le Bruissement de la langue. Essais critiques IV (Editions du Seuil, 1984).

'La mort de l'auteur', in R. Barthes (ed.), *Le Bruissement de la langue* (Editions du Seuil, 1984), 63–69.

L'aventure sémiologique (Editions du Seuil, 1985).

Critique et vérité (Editions du Seuil, 1999).
La préparation du roman. Cours au Collège de France (1978–1979 et 1979–1980) (Editions du Seuil, 2015).
Barthes, R., Bersani, L., Hamon, P., Riffaterre, M., and Watt, I., *Littérature et réalité* (Editions du Seuil, 1982).
Bennington, G., *Jacques Derrida* (Editions du Seuil, 1991).
Bergson, H., *La pensée et le mouvant* (Flammarion, 2014).
Berman, H., *Law and Revolution: The Formation of the Western Legal Tradition* (Harvard University Press, 1983).
Bourdieu, P., *Ce que parler veut dire. L'économie des échanges linguistiques* (Fayard, 1982).
'The Force of Law: Toward a Sociology of the Juridical Field', trans. Richard Terdiman (1987) 38 *Hastings Law Journal* 805.
'A Lecture on the Lecture', in P. Bourdieu, *In Other Words: Essays towards a Reflexive Sociology* (Stanford University Press, 1990).
Langage et pouvoir symbolique (Editions du Seuil, 2001).
Bourdieu, P., and Wacquant, L., *An Invitation to Reflexive Sociology* (Polity Press, 1992).
Britton, C. M., *Edouard Glissant and Postcolonial Theory: Strategies of Language and Resistance* (The University Press of Virginia, 1999).
Buchanan, I., *Deleuzism* (Duke University Press, 2000).
Butler, J., *Gender Trouble: Feminism and the Subversion of Identify*, 2nd edn (Routledge, 1990).
'Critically Queer' (1993) 1 *GLQ: A Journal of Lesbian and Gay Studies* 17.
Notes toward a Performative Theory of Assembly (Harvard University Press, 2018).
Canguilhem, G., *Idéologie et Rationalité. Dans l'Histoire des Sciences de la Vie* (Vrin, 1977).
Castoriadis, C., *L'Imaginaire comme tel* (Hermann Editeurs, 2007).
Cavallo, G., 'Between Volumen and Codex: Reading in the Roman World', in G. Cavallo and R. Chartier (eds.), *A History of Reading in the West*, trans. Lydia G. Cochrane (Polity Press, 1999), 65–89.
Césaire, A., *Discours sur le colonialisme* (Ed. Présence Africaine, 1955).
Chapoutot, J., *Le Grand Récit. Introduction à l'histoire de notre temps* (Presses Universitaires de France, 2021).
Châtelet, F., *Une histoire de la raison* (Editions du Seuil, 1992).
Chomsky, N., and Foucault, M., *The Chomsky-Foucault Debate on Human Nature* (The New Press, 2006).
Culler, J., *Literary Theory: A Very Short Introduction* (Oxford University Press, 1997).
Structuralist Poetics: Structuralism, Linguistics, and the Study of Literature (Routledge, 2002).

On Deconstruction: Theory and Criticism after Structuralism (Routledge, 2008).
Davies, B., and Bansel, P., 'The Time of Their Lives? Academic Workers in Neoliberal Time(s)' (2005) 14 *Health Sociology Review* 47.
Debord, G., *Commentaires sur la société du spectacle* (Gallimard, 1992).
Debray, R., *Le Scribe* (Editions Grasset et Fasquelle, 1980).
Vie et mort de l'image (Gallimard, 1992).
de Certeau, M., *L'écriture de l'histoire* (Gallimard, 1975).
La faiblesse de croire (Editions du Seuil, 1987).
L'invention du quotidien. 1. Arts de faire (Gallimard, 1990).
Histoire et psychanalyse entre science et fiction (Gallimard, 2016).
Deleuze, G., *La philosophie critique de Kant* (Presses Universitaires de France, 1963).
Proust et les signes (Presses Universitaires de France, 1964).
Différence et répétition (Presses Universitaires de France, 1968).
Critique et Clinique (Editions de Minuit, 1993).
Deleuze, G., and Guattari, F., *Qu'est-ce que la philosophie ?* (Editions de Minuit, 2019).
Deleuze, G., and Parnet, C., *Dialogues* (Champs essais, 1996).
de Man, P., *The Resistance to Theory* (University of Minnesota Press, 1986).
Derrida, J., *De la Grammatologie* (Editions de Minuit, 1967).
L'écriture et la différence (Editions du Seuil 1967).
Marges de la Philosophie (Editions de Minuit, 1972).
Positions (Editions de Minuit 1972).
Glas (Galilée, 1974).
La carte postale. De Socrate à Freud et au-delà (Flammarion, 1980).
'Des Tours de Babel', trans. J. F. Graham, in J. F. Graham (ed.), *Difference in Translation* (Cornell University Press, 1985), 165–207.
'Letter to a Japanese Friend', in D. Wood and R. Bernasconi (eds.), *Derrida and Différance* (Northwestern University Press, 1988), 1–5.
Papier Machine (Galilée, 2001).
The Beast and the Sovereign, vol 1 (University of Chicago Press, 2011).
The Beast and the Sovereign, vol 2 (University of Chicago Press, 2011).
Le dernier des Juifs (Galilée, 2014).
Théorie et pratique. Cours de l'ENS-Ulm 1975–1976 (Galilée, 2017).
Hospitalité. Volume 1 (Séminaire 1995–1996) (Editions du Seuil, 2021).
Derrida, J., and Ferraris, M., *A Taste for the Secret* (Polity Press, 2001).
Descola, P., *Par-delà nature et culture* (Gallimard, 2005).
Descombes, V., *Le Même et l'Autre. Quarante-cinq Ans de Philosophie Française (1933–1978)* (Editions de Minuit, 1979).
de Sutter, L., 'Pour une clinique', in L. de Sutter (ed.), *Postcritique* (Presses Universitaires de France, 2019), 209–238.
Superfaible. Penser aux XXIe siècle (Climats, 2023).

Dillon, B., *Essayism* (Fizcarraldo Editions, 2017).

Du Bois, W. E. B., *The World and Africa* (Oxford University Press, 2007).

Dufourmantelle, A., *Défense du secret* (Payot & Rivages, 2019).

Dumézil, G., *L'Idéologie des trois fonctions dans les épopées des peuples indo-européens* (Gallimard, 1968).

Types épiques indo-européens: Un héros, un sorcier, un roi, Paris (Gallimard, 1971).

Histoires romaines (Gallimard, 1973).

Eagleton, T., *The Function of Criticism* (Verso, 2005).

Fanon, F., *A Dying Colonialism*, trans H. Chevalier (Monthly Review Press, 1965).

The Wretched of the Earth, trans R. Philcox (Grove Press, 2004).

Felski, R., *The Limits of Critique* (University of Chicago Press, 2015).

Fenster, M., 'The Opacity of Transparency' (2006) 91 *Iowa Law Review* 885.

Feyerabend, P., *Against Method* (New Left Books, 1975).

Fish, S., *Is there a text in this class?* (Harvard University Press, 1980).

Foucault, M., *Naissance de la clinique* (Presses Universitaires de France, 1963).

Les mots et les choses (Gallimard, 1966).

L'archéologie du savoir (Gallimard, 1969).

L'ordre du discours (Gallimard, 1971).

Histoire de la Sexualité I. La volonté de savoir (Gallimard, 1976)

'Question of Method', in G. Burchell, C. Gordon, and P. Miller (eds.), *The Foucault Effect: Studies in Governmentality* (University of Chicago Press, 1991), 73–86.

'Il faut défendre la société'. Cours au Collège de France, 1976 (Gallimard, 1997).

Les anormaux. Cours au Collège de France, 1974–1975 (Gallimard, 1999).

Dits et écrits, I (1954–1975) (Gallimard, 2001).

Dits et écrits, II (Gallimard, 2001).

L'Herméneutique du Sujet. Cours au Collège de France, 1981–1982 (Editions du Seuil, 2001).

Naissance de la biopolitique. Cours au Collège de France (1978–1979) (Gallimard/Seuil, 2004).

Sécurité, Territoire, Population. Cours au Collège de France. 1977–1978 (Gallimard, 2004).

Le gouvernement de soi et des autres. Cours au Collège de France (1982–1983) (Gallimard/Seuil, 2008).

Leçons sur la volonté de savoir. Cours au Collège de France 1970–1971 (Gallimard/Seuil, 2011).

Qu'est-ce que la critique? (Vrin, 2015).

Histoire de la Sexualité IV. Les aveux de la chair (Gallimard, 2018).

Le Discours Philosophique (Gallimard/Seuil, 2023).

Freud, S., *Totem and Tabou*, 2nd edn (Routledge, 2001).

The Unconscious (Penguin Classics, 2005).

Fromm, E., *Escape from Freedom* (Henry Holt, 1969).

Gadamer, H.-G., *Truth and Method* (Bloomsbury, 2013).

Glissant, E., *Le discours antillais* (Editions du Seuil, 1981).

Poétique de la relation (Gallimard, 1990).

Goldmann, L., *Pour une sociologie du roman* (Gallimard, 1964).

Gramsci, A., *Selections from the Prison Notebooks*, trans. and ed. Q. Hoare and G. Nowell Smith (Lawrence and Wishart, 2003).

Guillaumin, C., *L'idéologie raciste. Genèse et langage actuel* (Gallimard, 2002).

Harcourt, B. *Exposed* (Harvard University Press, 2015).

Harland, R., *Superstructuralism: The Philosophy of Structuralism and Post-Structuralism* (Routledge, 1987).

Hartman, Y., and Darab, S., 'A Call for Slow Scholarship: A Case Study on the Intensification of Academic Life and Its Implications for Pedagogy' (2021) 34 *Review of Education, Pedagogy, and Cultural Studies* 49.

Hartog, F., *Régime d'historicité. Présentisme et expérience du temps* (Editions du Seuil, 2003).

Hunter, I., *Rethinking the School: Subjectivity, Bureaucracy, Criticism* (Allen & Unwin, 1994).

Jakobson, R., 'On Linguistic Aspects of Translation', in A. Fang and R. Brower (eds.), *On Translation* (Harvard University Press, 1959), 232–239.

Jullien, F., *La pensée chinoise. En vis-à-vis de la philosophie* (Gallimard, 2015).

L'incommensurable (L'observatoire, 2022).

Koselleck, R., *Kritik und Krise* (Verlag Karl Alber, 1959).

Le Règne de la Critique (Éditions de Minuit, 1979).

Kuus, M., 'For Slow Research' (2015) 39 *International Journal of Urban and Regional Research* 838.

Latour, B., *Nous n'avons jamais été modernes. Essai d'anthropologie symétrique* (La Découverte, 1997).

Pasteur: Guerre et paix des microbes (La Découverte, 2001).

La fabrique du droit. Une ethnographie du Conseil d'Etat (La Découverte, 2004).

'Why Has Critique Run out of Steam? From Matters of Facts to Matters of Concern' (2004) 30 *Critical Inquiry* 225.

La Science en action. Introduction à la sociologie des sciences (La Découverte, 2005).

Le Goff, J., 'L'homme médiéval', in J. Le Goff (ed.), *L'Homme médiéval* (Editions du Seuil, 1989), 9–28.

Legendre, P., *De la Société comme Texte. Linéaments d'une Anthropologie dogmatique* (Fayard, 2001).

Sur la question dogmatique en Occident. Aspect théoriques (Fayard, 1999).

Lecercle, J.-J., *De l'interpellation. Sujet, langue, idéologie* (Editions Amsterdam, 2019).

Lévi-Strauss, C., *Structural Anthropology, Vol. II*, trans. M. Layton (University of Chicago Press, 1976).

Levinas, E., *De l'existence à l'existant* (Vrin, 2013).

Lordon, F., *La société des affects. Pour un structuralisme des passions* (Editions du Seuil, 2013).

Lorenzini, D., *La force du vrai. De Foucault à Austin* (Le bord de l'eau, 2017).

Love, H., 'Truth and Consequences: On Paranoid Reading and Reparative Reading' (2010) 52 *Criticism* 235.

Lukács, G., *The Theory of the Novel: A Historico-philosophical Essay on the Forms of Great Epic Literature* (Merlin Press, 1971).

Lyons, M., 'New Readers in the Nineteenth Century: Women, Children, Workers', in G. Cavallo and R. Chartier (eds.), *A History of Reading in the West*, trans. L. G. Cochrane (Polity Press, 1999), 313–344.

Lyotard, J.-F., *La Condition Postmoderne* (Editions de Minuit, 1979).

Macé, M., *Façons de lire, manières d'être* (Gallimard, 2022).

MacIntyre, A., *Three Rival Version of Moral Inquiry: Encyclopaedia, Genealogy, and Tradition* (University of Notre Dame Press, 1990).

Malabou, C., and Derrida, J., *La Contre-Allée* (Paris: La Quinzaine Littéraire, 1999).

McLean, I., and Hewitt, F. (eds.), *Condorcet: Foundations of Social Choice and Political Theory* (Edward Elgar, 1994).

Mitchell, T., *Colonising Egypt* (Cambridge University Press, 1991).

Questions Of Modernity (University of Minnesota Press 2000).

Mountz, A., Bonds, A., Mansfield, B., Loyd, J., Hyndman, J., Walton-Roberts, M., and Curran, W., 'For Slow Scholarship: A Feminist Politics of Resistance through Collective Action in the Neoliberal University' (2015) 14 *An International Journal for Critical Geographies* 1235.

Murdoch, A., 'Edouard Glissant's Creolized World-Vision: From Resistance and Relation to Opacité' (2013) 26 *Callaloo* 875.

Nancy, J.-L., *Hegel, L'inquiétude du négatif* (Galilée, 2018).

Polanyi, M., *Personal Knowledge: Towards a Post-Critical Philosophy* (University of Chicago Press, 1958).

Rabau, S., *L'intertextualité* (Flammarion, 2002).

Rancière, J., *Les mots de l'histoire. Essai de poétique du savoir* (Editions du Seuil, 1992).

Le partage du sensible. Esthétique et politique (La Fabrique éditions, 2000).

L'inconscient esthétique (Galilée, 2001).

Le spectateur émancipé (La Fabrique éditions, 2008).

Ricoeur, P., *Histoire et vérité* (Editions du Seuil, 1955).

De l'interprétation. Essai sur Freud (Editions du Seuil, 1965).

Freud and Philosophy: An Essay on Interpretation, trans D. Savage (Yale University Press, 1970).

Temps et récit, Volume 1, L'intrigue et le récit historique (Editions du Seuil, 1983).

Temps et récit, Volume 2, La configuration dans le récit de fiction (Editions du Seuil, 1984).

La mémoire, l'histoire, l'oubli (Editions du Seuil, 2000).

Rose, N., *Governing the Soul: The Shaping of the Private Self* (Free Association Books, 1999).

Said, E., *The World, the Text, and the Critic* (Harvard University Press, 1983).

Culture and Imperialism (Vintage books, 1994).

Reflections on Exile and Other Literary and Cultural Essays (Granta, 2001).

Salmon, P., *An Event Perhaps* (Verso, 2020).

Samier, E., 'The Evolution of the Modern University: From Scholarship to Disenchanted Economic Handmaiden' (2010) 8 *Policy Futures in Education* 238.

Sapir, E., *Language: An Introduction to the Study of Speech* (Ishi Press, 2014).

Sarraute, N., *Tropisms and the Age of Suspicion* (Calder, 1963).

L'Ère du Soupçon (Gallimard, 1987).

Sedgwick, E. K., 'Paranoid Reading and Reparative Reading; or, You're So Paranoid, You Probably Think This Introduction Is about You', in E. Kosofsky Sedgwick (ed.), *Novel Gazing: Queer Readings in Fiction* (Duke University Press, 1997), 1–38.

Epistemology of the Closet (University of California Press, 2008).

Shatz, A., *The Rebel's Clinic: The Revolutionary Life of Frantz Fanon* (Farrar, Straus and Giroux, 2024).

Sloterdijk, P., *Critique of Cynical Reason* (University of Minnesota Press, 1987).

Spivak, G. C., *In Other Worlds: Essays in Cultural Politics* (Routledge, 2006).

Steiner, G., *Errata: An Examined Life* (Weidenfeld and Nicholson, 1997).

After Babel: Aspects of language and translation, 3rd edn (Oxford University Press, 1998).

Supiot, A., *Homo Juridicus. Essai sur la fonction anthropologique du Droit* (Editions du Seuil, 2005).

Vergès, F., *Un féminisme décolonial* (La fabrique, 2019).

Veyne, P., *Comment on écrit l'histoire* (Editions du Seuil, 1971).

Les Grecs ont-ils cru à leurs mythes? Essai sur l'imagination constituante (Editions du Seuil, 1983).

Foucault. Sa pensée, sa personne (Albin Michel, 2008).

Vigarello, G., 'Joie, tristesse, terreur . . . La mécanique classique des humeurs', in G. Vigarello (ed.), *Histoire des émotions. 1. De L'Antiquité aux Lumières* (Editions du Seuil, 2016).

Vismann, C., 'The Archive and the Beginning of Law', in P. Goodrich, F. Hoffmann, M. Rosenfeld, and C. Vismann (eds.), *Derrida and Legal Philosophy* (Palgrave, MacMillan, 2008), 99–114.

'Cultural Techniques and Sovereignty' (2013) 30 *Theory, Culture & Society* 83.

Files. Law and Media, Technology, trans. G. Winthrop-Young (Stanford University Press, 2008)

Wade, S., *Foucault in California* (Heyday, 2019).

Werner, M., and Zimmermann, B., 'Beyond Comparison: Histoire Croisée and the Challenge of Reflexivity' (2006) 45 *History and Theory* 30.

White, H., *Tropics of Discourse: Essays in Cultural Criticism* (Johns Hopkins University Press, 1978).

The Content of the Form: Narrative Discourse and Historical Representation (John Hopkins University Press, 1987)

Wittmann, R., 'Was There a Reading Revolution at the End of the Eighteenth Century', in G. Cavallo and R. Chartier (eds.), *A History of Reading in the West*, trans. L. G. Cochrane (Polity Press, 1999), 284–312.

International Law, Legal Theory, and Related Works

Aalberts, T., and Venzke, I., 'Moving Beyond Interdisciplinary Turf Wars: Towards an Understanding of International Law as Practice', in J. d'Aspremont, T. Gazzini, A. Nollkaemper, and W. Werner (eds.), *International Law as a Profession* (Cambridge Univeristy Press, 2017), 287–310.

Abebe, D., Chilton, A., and Ginsburg, T., 'The Social Science Approach to International Law' (2021) 22 *Chicago Journal of International Law* 1.

Abott, K. W., and Snidal, D., 'Hard and Soft Law in International Governance' (2000) 54 *International Organization*, 421.

Acker, S., and Armenti, C., 'Sleepless in Academia' (2004) 16 *Gender and Education* 3.

Ahlborn, C., 'The Rules of International Organizations and the Law of International Responsibility' (2011) 8 *International Organizations Law Review* 397.

Boyle, A., and McCall-Smith, K., 'Transparency in International Law-making', in A. Bianchi and A. Peters (eds.), *Transparency in International Law* (Cambridge University Press, 2013), 419–435.

Alexandrowicz, C. H., *An Introduction to the History of the Law of Nations in the East Indies* (Clarendon Press, 1967).

The Law of Nations in Global History (Oxford University Press, 2017).

Alford, R. P., 'The Proliferation of International Courts and Tribunals: International Adjudication in Ascendance' (2000) 94 *ASIL Proceedings* 160.

Allott, P., 'Language, Method and the Nature of International Law' (1971) 45 *British Yearbook of International Law* 79.

'The True Function of Law in the International Community' (1998) 5 *Global Legal Studies Journal* 391.

'The Concept of International Law' (1999) 10 *European Journal of International Law* 31.

Altwicker, T., 'International Legal Scholarship and the Challenge of Digitalization' (2019) 18 *Chinese Journal of International Law* 217.

Amaya-Castro, J.-M., and El Menyawi, H., 'Moving Away from Moving Away: A Conversation about Jacques Derrida and Legal Scholarship' (2005) 6 *German Law Journal* 101.

Anand, R. P., *Origin and Development of the Law of the Sea: History of International Law Revisited* (Martinus Nijhoff, 1983).

Anghie, A., 'Francisco De Vitoria and the Colonial Origins of International Law' (1996) 5 *Social and Legal Studies* 321.

Imperialism, Sovereignty and the Making of International Law (Cambridge University Press, 2004).

'The Evolution of International Law: Colonial and Postcolonial Realities' (2006) 27 *Third World Quarterly* 740.

'Rethinking International Law: A TWAIL Retrospective' (2023) 34 *European Journal of International Law* 7.

Arangio-Ruiz, A., 'Le domaine reservé. L'organisation internationale et le rapport entre le droit international et le droit interne. Cours générale de droit international public' (1990-IV) 225 *Collected Courses* 29.

Arsanjani, M., Cogan, J. K., Sloane, R. D., and Wiessner, S. (eds.), *Looking to the Future: Essays on International Law in Honor of W. Michael Reisman* (Brill, 2011).

Azaria, D., '*Secret Treaties in International Law and the Faith of States in Decentralized Enforcement*' (2017) *American Journal of International Law Unbound* 469.

Baker, C. D., 'Tolerance of International Espionage: A Functional Approach' (2003) 19 *American University International Law Review* 1091.

Baker, K. M., *Origins of Social Science: Condorcet. From Natural Philosophy to Social Mathematics* (University of Chicago Press, 1975).

Balkin, J. M., 'Deconstructive Practice and Legal Theory' (1987) 96 *Yale Law Journal* 743.

'Deconstruction's Legal Career' (2005) 27 *Cardozo Law Review* 719.

Barreto, J.-M., 'Cerberus: Rethinking Grotius and the Westphalian System', in M. Koskenniemi, W. Rech and M. Jimenez Fonseca (eds.), *International Law and Empire* (Oxford University Press, 2017), 149–176.

Barsalou, O., 'La doctrine de l'objecteur persistant en droit international' (2006) 19 *Revue Québécoise de droit international* 1.

Baxi, U., 'The Colonialist Heritage', in P. Legrand and R. Munday (eds.), *Comparative Legal Studies: Traditions and Transitions* (Cambridge University Press, 2003).

Baxter, R., 'International Law and Her Infinite Variety' (1980) 29 *International and Comparative Law Quarterly* 549.

Becker Lorca, A., 'Universal International Law: Nineteenth-Century Histories of Imposition and Appropriation' (2010) 51 *Harvard International Law Journal* 475.

Mestizo International Law: A Global Intellectual History 1842–1933 (Cambridge University Press, 2014).

Beckett, J., '"Rebel without a Cause" Martti Koskenniemi and the Critical Legal Project' (2006) 7 *German Law Review* 1045.

'The Politics of International Law – Twenty Years Later: A Reply', in EJIL: TALK!, 19 May 2009. www.ejiltalk.org/the-politics-of-international-law-twenty-years-later-a-reply/.

Bederman, D. J., *The Spirit of International Law* (University of Georgia Press, 2002).

International Law in Antiquity (Cambridge University Press, 2004).

Beneyto, J. M., and Kennedy, D. W., *New Approaches to International Law: The European and the American Experiences* (Springer, 2013).

Bennouna, M., 'How to Cope with the Proliferation of International Courts and Coordinate Their Action', in A. Cassese (ed.), *Realizing Utopia: The Future of International Law* (Oxford University Press, 2012), 287–294.

Benton, V., 'Made in Empire: Finding the History of International Law in Imperial Locations' (2018) 31 *Leiden Journal of International Law* 473.

Benvenisti, E., *The International Law of Occupation*, 2nd edn (Oxford University Press, 2012).

'Comments on the Systemic Vision of National Courts as Part of an International Rule of Law' (2012) 4 *Jerusalem Review of Legal Studies* 42.

Berman, N., 'In the Wake of Empire' (1999) 14 *American University International Law Review* 1515.

Besson, S., 'International Legal Theory Qua Practice of International Law', in J. d'Aspremont, T. Gazzini, A. Nollkaemper, and W. Werner (eds.), *International Law as a Profession* (Cambridge University Press, 2017), 268–284.

(ed.), 'International Courts and the Jurisprudence of Statehood' (2019) 9 *Transnational Legal Theory* 30.

(ed.), *Theories of International Responsibility Law* (Cambridge University Press, 2022).

'Democratic Representation within International Organizations: From International Good Governance to International Good Government' (2022) 19 *International Organizations Law Review* 489.

Consenting to International Law (Cambridge University Press, 2023).

Bhabba, H. K., *The Location of Culture* (Routledge, 1994).

Bianchi, A., 'The International Regulation of the Use of Force: The Politics of Interpretive Method' (2009) 22 *Leiden Journal of International Law* 665.

'Fear's Legal Dimension: Counterterrorism and Human Rights', in L. Boisson de Chazournes and M. Kohen (eds.), *International Law and the Quest for Its*

Implementation – Le droit international et la quête de sa mise en oeuvre: Liber Amicorum Vera Gowlland-Debbas (Brill, 2010), 170–189.

'Textual Interpretation and (International) Law Reading: The Myth of (In) determinacy and the Genealogy of Meaning', in P. Bekker (ed.), *Making Transnational Law Work in the Global Economy – Essays in Honour of Detlev Vagts* (Cambridge University Press, 2010), 34–56.

'On Power and Illusion: The Concept of Transparency in International Law', in A. Bianchi and A. Peters (eds.), *Transparency in International Law* (Cambridge University Press, 2013), 1–20.

International Law Theories. An Inquiry into Different Ways of Thinking (Oxford University Press, 2016)

Bianchi, A., Peat, D., and Windsor, M. R. (eds.), *Interpretation in International Law* (Oxford University Press, 2015).

Bianchi, A., and Saab, A., 'Fear and International Law-making: An Exploratory Inquiry' (2019) 32 *Leiden Journal of International Law* 351.

Bianchi, A., and Zarbiyev, F., *Demystifying Treaty Interpretation* (Cambridge University Press 2024).

Bos, M., *A Methodology of International Law* (T.M.C. Asser Instituut, 1984)

Boyle, A., and Chinkin, C., *The Making of International Law* (Oxford University Press, 2007)

Boyle, A., 'Some Reflections on the Relationship of Treaties and Soft Law' (1999) 48 *International Law and Comparative Law Quarterly* 901.

Brölmann, C., *The Institutional Veil in Public International Law: International Organisations and the Law of Treaties* (Hart, 2007)

Brower, C. N., 'Evidence before International Tribunals: The Need for Some Standard Rules' (1994) 28 *International Lawyer* 47.

Brown, C., 'The Proliferation of International Courts and Tribunals: Finding Your Way through the Maze' (2002) 21 *Melbourne Journal of International Law* 453.

Brownlie, I., 'International Law at the Fiftieth Anniversary of the United Nations: General Course on Public International Law' (1995) 255 *Collected Courses* 9.

Brunnée J., and Toope, S. J., 'International Law and Constructivism, Elements of an International Theory of International Law' (2000–2001) 39 *Columbia Journal of Transnational law* 19.

'Constructivism and International Law', in J. L. Dunoff and M. A. Pollack (eds.), *Interdisciplinary Perspectives on International Law and International Relations: The State of the Art* (Cambridge University Press, 2012), 119–145.

Brunnée, J., and Hey, E., 'Transparency and International Environmental Institutions', in A. Bianchi and A. Peters (eds.), *Transparency in International Law* (Cambridge University Press, 2013), 23–48.

Buchan, R., *Cyber Espionage and International Law* (Hart, 2018).

Buergenthal, T., 'Proliferation of International Courts and Tribunals: Is It Good or Bad?' (2001) 14 *Leiden Journal of International Law* 267.

Caddell, R., 'Secret Treaties' (2006) *Max Planck Encyclopedias of International Law*.

Carty, A., *Post-Modern Law: Enlightement, Revolution and the Death of Man* (Edinburgh University Press, 1990).

'The Corfu Channel Case – And the Missing Admiralty Orders' (2004) 3 *The Law and Practice of International Courts and Tribunals* 1.

The Philosophy of International Law (Edinburgh University Press, 2007).

The Decay of International Law. A Reappraisal of the Limits of Legal Imagination in International Affairs, with a New Introduction (Manchester University Press, 2019).

Cass, D. Z., 'Navigating the Newstream: Recent Critical Scholarship in International Law' (1996) 65 *Nordic Journal of International Law* 341.

Charlesworth, H., and Chinkin, C., *The Boundaries of International Law: A Feminist Analysis* (Manchester University Press, 2000).

Charlesworth, H., 'The Sex of the State in International Law', in N. Naffine and R. Owens (eds.), *Sexing the Subject of Law* (LBC Information Services, 1997), 25–42.

'Feminist Ambivalence about International Law' (2005) 11 *International Legal Theory* 1.

'Prefiguring Feminist Judgment in International Law', in T. Lavers and L. Hodson (eds.), *Feminist Judgments in International Law* (Hart, 2019), 34–48.

Charney, J., 'Universal International Law' (1993) 87 *American Journal of International Law* 529.

Chesterman, S., 'The Spy Who Came in from the Cold War: Intelligence and International Law' (2006) 27 *Michigan Journal of International Law* 1071.

Chimni, B. S., 'Third World Approaches to International Law: A Manifesto' (2006) 8 *International Community Law Review* 18.

International Law and World Order: A Critique of Contemporary Approaches, 2nd edn (Cambridge University Press, 2017).

'New Approaches to International Law: The Critical Scholarship of David Kennedy and Martti Koskenniemi', in B. S. Chimni (ed.), *International Law and World Order: A Critique of Contemporary Approaches* (Cambridge University Press, 2017), 246–357.

Chinkin, C., Wight, S., and Charlesworth, H., 'Feminist Approaches to International Law' (1991) 85 *American Journal of International Law* 613.

Chinkin, C., 'The Challenge of Soft Law: Development and Change in International Law' (1989) 38 *International Law and Comparative Quarterly* 850.

Coates, B. A., *Legalist Empire: International Law and American Foreign Relations in the Early Twentieth Century* (Oxford University Press, 2016).

Cohen-Jonathan, G., and Kovar, R., 'L'espionnage en temps de paix' (1960) 6 *Annuaire Français de Droit International* 239.

Collins, R., 'Classical Positivism in International Law Revisited', in J. d'Aspremont and J. Kammerhofer (eds.), *International Legal Positivism in a Post-Modern World* (Cambridge University Press, 2014).

Corten, O., *Sociologies du droit* (Dalloz, 2023).

Cot, J.-P., Pellet, A., and Forteau, M., *La Charte des Nations Unies, Commentaire article par article*, 3rd edn (Economica, 2005)

Cover, R., 'The Supreme Court, 1982 Term – Foreword: Nomos and Narrative', 97 *Harvard Law Review* 4.

Craven, M., Fitzmaurice, M., and Vogiatzi, M. (eds.), *Time, History and International Law* (Brill 2007).

Craven, M., 'Introduction: International Law and Its Histories', in M. Craven, M. Fitzmaurice and M. Vogiatzi (eds.), *Time, History and International Law* (Brill 2007), 1–25.

'The Invention of a Tradition: Westlake, the Berlin Conference and the Historicisation of International Law', in L. Nuzzo and M. Vec, *Constructing International Law: The Birth of a Discipline* (Klostermann, 2012), 1–30.

'Theorizing the Turn to History in International Law', in A. Orford and F. Hoffmann (eds.), *The Oxford Handbook of the Theory of International Law* (Oxford University Press, 2016).

Crawford, J., 'International Law as Discipline and Profession' (2012) 106 *ASIL Proceedings* 471.

Critchley, S., 'Derrida's Influence on Philosophy . . . and on My Work' (2005) 6 *German Law Journal* 25.

D'Amato, A., *The Concept of Custom in International Law* (Cornell University Press, 1971).

'What "Counts" as Law?', in N. G. Onuf (ed.), *Law-Making in the Global Community* (Carolina Academic Press, 1982), 83–99.

d'Aspremont, J., 'The Recommendations Made by the International Court of Justice' (2007) 56 *International and Comparative Law Quarterly* 185.

'The Foundations of the International Legal Order' (2007) 18 *Finnish Yearbook of International Law* 219.

L'Etat non-démocratique en droit international (Pedone, 2008).

'Softness in International Law: A Self-Serving Quest for New Legal Materials' (2008) 9 *European Journal of International Law* 1075.

Formalism and the Sources of International Law: A Theory of the Ascertainment of Legal Rules (Oxford University Press, 2011).

'The Politics of Deformalization in International Law' (2011) 3 *Goettingen Journal of International Law* 503.

'Wording in International Law' (2012) 25 *Leiden Journal of International Law* 575.

'The Idea of "Rules" in the Sources of International Law' (2014) 84 *British Yearbook of International Law* 103.

'The Law of International Organizations and the Art of Reconciliation: From Dichotomies to Dialectics' (2014) 11 *International Organizations Law Review* 428.

Epistemic Forces in International Law – Foundational Doctrines and Techniques of International Legal Argumentation (Edward Elgar, 2015).

'If International Judges Say So, It Must Be True: Empiricism or Fetishism?' (2015) 4/9 *European Society of International Law Reflections* 111.

'Martti Koskenniemi, the Mainstream and Self-Reflectivity' (2016) 29 *Leiden Journal of International Law* 29.

International Law as a Belief System (Cambridge University Press, 2017).

'The Professionalization of International Law', in J. d'Aspremont, T. Gazzini, A. Nollkaemper, and W. Werner, *International Law as a Profession* (Cambridge University Press, 2017), 19–42.

'The International Court of Justice and the Irony of System-Design' (2017) 8 *Journal of International Dispute Settlement* 366.

'What Was Not Meant to Be: General Principles of Law as a Source of International Law', in R. Pisillo Mazzeschi and P. De Sena (eds.), *Global Justice, Human Rights, and the Modernization of International Law* (Brill, 2018), 327–348.

'The International Law of Statehood and Recognition: A Post-Colonial Invention', in Giuliana Ziccardi Capaldo (ed.), *The Global Community Yearbook of International Law and Jurisprudence 2018* (Oxford University Press, 2019), 139–152.

'International Law, Universality, and the Dream of Disrupting from the Centre' (2018) 7/7 *European Society of International Law Reflections*, https://esil-sedi.eu/esil-reflection-international-law-universality-and-the-dream-of-disrupting-from-the-centre/.

The Critical Attitude and the History of International Law (The Brill, 2019).

'Bindingness', in J. d'Aspremont and S. Singh (eds.), *Concepts for International Law, Contribution to Disciplinary Thought* (Edward Elgar, 2019), 67–82.

'Critical Histories of International Law and the Repression of Disciplinary Imagination' (2019) 7 *London Review of International Law* 89.

'Three International Lawyers in a Hall of Mirrors' (2019) 32 *Leiden Journal of International Law* 367.

'Critical Histories of International Law and the Repression of Disciplinary Imagination' (2019) 7 *London Review of International Law* 89.

'The Control over Knowledge by International Courts and Arbitral Tribunals', in T. Schultz and F. Ortino (eds.), *Oxford Handbook of International Arbitration* (Oxford University Press, 2020), 328–346.

'Current Theorizations About the Treaty', in D. B. Hollis (ed.), *The Oxford Guide to Treaties*, 2nd edn (Oxford University Press, 2020), 46–58.

'International Law, Theory, and History: Ordering through Distinctions', in J. d'Aspremont (ed.), *The History and Theory of International Law*, vol 1 (Edward Elgar, 2020), 1–27.

'Comparativism and Colonizing Thinking in International Law' (2020) 57 *Canadian Yearbook of International Law* 89.

'Turntablism in the History of International Law' (2020) 22 *Journal of the History of International Law* 472.

After Meaning: The Sovereignty of Forms in International Law (Edward Elgar, 2021).

The Discourse on Customary International Law (Oxford University Press, 2021).

'A Worldly Law in a Legal World', in A. Bianchi and M. Hirsch (eds.), *International Law's Invisible Frames: Social Cognition and Knowledge Production in International Legal Processes* (Oxford University Press, 2021), 110–127.

'International Law as a Crisis Discourse: The Peril of Wordlessness', in M. Mbengue and J. d'Aspremont (eds.), *Crisis Narratives in International Law* (Brill, 2021), 17–33.

'International Legal Methods: Working for a Tragic and Cynical Routine', in R. Deplano and N. Tsagourias (eds.), *Handbook on Research Methods in International Law* (Edward Elgar, 2021), 42–59.

'The Law of Statehood as a Constellation of Hybrids', in J. Vidmar, S. McGibbon, and L. Raible (eds.), *Research Handbook on Secession* (Edward Elgar, 2022), 29–41.

'Time Travel in the Law of International Responsibility', in S. Besson (ed.), *Theories of International Responsibility Law* (Cambridge University Press, 2022), 252–276.

'International Law and the Rage against Scienticism' (2022) 33 *European Journal of International Law* 679.

'Two Attitudes towards Textuality in International Law: The Battle for Dualism' (2022) 42 *Oxford Journal of Legal Studies* 963.

The Experiences of International Organizations: A Phenomenological Approach to International Institutional Law (Edward Elgar, 2023).

'Consenting to International Law in Five Moves', in S. Besson (ed.), *Consent in International Law* (Cambridge University Press, 2023), 117–134.

'The International Court of Justice as the Master of the Sources', in C. Espósito and K. Parlett (eds.), *The Cambridge Companion to the International Court of Justice* (Cambridge University Press, 2023), 210–228.

'The Love for International Organizations' (2023) 20 *International Organizations Law Review* 111.

'The Chivalric Pursuit of Coherence in International Law' (2024) 37 *Leiden Journal of International Law* 191.

'International Legal Positivism and the European Quest for Scientificity', in A. van Aaken, P. d'Argent, L. Mälksoo, and J. J. Vasel (eds.), *Oxford Handbook of International Law in Europe* (Oxford University Press, 2025), 253–272.

'International Law and Its Critical Misrepresentations' (2024) 2 *Journal du Droit Transnational.*

d'Aspremont, J., and Dopagne, F., 'Two Constitutionalisms in Europe: Pursuing an Articulation of the European and International Legal Orders' (2008) 68 *Heidelberg Journal of International Law* (ZaÖRV) 939.

d'Aspremont, J., and Mbengue, M. M., 'Strategies of Engagement with Scientific Fact-Finding in International Adjudication' (2014) *Journal of International Dispute Settlement* 240.

d'Aspremont, J., and Singh, S. (eds.), *Concepts for International Law: Contributions to Disciplinary Thought* (Edward Elgar, 2019).

de la Rasilla del Moral, I., 'Martti Koskenniemi and The Spirit of the Beehive in International Law' (2010) 10 *Global Jurist* 1.

'The Ambivalent Shadow of the Pre-Wilsonian Rise of International Law' (2014) 7 *European Law Review* 2.

de Nanteuil, A., 'La transparence en droit international: Réflexions sur une exigence encore incertaine' (2015) 61 *Annuaire français de droit international* 809.

de Saussure, F., *Course in General Linguistics*, Charles Bally and Albert Sechehaye (eds.) (Open Court, 1986).

Degan, V., *Sources of International Law* (Kluwer Law International, 1997).

Delaney, J., and Barstow Magraw, D., 'Procedural Transparency', in P. Muchlinski, F. Ortino, and C. Schreuer (eds.), *Oxford Handbook of International Investment Law* (Oxford University Press, 2008), 721–788.

Delimatsis, P., 'Institutional Transparency in the WTO', in A. Bianchi and A. Peters (eds.), *Transparency in International Law* (Cambridge University Press, 2013), 104–128.

Desautels-Stein, J., 'Structuralist Legal Histories' (2015) 78 *Law and Contemporary Problems* 37.

'International Legal Structuralism: A Primer' (2016) 8 *International Theory* 201.

The Right to Exclude: A Critical Race Approach to Sovereignty, Borders, and International Law (Oxford Universtiy Press, 2023).

Desautels-Stein, J., and Rasulov, A., 'Deep Cuts: Four Critiques of Legal Ideology' (2021) 31 *Yale Journal of Law & the Humanities* 435.

Devaney, J. G., 'A Coherence Framework for Fact-finding before the International Court of Justice' (2023) 36 *Leiden Journal of International Law* 1073.

Donaldson, M., 'The Survival of the Secret Treaty: Publicity, Secrecy, and Legality in the International Order' (2017) 111 *American Journal of International Law* 575.

Donaldson, M., and Kingsbury, B., 'Power and the Public: The Nature and Effects of Formal Transparency Policies in Global Governance Institutions', in A. Bianchi and A. Peters (eds.), *Transparency in International Law* (Cambridge University Press, 2013), 502–533.

Dopagne, F., 'Retour sur un "Classique" - M. Virally, "La notion de fonction dans la théorie de "l'organization internationale"' (2011) *Revue Générale de Droit International Public* 285.

Dumberry, P., 'Incoherent and Ineffective: The Concept of Persistent Objector Revisited' (2010) 59 *International and Comparative Law Quarterly* 779.

Dunoff, J., 'From Interdisciplinarity to Counterdisciplinarity: Is There Madness in Martti's Method?' (2013) 27 *Temple Journal of International and Comparative Law* 309.

Dunoff, J., and Pollack, M. A., 'Introduction to International Legal Theory: Taking Stock, Looking Ahead', in J. L. Dunoff and M. A. Pollack (eds.), *International Legal Theory: Foundations and Frontiers* (Cambridge University Press, 2022), 3–36.

Dupuy, P.-M., 'L'unité de l'ordre juridique international: cours général de droit international public' (2002) 297 *Collected Courses* 9.

Dupuy, R.-J., 'Declaratory Law and Programmatory Law: From Revolutionary Custom to "Soft Law"', in R. J. Akkerman, P. J. van Krieken, and C. O. Pannenborg (eds.), *Declarations on Principles. A Quest for Universal Peace. Liber Amicorum discipulorumque Prof. Dr. Bert. V.A. Röling* (Sijthoff, 1977), 247–257.

Ebbesson, J., 'Global or European Only? International Law on Transparency in Environmental Matters for Members of the Public', in A. Bianchi and A. Peters (eds.), *Transparency in International Law* (Cambridge University Press, 2013), 49–74.

Ehring, L., 'Public Access to Dispute Settlement Hearings in the World Trade Organization' (2008) 11 *Journal of International Economic Law* 1021.

Elías, T. O., *Africa and the Development of International Law* (Sijthoff, 1972).

Elias, C. L., and Lim, O., *The Paradox of Consensualism in International Law* (Kluwer Law International, 1998).

Engle, K., Nesiah, V., and Otto, D., 'Feminist Approaches to International Law', in J. L. Dunoff and M. A. Pollack (eds.), *International Legal Theory. Foundations and Frontiers* (Cambridge University Press, 2022), 174–202.

Erlanger, H., Garth, B., Larson, J., Mertz, E., Nourse, V., and Wilkins, D., 'New Legal Realism Symposium: Is It Time for a New Legal Realism?' (2005) 2 *Wisconsin Law Review* 335.

Esquirol, J., 'Making the Critical Moves: A Top Ten in Progressive Legal Scholarship' (2021) 92 *University of Colorado Law Review* 1089.

Falk, R., *The End of World Order: Essays on Normative International Relations* (Holmes & Meier, 1983).

Fallah, S. M., 'The Admissibility of Unlawfully Obtained Evidence before International Courts and Tribunals' (2020) 19 *The Law and Practice of International Courts and Tribunals* 147.

Fassbender, B., and Peters, A., *The Oxford Handbook of the History of International Law* (Oxford University Press, 2012).

Fidler, D. P., 'Revolt against or from within the West? TWAIL, the Developing World, and the Future Direction of International Law' (2003) 2 *Chinese Journal of International Law* 29.

Fitzmaurice, G., 'Some Problems Regarding the Formal Sources of International Law', in *Symbolae Verzijl* (Martinus Nijhoff, 1958), 153–176.

Florini, A., 'The End of Secrecy' (1998) 112 *Foreign Policy* 50.

Forray, V., and Pimont, S., *Décrire le droit … et le transformer. Essai sur la décriture du droit* (Dalloz, 2017).

Forteau, M., 'L'Etat selon le droit international: Une figure à géométrie variable' (2007) 4 *Revue générale de droit international public* 737.

Franck, T., *Fairness in International Law and Institutions* (Clarendon Press, 1995).

Frankenberg, G., 'Critical Comparisons: Re-thinking Comparative Law' (1985) 26 *Harvard International Law Journal* 411.

Galindo, F., 'Martti Koskenniemi and the Historiographical Turn in International Law' (2005) 16 *European Journal of International Law* 539.

Garcia-Salmones, M., *The Project of Positivism in International Law* (Oxford University Press, 2013).

Gattini, A., 'Evidentiary Issues in the ICJ's Genocide Case' (2007) 5 *Journal of International Criminal Justice* 889.

Gattini A., and Cortesi, G., 'Some New Evidence on the ICJ's Treatment of Evidence: The Second Genocide Case' (2015) 28 *Leiden Journal of International Law* 899.

Gautier, P., *Essai sur la définition des traités entre Etats* (Bruylant, 1993).

Goldmann, G. 'The Ambiguity of Colonial International Law: Three Approaches to the Namibian Genocide' (2024) 37 *Leiden Journal of International Law* 1.

Goodrich, P., 'Law and Modernity' (1986) 49 *The Modern Law Review* 545.

'Europe in America: Grammatology, Legal Studies, and the Politics of Transmission' (2001) 101 *Columbia Law Review* 2033.

Goodrich, P., Hoffmann, F., Rosenfeld, M., and Vismann, C., 'Introduction: A Philosophy of Legal Enigmas', in P. Goodrich, F. Hoffmann, M. Rosenfeld, and C. Vismann (eds.), *Derrida and Legal Philosophy* (Palgrave MacMillan, 2008), 1–20.

Gosnell, C., 'Admissibility of Evidence', in K. Khan, C. Buisman, and C. Gosnell (eds.), *Principles of Evidence in International Criminal Justice* (Oxford University Press, 2010), 375–444.

Gray, C., *International Law and the Use of Force*, 3rd edn (Oxford University Press, 2008).

Grewe, W., *The Epochs of International Law*, trans. M. Byers (de Gruyter, 2000).

Guillaume, G., 'La Cour Internationale de Justice. Quelques propositions concrètes à l'occasion du cinquantenaire' (1996) 100 *Revue générale de droit International Public* 323.

Habermas, J., *The Philosophical Discourse of Modernity. Twelve Lectures*, trans. F. Lawrence (Polity Press, 1987).

Haskell, J., 'Hugo Grotius in the Contemporary Memory of International Law: Secularism, Liberalism, and the Politics of Restatement and Denial', in J. M. Beneyto, D. Kennedy, J. Corti Varela, and J. Haskell (eds.), *New Approaches to International Law: The European and the American Experiences* (T.M.C Asser /Springer, 2012).

Haskell, J., and Rasulov, A., 'International Law and the Turn to Political Economy' (2018) 31 *Leiden Journal of International Law* 243.

Hernandez, G., 'Interpretation', in J. Kammerhofer and J. d'Aspremont (eds.), *International Legal Positivism in a Postmodern World* (Cambridge University Press, 2014), 317–348.

'The Responsibility of the International Legal Academic: Situating the Grammarian within the "Invisible College"', in J. d'Aspremont, T. Gazzini, A. Nollkaemper, and W. Werner (eds.), *International Law as a Profession* (Cambridge University Press, 2017), 160–188.

Hertogen, A., 'Letting Lotus Bloom' (2015) 26/4 *European Journal of International Law* 901.

Higgins, R., *Problems and Process: International Law and How We Use It* (Oxford University Press, 1995).

Hinojosa Martinez, L. M., 'Transparency in International Financial Institutions', in A. Bianchi and A. Peters (eds.), *Transparency in International Law* (Cambridge Univeristy Press, 2013), 77–104.

Hoffmann, F., 'Epilogue: In Lieu of Conclusion' (2005) 6 *German Law Journal* 197.

Holtermann, J. V. H., and Rask Madsen, M., 'Toleration, Synthesis or Replacement? The "Empirical Turn" and Its Consequences for the Science of International Law' (2016) 29 *Leiden Journal of International Law* 1001.

Hood, C., 'Transparency in Historical Perspective', in C. Hood and D. Heald (eds.), *Transparency: The Key to Better Governance?* (Oxford University Press, 2006), 2–23.

Hovell, D., 'The Elements of International Legal Positivism' (2022) 75 *Current Legal Problems* 71.

Hume, D., *A Treatise of Human Nature* (Oxford University Press, 2011).

Jacobs, F., 'Judicial Dialogue and the Cross-Fertilization of Legal System: The European Court of Human Rights' (2008) 38 *Texas International Law Journal* 547.

Jacqué, J.-P., *Elements pour une théorie de l'acte juridique en Droit international public* (LGDJ, 1972).

Jeffery, R., *Hugo Grotius in International Thought* (Palgrave MacMillan, 2006).

Jenks, C.W., *The Common Law of Mankind* (Stevens & Sons, Ltd, 1958).

Jennings, R. Y., 'Nullity and Effectiveness in International Law', in *Cambridge Essays in International Law: Essays in honour of Lord McNair* (Stevens & Sons, Ltd, 1965), 64–82.

'What Is International Law and How Do We Tell It When We See It?' (1981) 37 *Schweizerisches Jahrbuch fur Internationales Recht* 59.

'The Identification of International Law', in B. Cheng (eds.), International Law: Teaching and Practice (Stevens & Sons, Ltd 1982), 3–18.

Johns, F., 'Critical International Legal Theory', in J. L. Dunoff and M. A. Pollack (eds.), *International Legal Theory. Foundations and Frontiers* (Cambridge University Press, 2022), 133–152.

Johnstone, I., and Ratner, S. R., 'International Legal Argumentation: Practice in Need of a Theory', in I. Johnstone and S. R. Ratner (eds.), *Talking International Law: Legal Argumentation Outside the Courtroom* (Oxford University Press, 2021), 3–24.

Jouannet, E., 'Présentation critique', in M. Koskenniemi (eds.), *La Politique du Droit International* (Pedone, 2007), 7–46.

'Universalism and Imperialism: The True-False Paradox of International Law?' (2007) 18 *European Journal of International Law* 379.

'A Critical Introduction', in M. Koskenniemi, *The Politics of International Law* (Hart, 2011), 1–32.

Kelsen, H., 'Theorie du droit international public'(1953-III) 84 *Collected Courses* 1.

Kennedy, D. W., 'Critical Theory, Structuralism and Contemporary Legal Scholarship' (1985–1986) 21 *New England Law Review* 209.

International Legal Structures (Nomos, 1987).

'A New Stream of International Law Scholarship' (1988) 7 *Wisconsin International Law Journal* 1.

'The Disciplines of International Law and Policy' (1999) 12 *Leiden Journal of International Law* 9.

'When Renewal Repeats: Thinking against the Box' (2000) 32 *New York University Journal of International Law and Politics* 335–499.

'Tom Franck and the Manhattan School' (2003) 35 *New York University Journal of International Law and Politics* 397.

Of War and Law (Princeton University Press, 2006).

'The Hermeneutic of Suspicion in Contemporary American Legal Thought' (2014) 25 *Law Critique* 91.

A World of Struggle: How Power, Law, and Expertise Shape Global Political Economy (Princeton University Press, 2016).

Kidd White, E., 'Images of Reach, Range, and Recognition: Thinking about Emotions in the Study of International Law', in S. A. Bandes, J. Lynee Madeira, K. Temple, and E. Kidd White (eds.), *Research Handbook on Law and Emotion* (Edward Elgar, 2021), 35–69.

Kingsbury, B., 'Is the Proliferation of International Courts and Tribunals a Systemic Problem?' (1999) 31 *New York University Journal of International Law and Politics* 679.

'The Concept of "Law" in Global Administrative Law' (2009) 20 *European Journal of International Law* 1.

Kingsbury, B., Krisch, K., and Stewart, R. B., 'The Emergence of Global Administrative Law' (2005) 68 *Law and Contemporary Problems* 15.

Kish, J., *International Law and Espionage* (Martinus Nijhoff, 1995).

Kiss, A., 'Les traités-cadres: Une technique juridique caractéristique du droit international de l'environnement' (1993) 39 *Annuaire français de droit international* 792.

Klaaren, J., 'The Human Right to Information and Transparency', in A. Bianchi and A. Peters (eds.), *Transparency in International Law* (Cambridge University Press, 2013).

Klabbers, J., *The Concept of Treaty in International Law* (Kluwer Law International, 1996).

'The Relative Autonomy of International Law and The Forgotten Politics of Interdisciplinarity' (2004) 1 *Journal of International Law and International Relations* 35.

'Two Concepts of International Organization' (2005) 2 *International Organizations Law Review* 277.

'Constitutionalism and the Making of International Law' (2008) 5 *NoFo* 84.

'The Paradox of International Institutional Law' (2008) 5 *International Organization Law Review* 151.

'Two Contending Approaches to the Law of International Organizations', in J. Klabbers and A. Wallendahl (eds.), *Research Handbook on International Organizations Law: Between Functionalism and Constitutionalism* (Edward Elgar, 2010), 1–28.

'The Ethics of Inter-disciplinarity and the Academic Industry' (on file with the author).

Klein, P., and Corten, O. (eds.), *Les Conventions de Vienne sur le Droit des Traités. Commentaire article par article* (Bruylant, 2006).

Kleinlein, T., 'International Legal Thought: Creation of a Tradition and the Potential of Disciplinary Self-Reflection', in G. Ziccardi Capaldo, *The Global Community: Yearbook of International Law and Jurisprudence 2016* (Oxford University Press, 2016), 811–828.

Knop, K., 'Borders of the Imagination: The State in Feminist International Law' (1994) 88 *Proceedings of the Annual Meeting (American Society of International Law)* 14.

Koch, C., 'Judicial Dialogue for Legal Multiculturalism' (2004) 25 *Michigan Journal of International Law* 979.

Kochi, T., *The Other's War: Recognition and the Violence of Ethics* (Birkbeck Law Press, 2009).

Kohen, M. G. (ed.), *Secession: International Law Perspectives* (Cambridge University Press, 2006).

Koskenniemi, M., 'Theory: Implications for the Practitioner', in P. Allott, T. Carty, M. Koskenniemi, and C. Warbrick, *Theory and International Law: An Introduction* (The British Institute of International and Comparative Law and International Law Group, Society of Public Teachers of Law, 1991), 41–75.

'Repetition as Reform' (1998) 9 *European Journal of International Law* 405.

'Between Commitment and Cynicism: Outline for a Theory of International Law as Practice', in *Collection of Essays by Legal Advisers of States, Legal Adviser of International Organizations and Practitioners in the Field of International Law* (Office of Legal Affairs, United Nations, 1999), 495–523.

'Letter to the Editors of the Symposium' (1999) 93 *American Journal of International Law* 351.

The Gentle Civilizer of Nations: The Rise and Fall of International Law 1870–1960 (Cambridge University Press, 2002).

'What Is International Law For?', in M. D. Evans (ed.), *International Law* (Oxford University Press, 2003), 89–114.

From Apology to Utopia: The Structure of International Legal Argument (Cambridge University Press, 2005).

'What Is International Law For?', in M. D. Evans (ed.), *International Law*, 2nd edn (Oxford: Oxford University Press, 2006), 57–82.

'Constitutionalism as Mindset: Reflections on Kantian Themes about International Law and Globalization' (2006) 8 *Theoretical Inquiries in Law* 9.

'Constitutionalism, Managerialism and the Ethos of Legal Education' (2007) 1 *European Journal of Legal Studies* 1.

'The Fate of International Law: Between Technique and Politics' (2007) 70 *Modern Law Review* 1.

'Into Positivism: Georg Friedrich von Martens (1756–1821) and Modern International Law' (2008) 15 *Constellations* 189.

'The Politics of International Law – 20 Years Later' (2009) 20 *European Journal of International Law* 7.

'Miserable Comforters: International Relations as New Nature Law' (2009) 15 *European Journal of International Relations* 395.

'Law, Teleology and International Relations: An Essay in Counterdisciplinarity' (2011) 26 *International Relations* 3.

'The Mystery of Legal Obligation' (2011) 3 *International Theory* 319.

'Histories of International Law: Significance and Problems for a Critical View' (2013) 27 *Temple International and Comparative Law Journal* 215.

'International Law and the Emergence of Mercantile Capitalism: Grotius to Smith', in P.-M. Dupuy and V. Chetail (eds.), *The Roots of International Law: Liber Amicorum Peter Haggenmacher* (Martinus Nijhoff, 2014), 3–37.

'Between Commitment and Cynicism: Outline for a Theory of International Law as Practice', in J. d'Aspremont, T. Gazzini, A. Nollkaemper, and W. Werner (eds.), *International Law as a Profession* (Cambridge University Press, 2017).

'Imagining the Rule of Law: Rereading the Grotian "Tradition"' (2019) 30 *European Journal of International Law* 17.

To the Uttermost Parts of the Earth (Cambridge University Press, 2021).

Koskenniemi, M., and Schmitt, C., 'Hans Morgenthau and the Image of Law in International Relations', in M. Byers (ed.) *The Role of Law in International Politics: Essays in International Relations and International Law* (Oxford University Press, 2000), 17–34.

Krisch, N., *Beyond Constitutionalism: The Pluralist Structure of Postnational Law* (Oxford University Press, 2010).

Kumm, M., 'The Legitimacy of International Law: A Constitutionalist Framework of Analysis' (2004) 15 *European Journal of International Law* 917.

Lafouasse, F., *L'espionnage dans le droit international* (Nouveau Monde Éditions, 2012).

Laghmani, S., 'Les Origines du droit international public et le concept de discours fondateur', in P.-M. Dupuy and V. Chetail (eds.), *The Roots of International Law. Liber Amicorum Peter Haggenmacher* (Martinus Nijhoff, 2014), 449–464.

Lando, M., 'Secret Custom *or* the Impact of Judicial Deliberations on the Identification of Customary International Law' (2022) 81 *The Cambridge Law Journal* 550.

Lauterpacht, H., *The Function of Law in the International Community* (Oxford: Clarendon Press, 1933).

'The Grotian Tradition in International Law' (1946) 23 *The British Yearbook of International Law* 1.

'Restrictive Interpretation and the Principle of Effectiveness in the Interpretation of Treaties' (1949) 26 *British Yearbook of International Law* 48.

'Some Observations on the Prohibition of "Non Liquet" and the Completeness of the Law', in *Symbolae Verzijl* (Martinus Nijhoff, 1958), 196–221.

The Function of Law in the International Community (Oxford University Press, republished in 2010).

Legrand, P., 'The Same and the Different', in Pierre Legrand and Roderick Munday (eds.), *Comparative Legal Studies: Traditions and Transitions* (Cambridge University Press, 2003), 240–311.

'Comparative Legal Studies and the Matter of Authenticity' (2006) 1 *Journal of Comparative Law* 365.

'"Il n'y a pas de hors-texte": Intimations of Jacques Derrida as Comparatist-at-Law', in P. Goodrich, F. Hoffmann, M. Rosenfeld, and C. Vismann (eds.), *Derrida and Legal Philosophy* (Palgrave MacMillan, 2008), 191–210.

'Foreign Law: Understanding Understanding' (2011) 6 *Journal of Comparative Law* 67.

Negative Comparative Law: A Strong Programme for Weak Thought (Cambridge University Press, 2022).

Lesaffer, R., 'The Classical Law of Nations (1500–1800)', in A. Orakhelashvili (ed.), *Research Handbook on the Theory and History of International Law* (Edward Elgar 2011), 408–440.

Lythgoe, G., *The Rebirth of Territory* (Cambridge University Press, 2024).

Macaulay, S., 'The New versus the Old Legal Realism: Things Ain't What They Used to Be' (2005) 2 *Wisconsin Law Review* 365.

Mainetti, V., 'Les traités secrets en droit international', in P. Zen Ruffinen (ed.), *Les secrets et le droit* (Schulthess, 2004).

Maupin, J., 'Transparency in International Investment Law: The Good, the Bad and the Murky', in A. Bianchi and A. Peters (eds.), *Transparency in International Law* (Cambridge University Press, 2013), 142–171.

Mbengue, M. M. and d'Aspremont, J. (eds.), *Crisis Narratives in International Law* (Brill, 2022).

Mbengue, M. M., and Tignino, M., 'Public Participation and Amicus Curiae in Water Disputes', in E. Brown Weiss, L. Boisson de Chazournes, and N. Bernasconi-Osterwalder (eds.), *Fresh Water and International Economic Law* (Oxford University Press, 2005), 307–405.

McDougal, M. S., 'International Law and the Future' (1979) 50 *Mississippi Law Journal* 259.

Megret, F., 'International Law as Law', in J. Crawford and M. Koskenniemi (eds.), *Cambridge Companion to International Law* (Cambridge University Press, 2012), 67–92.

Miéville, C., *Between Equal Rights: A Marxist Theory of International Law* (Haymarket Books, 2006).

Milanovic, M., 'Human Rights Treaties and Foreign Surveillance: Privacy in the Digital Age' (2015) 56 *Harvard International Law Journal* 81.

Monateri, P. G., 'Black Gaius: A Quest for Multicultural Origins of the "Western Legal Tradition"' (2000) 51 *Hastings Law Journal* 479.

Montejo, B., 'The Notion of "Effective Control" under the Articles on the Responsibility of International Organizations', in M. Ragazzi (ed.),

Responsibility of International Organizations: Essays in Memory of Sir Ian Brownlie (Martinus Nijhoff, 2013), 387–404.

Morgan, E., *The Aesthetics of International Law* (University of Toronto Press, 2007).

Morgenthau, H., *Politics among Nations* (Alfred A. Knopf, 1950).

Moulin, T., *Cyber-espionage in International Law: Silence Speaks* (Manchester University Press, 2023).

Muir Watt, H., 'Globalization and Comparative Law', in M. Reimann and R. Zimmermann (eds.), *The Oxford Handbook of Comparative Law* (Oxford University Press, 2007), 579–608.

Muller, A.S., Rai, D., and Thuránszky, J. M. (eds.), *The International Court of Justice: Its Future Role after Fifty Years* (Martinus Nijhoff, 1997).

Mutua, M., 'Savages, Victims and Saviors: The Metaphor of Human Rights' (2001) 42 *Harvard International Law Journal* 201.

'What Is TWAIL?' (2000) 94 *American Society of International Law Proceedings* 31.

Navarrete, I., 'L'espionnage en temps de paix en droit international public' (2016) 53 *Canadian Yearbook of International Law* 1.

Neff, S. C., *Justice among Nations: A History of International Law* (Harvard University Press, 2014).

Neumann, T., and Simma, B., 'Transparency in International Adjudication', in A. Bianchi and A. Peters (eds.), *Transparency in International Law* (Cambridge University Press, 2013), 436–476.

Nourse, V., and Shaffer, G., 'Varieties of New Legal Realism: Can A New World Order Prompt a New Legal Theory' (2009) 95 *Cornell Law Review* 61.

Nouvel, Y., 'Les relations économiques internationales à l'heure de la transparence', in J.-M. Sorel (ed.), *Le droit international économique à l'aube du xxie siècle. En hommage aux professeurs Dominique Carreau et Patrick Juillard* (Pedone, 2009), 211–230.

Nuzzo, L., 'The Birth of an Imperial Location: Comparative Perspectives on Western Colonialism in China' (2018) 31 *Leiden Journal of International Law* 569.

Obregon, L., 'Empire, Racial Capitalism and International Law: The Case of Manumitted Haiti and the Recognition Debt' (2018) 31 *Leiden Journal of International Law* 597.

Onuf, N., *World of Our Making: Rules and Rules in Social Theory and International Relations* (University of South Carolina Press, South Carolina, 1989).

'The Constitution of International Society' (1994) 5 *European Journal of International Law* 1.

Oppenheim, L., 'The Science of International Law: Its Task and Method' (1908) 2 *American Journal of International Law* 313.

Orakhelashvili, A., *The Interpretation of Acts and Rules in Public International Law* (Oxford University Press, 2008).

Orford, A., *Reading Humanitarian Intervention. Human Rights and the Use of Force in International Law* (Cambridge University Press, 2003).

International Law and Its Others (Cambridge University Press, 2006).

'On International Legal Method' (2013) 1 *London Review of International Law* 166.

'Scientific Reason and the Discipline of International Law' (2014) 25 *European Journal of International Law* 369.

'International Law and the Limits of History', in W. Werner, M. de Hoon and A. Galan (eds.), *The Law of International Lawyers: Reading Martti Koskenniemi* (Cambridge University Press, 2015), 297–320.

'Scientific Reason and the Discipline of International Law', in J. d'Aspremont, T. Gazzini, A. Nollkaemper, and W. Werner (eds.), *International Law as a Profession* (Cambridge University Press, 2017), 93–114.

International Law and the Politics of History (Cambridge University Press, 2021).

Otto, D., 'Resisting the Heteronormative Imaginary of the Nation-State. Rethinking Kinship and Border protection', in D. Otto (ed.), *Queering International Law: Possibilities, Alliances, Complicities* (Routledge, 2018), 222–240.

Pahuja, S., 'The Postcoloniality of International Law' (2005) 46 *Harvard International Law Journal* 459.

Decolonising International Law: Development, Economic Growth and the Politics of Universality (Cambridge University Press, 2011).

'Decolonization and the Eventness of International Law', in F. Johns, R. Joyce, and S. Pahuja (eds.), *Events: The Force of International Law* (Routledge, 2011), 91–106.

Paparinski, M., *The International Minimum Standard and Fair and Equitable Treatment* (Oxford University Press, 2013).

Parfitt, R., *The Process of International Legal Reproduction. Inequality, Historiography, Resistance* (Cambridge University Press 2019).

Pellet, A., 'Article 38', in A. Zimmermann, C. J. Tams, K. Oellers-Frahm, and C. Tomuschat (eds.), *The Statute of the International Court of Justice* (Oxford University Press, 2002), 731–870.

'Complementarity of International Treaty Law, Customary Law and Non-Contractual Law-Making' in R. Wolfrum and V. Röben (eds.), *Developments of International Law in Treaty Making* (Springer, 2005), 411–424.

'Lotus que de sottises on profère en ton nom! Remarques sur le concept de souveraineté dans la jurisprudence de la Cour mondiale', in E. Belliard (ed.), *Mélanges en l'honneur de Jean-Pierre Puissochet : l'État souverain dans le monde d'aujourd'hui* (Pedone, 2008), 114–151.

'Cours général: Le droit international entre souveraineté et communauté internationale' (2007) *Anuário Brasileiro de Direito Internacional* II.

Peters, A., 'Towards Transparency as a Global Norm', in A. Bianchi and A. Peters (eds.), *Transparency in International Law* (Cambridge University Press, 2013), 534–607.

'International Legal Scholarship Under Challenge', in J. d'Aspremont, T. Gazzini, A. Nollkaemper, and W. Werner (eds.), *International Law as a Profession* (Cambridge University Press, 2017), 111–159.

Picker, C. B., Bunn, I., and Arner, D. (eds.), *International Economic Law - The State and Future of the Discipline* (Hart, 2008).

Piotrowski, S. J., *Transparency and Secrecy: A Reader Linking Literature and Contemporary Debate* (Lexington Books, 2010).

Prost, M., *The Concept of Unity in Public International Law* (Hart, 2012).

Purcell, K., 'Faltering at the Critical Turn to History: "Juridical Thinking" in International Law and Genealogy as History, Critique, and Therapy' (2016) 2/15 *Jean Monnet Working Paper Series* 1.

Raič, D., *Statehood and the Law of Self-Determination* (Kluwer Law International, 2002).

Rajkovic, N., 'Rules, Lawyering, and the Politics of Legality: Critical Sociology and International Law's Rule' (2014) 27 *Leiden Journal of International Law* 331.

Rasulov, A., 'New Approaches to International Law: Images of a Genealogy', in M. Jose Beneyto and D. Kennedy (eds.), *New Approaches to International Law: The European and the American Experiences* (T.M.C Asser/Springer, 2012).

'From Apology to Utopia and the Inner Life of International Law' (2016) 29 *Leiden Journal of International Law* 641.

'What Is Critique? Towards a Sociology of Disciplinary Heterodoxy in Contemporary International Law', in J. d'Aspremont, T. Gazzini, A. Nollkaemper, and W. Werner (eds.), *International Law as a Profession* (Cambridge University Press, 2017), 189–221.

'A Marxism for International Law: A New Agenda' (2018) 29 *European Journal of International Law* 631.

'Imperialism', in J. d'Aspremont and S. Singh (eds.), *Concepts for International Law: Contributions to Disciplinary Thought* (Edward Elgar, 2019), 422–446.

Raustiala, K., 'Form and Substance in International Agreements' (2005) 99 *American Journal of International Law* 581.

Rech, W., 'Ideology', in J. d'Aspremont and S. Singh (eds.), *Concepts for International Law: Contributions to Disciplinary Thought* (Edward Elgar, 2019), 339–412.

Rech, W., and Jimenez Fonseca, M. (eds.), *International Law and Empire* (Oxford University Press, 2017).

Reed L., and Jacovides, A., 'Great Expectations: Where Does the Proliferation of International Dispute Resolution Leave International Law' (2002) 96 *ASIL Proceedings* 219.

Reisman, W. M., 'The View from the New Haven School of International Law' (1992) 86 *ASIL Proceedings* 118.

Reisman, W. M., and Skinner, C. P., *Fraudulent Evidence before Public International Tribunals: The Dirty Stories of International Law* (Cambridge University Press, 2014).

Reisman, W. M., Wiessner, S., and Willard, A., 'The New Haven School: A Brief Introduction' (2007) 32 *Yale Journal of International Law* 576.

Reuter, P., 'Le droit au secret et les institutions internationales' (1956) 2 *Annuaire français de droit international* 46.

Riddell, A., and Plant, B., *Evidence before the International Court of Justice* (British Institute of International and Comparative Law, 2016).

Roberts, A., 'Traditional and Modern Approaches to Customary International Law: A Reconciliation' (2001) 95 *American Journal of International Law* 757.

Is International Law International? (Oxford University Press, 2017).

Roberts, A., Stephan, P. B., Verdier, P.-H., and Versteeg M., 'Comparative International Law: Framing the Field' (2015) 109 *American Journal of International Law* 467.

(eds.), *Comparative International Law* (Oxford University Press, 2018).

Rodell, F., 'Goodbye to Law Reviews' (1936) 23 *Virginia Law Review* 38.

'Goodbye to Law Reviews – Revisited' (1962) 48 *Virginia Law Review* 279.

Saab, A., 'Emotions and International Law' (2021) 10/3 *ESIL Reflections*, https://esil-sedi.eu/esil-reflection-emotions-and-international-law/.

Sands, P., *East West Street: On the Origins of Genocide and Crimes against Humanity* (Weidenfeld & Nicolson, 2016).

Schachter, O., 'The Twilight Existence of Non-binding International Agreements' (1977) 71 *American Journal of International Law* 296.

Schlag, P., '"Le Hors de Texte, C'est Moi": The Politics of Form and the Domestication of Deconstruction' (1990) 11 *Cardozo Law Review* 1631.

'Normative and Nowhere to Go' (1990) 43 *Stanford Law Review* 167.

'The Aesthetics of American Law' (2002) 115 *Harvard Law Review* 1047.

'Spam Jurisprudence, Air Law, and the Rank of Anxiety of Nothing Happening (A Report on the State of the Art)' (2009) 97 *Georgia Law Journal* 803.

'The Law Review Article' (2017) 88 *University of Colorado Law Review* 1043.

Schrijver, N., 'The Future of the United Nations' (2006) 10 *Max Planck Yearbook of United Nations Law* 1.

Schwarzenberger, G., 'Myths and Realities in Treaty Interpretation' (1968) 9 *Virginia Journal of International Law* 1.

Scobbie, I., 'The Theorist as Judge: Hersch Lauterpacht's Concept of the International Judicial Function' (1997) 8 *European Journal of International Law* 264.

Scott, D. M., 'History as Deconstruction, History as Reconstruction: Time and Structure in Critical International Law' (2022) 35 *Hague Yearbook of International Law* 109.

Shaffer, G., and Ginsburg, T., 'The Empirical Turn in International Legal Scholarship' (2012) 106 *American Journal of International Law* 1.

Shaffer, G., 'A New Legal Realism: Method in International Economic Law Scholarship', in C. B. Picker, I. Bunn, and D. Arner (eds.), *International Economic Law – The State and Future of the Discipline* (Hart, 2008), 29–42.

Shahabuddin, M., 'The "Standard of Civilization" in International Law: Intellectual Perspectives from Pre-war Japan' (2019) 32 *Leiden Journal of International Law* 13.

Minorities and the Making of Postcolonial States in International Law (Cambridge Universtiy Press, 2021).

Shirlow, E., 'Three Manifestations of Transparency in International Investment Law: A Story of Sources, Stakeholders and Structures' (2017) 8 *Göttingen Journal of International Law* 73.

Simma, B., and Alston, P., 'The Sources of Human Rights Law: Custom, Jus Cogens and General Principles' (1988–1989) 12 *Australian Yearbook of International Law* 82.

Simma, B., 'Universality of International Law from the Perspective of a Practitioner' (2009) 20 *European Journal of International Law* 265.

Simpson, G., *The Sentimental Life of International Law: Literature, Language, and Longing in World Politics* (Oxford University Press, 2021).

Sinclair, G. F., *To Reform the World: International Organizations and the Making of Modern States* (Oxford University Press, 2017).

Singh, S., 'International Legal Positivism and New Approaches to International Law', in J. Kammerhofer and J. d'Aspremont (eds.), *International Legal Positivism in a Postmodern World* (Cambridge University Press, 2014), 291–314.

Skouteris, T., *The Notion of Progress in International Law Discourse* (T.M.C. Asser/Springer, 2010).

Slaughter, A.-M., 'The Liberal Agenda for Peace: International Relations Theory and the Future of the United Nations' (1994) 4 *Transnational Law and Contemporary Problems* 377.

Sorel, J.-M., 'Article 31', in P. Klein and O. Corten (eds.), *Les Conventions de Vienne sur le Droit des Traités. Commentaire article par article* (Bruylant, 2006), 1321–1354.

Staggs Kelsall, M., 'Disordering International Law' (2022) 33 *European Journal of International Law* 729.

Straumann, B., '"Ancient Caesarean Lawyers" in a State of Nature: Roman Tradition and Natural Rights in Hugo Grotius's "De iure praedae"' (2006) 34 *Political Theory* 328.

Sur, S., *L'interprétation en droit international public* (LGDJ, 1974).

Sutton, R., 'How the Emotions and Perceptual Judgments of Frontline Actors Shape the Practice of International Humanitarian Law', in S. A. Bandes, J. Lynee Madeira, K. Temple, and E. Kidd White (eds.), *Research Handbook on Law and Emotion* (Edward Elgar, 2021), 477–491.

'Read the Room: Legal and Emotional Literacy in Frontline Humanitarian Negotiations' (2021) 24 *Yearbook of International Humanitarian Law* 103.

Sutton, R., and Paddon Rhoads, E., 'Empathy in Frontline Humanitarian Negotiations: A Relational Approach to Engagement' (2022) 7 *International Journal of Humanitarian Action* 23.

Suy, E., *Les actes juridiques unilatéraux en droit international public* (LGDJ, 1962).

Tasioulas, J., 'In Defence of Relative Normativity: Communitarian Values and the Nicaragua Case' (1996) 16 *Oxford Journal of Legal Studies* 85.

'Customary International Law and the Quest for Global Justice', in A. Perreau-Saussine and Murphy, J. B. (eds.), *The Nature of Customary Law* (Cambridge University Press, 2007), 307–335.

Tesón, F. R., 'The Kantian Theory of International Law'(1992) 92 *Columbia Law Review* 53.

Thierry, H., 'The European Tradition of International Law: Georges Scelle' (1990) 1 *European Journal International Law* 193.

Thirlway, H., 'The Proliferation of International Judicial Organs and the Formation of International Law', in W. Heere (ed.), *International Law and The Hague's 750th Anniversary* (T.M.C Asser Instituut 1999), 433–441.

Tondini, M., 'Espionage and International Law in the Age of Permanent Competition' (2018) 57 *The Military Law and the Law of War Review* 17.

Tourme Jouannet, E., *Le droit international, le capitalisme et la terre. Histoire des accaparements de terres d'hier à aujourd'hui* (Bruylant, 2021).

Tourme-Jouannet, E., 'Des Origines Coloniales du Droit International: A Propos du Droit des Gens Moderne au 18ème Siècle', in P.-M. Dupuy and V. Chetail (eds.), *The Roots of International Law: Liber Amicorum Peter Haggenmacher* (Martinus Nijhoff, 2014), 651–670.

Twining, W., 'Social Science and Diffusion of Law' (2005) 32 *Journal of Law and Society* 203.

Tzanakopoulos, A., 'Transparency in the Security Council', in A. Bianchi and A. Peters (eds.), *Transparency in International Law* (Cambridge University Press, 2013), 367–391.

Tzouvala, N., *Capitalism as Civilisation: A History of International Law* (Cambridge University Press, 2020).

'New Approaches to International Law: The History of a Project' (2016) 27 *European Journal of International Law* 215.

Unger, R. M., *Law in Modern Society: Toward a Criticism of Social Theory* (The Free Press, 1976).

Van Damme, I., *Treaty Interpretation by the WTO Appellate Body* (Oxford University Press, 2009).

Van Hoof, G. J. H., *Rethinking the Sources of International Law* (Kluwer Law International, 1983).

Venzke, I., *How Interpretation Makes International Law: On Semantic Change and Normative Twists* (Oxford University Press, 2012).

How the Practice of Interpretation Makes International Law: On Semantic Change and Normative Twists (Oxford University Press, 2012).

'Contemporary Theories and International Lawmaking', in C. Brölmann and Y. Radi (eds.), *Research Handbook on the Theory and Practice of International Lawmaking* (Edward Elgar, 2016), 66–86.

'International Law as an Argumentative Practice: On Wohlrapp's *The Concept of Argument*' (2016) 7 *Transnational Legal Theory* 9.

Venzke, I., and Heller, K. J., *Contingency in International Law: On the Possibility of Different Legal Histories* (Oxford University Press, 2021).

Verdier, P.-H., and Voeten, E., 'How Does Customary International Law Change? The Case of State Immunity' (2015) 59 *International Studies Quarterly* 209.

Verhoeven, J., *Droit international 1. Les nullités du droit des gens* (Pedone, 1981).

Vidmar, J., *Democratic Statehood in International Law: The Emergence of New States in Post-Cold War Practice* (Hart, 2013).

Vinuales, J. E., 'On Legal Inquiry', in D. Alland, V. Chetail, O. de Frouville, and J. E. Vinuales (eds.), *Unity and Diversity of International Law: Essays in Honour of Professor Pierre-Marie Dupuy* (Martinus Nijhoff, 2014).

Virally, M., 'La notion de fonction dans la théorie de l'organization internationales', in *Mélanges Offerts à Charles Rousseau: La Communauté Internationale* (Pedone, 1974), 277–300.

'A Propos de la "Lex Ferenda"', in D. Bardonnet (ed.), *Mélanges Reuter: le droit international: Unité et diversité* (Pedone, 1981), 519–533.

von Bernstorff, J., 'Sisyphus Was an International Lawyer. On Martti Koskenniemi's "From Apologia to Utopia" and the Place of Law in International Politics' (2006) 7 *German Law Journal* 1015.

'German Intellectual Historical Origins of International Legal Positivism', in J. Kammerhofer and J. d'Aspremont (eds.), *International Legal Positivism in a Post-Modern World* (Cambridge University Press, 2014), 50–80.

'The Relationship between Theory and Practice in International Law: Affirmative versus Reflexive Distance', in J. d'Aspremont, T. Gazzini, A. Nollkaemper, and W. Werner (eds.), *International Law as a Profession* (Cambridge University Press, 2017), 222–243.

von Bogdandy, A., and Venzke, I., 'In Whose Name? An Investigation of International Courts' Public Authority and Its Democratic Justification' (2012) 23 *European Journal of International Law* 7.

Weil, P., 'Towards Relative Normativity in International Law' (1983) 77 *American Journal of International Law* 413.

Weiler, J. H. H., 'The Rule of Lawyers and the Ethos of Diplomats: Reflections on the Internal and External Legitimacy of WTO Dispute Settlement' (2001) 35 *Journal of World Trade* 191.

Werner, W., 'The Never-ending Closure: Constitutionalism and International Law', in N. Tsagourias (ed.), *Transnational Constitutionalism: International and European Perspectives* (Cambridge University Press, 2007), 329–368.

Repetition and International Law (Cambridge University Press, 2022).

Werner, W., de Hoon, M., and Galán, A. (eds.), *The Law of International Lawyers: Reading Martti Koskenniemi* (Cambridge Universtiy Press, 2018).

White, N., *The Law of International Organizations* (Manchester University Press, 2005).

Winter. S. L., *A Clearing in the Forest: Law, Life and Mind* (University of Chicago Press, 2001).

Zarbiyev, F., *Le Discours interprétatif en droit international* (Bruylant, 2015).

'The "Cash Value" of the Rules of Treaty Interpretation' (2019) 32 *Leiden Journal of International Law* 33.

Zimmermann, A., Tomuschat, C., and Oellers-Frahm, K. (eds.), *The Statute of the International Court of Justice* (Oxford University Press, 2002).

Zoellner, C.-S., 'Transparency: An Analysis of an Evolving Fundamental Principle in International Economic Law' (2006) 27 *Michigan Journal of International Law* 579.

INDEX

Printed by Integrated Books International,
United States of America